Advances in African Economic, Social and Political Development

Africa is emerging as a rapidly growing region, still facing major challenges, but with a potential for significant progress – a transformation that necessitates vigorous efforts in research and policy thinking. This book series focuses on three intricately related key aspects of modern-day Africa: economic, social and political development. Making use of recent theoretical and empirical advances, the series aims to provide fresh answers to Africa's development challenges. All the socio-political dimensions of today's Africa are incorporated as they unfold and new policy options are presented. The series aims to provide a broad and interactive forum of science at work for policymaking and to bring together African and international researchers and experts. The series welcomes monographs and contributed volumes for an academic and professional audience, as well as tightly edited conference proceedings. Relevant topics include, but are not limited to, economic policy and trade, regional integration, labor market policies, demographic development, social issues, political economy and political systems, and environmental and energy issues.

All titles in the series are peer-reviewed. The book series is indexed in SCOPUS.

* * *

Giuseppe T. Cirella
Editor

Uncertainty Shocks in Africa

Impact and Equilibrium Strategies for Sound Economic and Social Development

Springer

Editor
Giuseppe T. Cirella
Faculty of Economics
University of Gdansk
Sopot, Poland

ISSN 2198-7262 ISSN 2198-7270 (electronic)
Advances in African Economic, Social and Political Development
ISBN 978-3-031-21884-2 ISBN 978-3-031-21885-9 (eBook)
https://doi.org/10.1007/978-3-031-21885-9

This Springer imprint is published by the registered company Springer Nature Switzerland AG
The registered company address is: Gewerbestrasse 11, 6330 Cham, Switzerland

ai miei

Foreword

It gives me great pleasure to accept Prof. Dr. Giuseppe T. Cirella's invitation to write this Foreword and to provide useful suggestions to better understand the scope of this book. As a welcomed addition to the Scopus-indexed Springer book series, *Advances in African Economic, Social and Political Development*, this book spans innovative COVID-19 era findings and pieces together several important case studies in the sciences and social sciences. Since human society survives from nature and civilization is sustained by natural resources and environmental services, mostly provided for free, nature's resilience, adaptability, and renewability evolve in a sustainable manner when human disturbances do not exceed the carrying capacity. As the world experienced the first 2 years of the COVID-19 pandemic, it witnessed economies decimated and brought to a standstill. The economic shocks affected the most viable, economically resilient countries and almost paralyzed those of low and medium-income. Although COVID-19 is yet to recede completely from our societies, as we still experience some flash waves, almost all countries have passed their peak periods faced in 2020 and 2021. Countries are now trying to rebuild economically and socially, in the wake of the colossal economic downturns experienced, just as they would, from a post-disaster socioeconomic recovery following most natural disasters that negatively impact and harm a community. Evidence has shown that low and medium-income countries, especially sub-Saharan Africa and East Asia, suffered huge economic woes during and directly after the pandemic, especially those that derive a large percentage of their gross domestic product from transport and tourism. This is not unconnected with the fact that apart from bad governance which precedes the pandemic, particularly in Africa, political crisis, security fragility, and economic weakness were already pronounced but were made worse by the advent of COVID-19.

In a corroborative contribution to post-pandemic socioeconomic recovery, this book is a cross-fertilization of ideas, models, empirical research, and opinions from well-rounded researchers who originate from or have extensive experience on the African continent. This book's title, "*Uncertainty shocks in Africa: Impact and equilibrium strategies for sound economic and social development*", is timely and focuses on two important interlinking parts to a prosperous post-pandemic Africa. The first part examines how new urban thinking can engender sustainable advancement, while the second comprehensively looks at how social development programmes and practices can bring post-COVID-19 community robustness for sustainable progress in Africa. Crossbreeding of ideas from experts on strategies for economic recovery from East to West Africa, how small and medium scale enterprises can survive post-COVID-19 shocks, and how strategies for building green cities and strategic urbanization combine to engender post-pandemic economic survival and resilience in Africa, is discussed in a germane and contemporary manner. Aside from the astronomical rise in intimate partner violence brought forth by COVID-19, this all-important book also offers strategies to tackle this as well as how modern contraceptives can be more readily available for economic and social wellbeing from a bottom-up, grassroots perspective. Linkages among several other aforementioned socioeconomic topics and how they can combine to help Africa achieve Agenda 2063 are brought to the fore of this book. The uncertainty shocks from the COVID-19 pandemic created different second-moment shocks that are both positive and negative, warranting a clear understanding of their impact and how future steps should be considered. In conclusion, this book is a must read for macro volatility researchers seeking robustly generated firsthand and empirical correlations for the future development of Africa and for future shocks shaped by the effects and experience from the COVID-19 crisis.

Paul O. Adekola Ph.D.

Department of Economics and
Development Studies, Demography and
Social Statistics Program, College of
Management and Social Sciences,
Covenant University, Ota, Nigeria

Centre for Economic Policy and
Development Research,
Covenant University,
Ota, Nigeria

Department of Life Sciences, Research
Centre for Anthropology and Health,
University of Coimbra,
Coimbra, Portugal

Preface

"*Uncertainty shocks in Africa: Impact and equilibrium strategies for sound economic and social development*" is a book that aims to integrate an interdisciplinary approach to understand how to best mitigate the COVID-19 crisis as well as reduce future shocks to the continent. Over the last half century, uncertainty appears to noticeably increase after major economic and political shocks occurred. The volatility and shock experienced from COVID-19 has been worldwide. This book focuses on the African experience, i.e., specific to economic and social impacts over the last 2 years, by examining the drop and rebound effect different African countries endured during the pandemic. Core expertise integrates aspects of economics, human geography, sociology, urban planning, and development studies, using scientific methods to explain the strain on societies as well as the goals for future sustainable practice. Experience from shocks can be used to react to a current situation as well as prepare for shortages. Case research explores the future carrying capacity of African communities and the economic impact caused from scarcity. This can aid in building stronger, more resilient economies with protective safeguards. This book adds to the knowledgebase of how to build a more robust Africa with sustainable solutions working in tandem with vibrant and robust economies. Common sense social strategies go hand in hand with trackable shocked economies via first- and second-moment reactions. Key topics from this book incorporate a new urban thinking for economic revival, developing sustainable economies post-COVID-19, understanding social practices during a crisis, and developing community robustness from the experience of shock events. Policymakers, academicians, and students wishing to advance their knowledge in African economic and social development as well as crises advancement from uncertainty shocks will find this book particularly valuable.

This book pieces together connections relating to lockdown measures, crisis causation, and shock impact most countries faced dating back to 2020. Specific to Africa, it explores how countries dealt with the COVID-19 crisis and how it, i.e., case-specifically, affected different aspects of different economies and social structures. Uncertainty shocks, in this setting, interrelate via an umbrella effect by overlaying related first- and second-moment reactions during the crisis. This book distinctively explores crises management in Africa by making sense of the cause and effect as well as reactionary results from a pre-, during, and post-pandemic perspective with the underlying goal of limiting the impact of future shocks. It tests the theories of impact shocks on selected African countries that experienced economic and social decline and, in a general sense, evaluates the impact of shocks via a sustainable growth and change approach. It is reasonable to state, the economic and social shocks discussed are not limited to economists and sociologists, instead, they magnify to include policymakers and everyday people. The COVID-19 era has produced an economic and social crisis that has spread throughout society with adverse effects on consumers, investors, community development, and societal wellbeing. An examination into the negative shocks on supply and demand and the left tail risk of moving forward is considered imperative for much of the continent's economies. The impact of the first-moment shock in 2020 and the economic shutdown is assessed and raises important questions about the future. What will be the genesis and long-term impact of permanent supply and demand difficulties in different African countries? Will it take the shape of economic uncertainty, or has the COVID-19 era become a launching pad that will drive new sustainable economic initiatives? Observing how human beings change the environment and, specifically, how population growth and urbanization negatively impact nature, recent shocked economies and social upheaval in Africa indicate a crossroads moment for the continent. This book facilitates learning from the crisis' supply and demand disruptions as well as social mishaps to better inform the economies and societies of Africa, and beyond, to take a longer view of how to protect from and prepare for future shocks at a generational level. This book is divided into two parts; first, it looks at shocked economies in terms of urban thinking and sustainable advancement, and second, it explores shocked social development and mechanisms to improve community robustness.

Part I opens with seven contributions that examine urbanization, macroeconomics, city development processes, green city strategies, and specific sectors of the economy such as finance and tourism. These contributions interconnect with the shocked economies concept by demonstrating how the COVID-19 pandemic paralyzed urban centers and the mobility of people. "Urbanization Motif, COVID-19, and Economic Revival: Exploratory Research from Addis Ababa, Ethiopia" uses primary and secondary data to undertake an empirical examination of the cityscape urbanization process Addis Ababa, Ethiopia, faced in the first year of the outbreak. From an economic viewpoint, sub-city district differences are analysed using the generalized method of moments estimator, the limited information maximum likelihood estimator, and an ordinary least squares regression model. Affected sectors include health services and tourism while information and technology, entertainment, and Internet-based industries fared better. The findings suggest that Addis Ababa's City Center recovered at a slower rate when compared to its outer sub-city districts. "Lessons for Sub-Saharan Africa: Using the Development Model from East Asia in Nigeria, 1965-2015" is primarily a historical look at how economic indicators in East Asia could benefit sub-Saharan Africa. In search of a common development model, an extensive examination of East Asia is compared from 1965 to 2015. This chapter centres on questions that try to identify positive indicators as well as reasons to how East Asia developed, the rapidity of the development, and if there is a unified development model. Secondary work explores the case of South Korea and Nigeria as representative countries of the two subregions. Recommendations centre on developing other sectors of the economy and increasing domestic demand to serve as a security measure. This can aid in protecting the economy from potential global market shocks, e.g., the COVID-19 crisis, strengthen budgetary control to improve fiscal solvency, and maintain a low external debt profile to reduce government expenditure on debt servicing. "Economic Shocks from COVID-19 and the Assessment of Micro, Small, and Medium-Sized Enterprises Emergence of Insurance Coverage in Urban South-West, Nigeria" focuses on the financial uncertainties which affected economic growth and investments in terms of micro, small, and medium-sized enterprises (MSMEs). Insurance coverage is one of the risk management tools that helps protect businesses from shocks and enables them to remain in business. This chapter examines the impact of the COVID-19 pandemic on MSMEs' level of production income and the uptake of insurance coverage in South-West, Nigeria. It recommends that insurance companies develop tailor-made products for MSMEs so as to make insurance more attractive, and given the high cost of premiums, offer flexible payments methods to increase uptake. "Shocks from the COVID-19 Crisis in Ethiopia" case researches the shock of the pandemic in Ethiopia from before the COVID-19 outbreak to the end of 2021. The economic shock of the pandemic is explored by examining the macroeconomy, poverty and food insecurity, and social conditions of the country with recommendations on how to best recovery. Linkages between economic and social measures are considered, including how to best deal with the pandemic's aftereffects and how to mitigate future economic shocks. "Green Buildings and Green City Strategies for the COVID-19 Pandemic Affected Tourism Industry in Rwanda" details the use of green buildings and green city strategies for the COVID-19 pandemic affected tourism industry in Rwanda. Recently adopted green buildings and green city policies, including newly developed city master plans and green building code, reflect on the tourism industry, regulating its influence on urban development and communities in the country. After surveying hotel suppliers and hotel managers in Rwanda's Musanze District, this chapter provides recommendations for actions on how Rwanda's secondary cities, that highly depend on tourism, can respond to the pandemic and set a path of sustainable and inclusive growth. "The African Union's Agenda 2063 and Africa's Tourism Industry" pieces together aspects of the African Union's Agenda 2063 framework that focuses on long-run sustainable tourism and economic development in Africa. It assesses how the tourism industry contributes to economic development and should prioritize destination readiness as a blueprint to moving forward. Agenda 2063 is broken down in terms of how a common tourism industry can exist in Africa and what factors highlight a Pan-African approach. Background knowledge on the topic is thoroughly explored and presented in a chronological order pre-COVID-19. Recent efforts have been made to develop the tourism industry post-COVID-19 using attractions, accommodation, and accessibility as key starting points.

Part II shifts the focus of uncertainty shocks in Africa towards the social dimension of developing mechanisms to improve community robustness and limit socio-economic differences, e.g., in informal settlements, as a result of the COVID-19 crisis. This part of the book is divided into three subsections: (1) three contributions are directly dedicated to wellbeing and household affairs (i.e., gender-based violence (GBV), contraceptive utilization, and housing), (2) two contributions focus on television programme choices, and (3) one contribution examines rural life. "Societal Shocks and Gender-Based Violence Among Vulnerable People in Kibera and Other Informal Settlements Around Nairobi, Kenya" begins by examining societal shocks and GBV among vulnerable people in Kibera and other informal settlements around Nairobi, Kenya. The main perpetrators of GBV are youthful males aged 18–33 years who are in the context of a family or intimate partner relationship. This chapter, specifically, looks at the social structures that increase the vulnerability of people living in Nairobi's slums in comparison to the other parts of the country using Johan V. Galtung's classification of direct, structural, and cultural violence framework. "Contraceptive Utilization Among Married Couples in Nigeria: Socio-Cultural Factors" investigates contraceptive utilization among married couples in Nigeria by comparing socio-cultural factors of 8061 married couples. Results show a clear regional difference in contraceptive use among married couples with the lowest rate from North-West (i.e., 7.2%) and highest from South-West (i.e., 36.8%). Factors that positively determine acceptance are education, wealth index, religion, age, and an ideal family size. "COVID-19 and the Built Environment: Informal Sector, Housing, and Shock Challenges in Nigeria" evaluates housing planning and design in residential areas with a specific focus on informal settlements throughout Nigeria. Problems such as lack of space, lack of adequate security, and light and noise pollution are reported to be problematic. It is recommended that the government continue to stimulate more public information on the pandemic, create job opportunities, and ensure better housing quality and standards for its citizenry, especially for the less fortunate. "Influence of the Big Brother Naija Lockdown 2020 Edition Reality TV Show on Nigerians' Value Orientation During the COVID-19 Lockdown Measures" investigates how Nigerians consumed the Big Brother Naija Lockdown 2020 edition reality TV show featured on Nigerian television during the period of the COVID-19 lockdown. Understanding whether the reality TV show affected their value orientation was examined using a semi-structured online questionnaire. It was found that Nigerians increased their viewership of the 2020 edition in comparison to previous years. Recommendations are offered to better understand why males did not watch the show as much as females as well as why they found the show more acceptable even though they watched it less. This chapter probes into prolonged social isolation and television exposure to better understand psychological impacts and associated influences during public health crises. "COVID-19 Television Audience Program Choices: Analysis of How Nigerians Consume Television During the Pandemic" is anchored on the uses and gratification theory and examines the key factors that influence viewers' selection and consumption of TV programmes during Nigeria's first phase of the COVID-19 lockdown. The results show that most respondents doubled their consumption of TV programmes to combat boredom, get information on COVID-19, and get spiritual inspiration. "Underlying Factors that Worsened the Vulnerability of Small-Holder Farmers During the COVID-19 Pandemic: Evidence from North-Central, Nigeria", to end, determines the underlying factors that worsened the vulnerability of small-holder farmers during the COVID-19 pandemic in North-Central, Nigeria. Proffering lasting solutions to the problems of low productivity, arising from the vulnerability to cope with shock events, is central to understanding how, why, and what occurred over the last 2 years. To better understand this, the socioeconomic characteristics of small-holder farmers were identified and interlinked with factors that impaired their vulnerability during the initial outbreak phase. The major factors that significantly worsened the vulnerability of the farmers is educational level, farming experience, access to finance, adoption of improved technologies, and access to extension services. In brief, the COVID-19 pandemic created financial uncertainties which affected economic growth and investments throughout different sectors of the economy—creating agricultural setbacks that should not be overlooked but rather highlighted—for future shock preparedness.

The inspiration of this book dates to the end of 2021 when much of the world started to experience some form of normalcy following the 2-year period of the COVID-19 pandemic. The work prepared for this book was originally intended for a global study on economic shocks, however due to several reasons pertaining to publication requirements, this African-centric book was put together to collate important findings from the continent. Socioeconomic development gains, i.e., decreasing poverty and inequality in rural and urban communities, are one of the central stories and motivation of the contributors. With economic transformation and rapid urbanization strongly intertwined in the continent's future, this book encourages the decision-making process and open-mindedness of Africa's next development phase and long-term success post-pandemic.

Sopot, Poland Giuseppe T. Cirella

Contents

Editor and Contributors

About the Editor

Prof. Dr. Giuseppe T. Cirella Professor of Human Geography, works at the Faculty of Economics, University of Gdansk, Sopot, Poland, where he received his equivalency Doctor of Habilitation (*Dr. Hab.*) in Economics and Finance. He specializes in economic development, environmental social science, and sustainability. His interdisciplinary background also includes socio-political research throughout Eastern Europe, Africa, and China. After completing a Doctor of Philosophy (*Ph. D.*) at Griffith University, Australia, within the Centre for Infrastructure Engineering and Management, on developing a sustainability-based index, he founded the Polo Centre of Sustainability in Italy. Notably, he has held professorships and scientific positions at Saint Petersburg State University, Russia; Inner Mongolia University of Science and Technology, China; Life University, Cambodia; and Free University of Bozen, Italy. In his early career, he worked with the Canadian International Development Agency in Indonesia as well as with Radarsat International in Brazil. He is also on the editorial board of a number of internationally renowned academic peer-reviewed journals.

Faculty of Economics, University of Gdansk, Sopot, Poland

Contributors

Birhanu G. Abebe Ethopian Institute of Architecture, Building Construction and City Development, Addis Ababa University, Addis Ababa, Ethiopia

Solomon T. Abebe Polo Centre of Sustainability, Imperia, Italy

Paul O. Adekola Department of Economics and Development Studies, Demography and Social Statistics Programme, Covenant University, Ota, Ogun State, Nigeria
Centre for Economic Policy and Development Research, Covenant University, Ota, Ogun State, Nigeria
Department of Anthropology, Research Centre for Anthropology and Health, Human Biology, Health and Society Unit, University of Coimbra, Coimbra, Portugal

Gideon A. Adeyemi Centre for Economic Policy and Development Research, Covenant University, Ota, Ogun State, Nigeria
Department of Civil Engineering, Covenant University, Ota, Ogun State, Nigeria

Dheeraj Arrabothu Global Green Growth Institute, Kigali, Rwanda

Andrew A. Ate Department of Mass Communication, Edo State University Uzairue, Iyamho, Edo State, Nigeria

Adeyemi E. Ayinde-Olawale Department of Planning, Research, and Development, Nigerian Agricultural Insurance Corporation, Abuja, Nigeria

Dominic E. Azuh Demography and Social Statistics Programme, Department of Economics and Development Studies, Covenant University, Ota, Ogun State, Nigeria
Centre for Economic Policy and Development Research, Covenant University, Ota, Ogun State, Nigeria

Giuseppe T. Cirella Faculty of Economics, University of Gdansk, Sopot, Poland

Peter E. Egielewa Department of Mass Communication, Edo State University Uzairue, Iyamho, Edo State, Nigeria

Bedane S. Gemeda Ethiopian Institute of Architecture, Building Construction and City Development, Addis Ababa University, Addis Ababa, Ethiopia

Fekede T. Gemeda College of Development Studies, Center for Environment and Development, Addis Ababa University, Addis Ababa, Ethiopia

Ilija Gubic Faculty of Architecture, University of Belgrade, Belgrade, Serbia

Adedoyin L. Ibitoye School of Business and Management, Management Development Institute of Singapore in Tashkent, Tashkent, Uzbekistan

Olalekan Ibitoye School of Business and Management, Management Development Institute of Singapore in Tashkent, Tashkent, Uzbekistan

Gakwaya P. Isingizwe Faculty of Economics, University of Gdansk, Sopot, Poland

Felix O. Iyalomhe Polo Centre of Sustainability, Imperia, Italy

Wyclife Ong'eta Mose School of Security, Diplomacy and Peace Studies, Kenyatta University, Nairobi, Kenya

Richard Ndicunguye Global Green Growth Institute, Kigali, Rwanda

Blessed F. Ngonso Department of Mass Communication, Edo State University Uzairue, Iyamho, Edo State, Nigeria

Idowu T. Ogunyemi Department of Planning, Research, and Development, Nigerian Agricultural Insurance Corporation, Abuja, Federal Capital Territory, Nigeria

Solomon A. Olatunji Department of Urban and Regional Planning, Federal University Oye-Ekiti, Oye-Ekiti, Nigeria

Adebanke Olawole-Isaac Demography and Social Statistics Programme, Department of Economics and Development Studies, Covenant University, Ota, Ogun State, Nigeria
Centre for Economic Policy and Development Research, Covenant University, Ota, Ogun State, Nigeria

Olajumoke I. Omodara Faculty of Economics, University of Gdansk, Sopot, Poland

Christian Orobello Faculty of Economics, University of Gdansk, Sopot, Poland

Andrzej Paczoski Faculty of Economics, University of Gdansk, Sopot, Poland

Michael J. Rosciszewski-Dodgson Faculty of Economics, University of Gdansk, Sopot, Poland

Chelsea R. Spring Faculty of Economics, University of Gdansk, Sopot, Poland

Adewale O. Yoade Department of Urban and Regional Planning, Wesley University Ondo, Ondo, Nigeria

List of Abbreviations

ACT	Access to COVID-19 Tools
AfCFTA	African Continental Free Trade Area
ATT	average treatment effects on the treated
BAY	Borno, Adamawa, and Yobe
CI	confidence interval
DHS	Demographic and Health Surveys
EABC	East African Business Council
ECOWAS	Economic Community of West African States
ERF	Economic Recovery Fund
EVI	Economic Vulnerability Index
FCT	Federal Capital Territory
FDI	foreign direct investment
GBMCS	Green Building Minimum Compliance System
GBV	gender-based violence
GDP	gross domestic product
GHG	greenhouse gas
GLS	generalized least squares
GMM	generalized method of moments
HCI	heavy and chemical industry
ICT	information and communication technology
ICU	intensive care unit
IDP	internally displaced person
ILO	International Labour Organization
IMF	International Monetary Fund
IUCD	intra-uterine contraceptive device
LGA	local government area
LIML	limited information maximum likelihood
MSMEs	Micro, small, and medium-sized enterprises
MSPRP	COVID-19 Multi-Sectoral Preparedness and Response Plan
NDHS	Nigerian Demographic and Health Survey
NLUDMP	National Land Use and Development Master Plan 2020-2050

OECD	Organisation for Economic Co-operation and Development
OLS	ordinary least squares
OR	odds ratio
PHCN	Power Holding Company of Nigeria
PPP	purchasing power parity
PSM	propensity score matching
RDB	Rwanda Development Board
RECs	Regional Economic Communities
RQ	research question
SAATM	Single African Air Transport Market
SDGs	United Nations Sustainable Development Goals
SMEs	small and medium-sized enterprises
TAP	Tourism Action Plan
TIFA	Trends and Insights for Africa
UK	The United Kingdom
UN	United Nations
UN-Habitat	United Nations Human Settlements Programme
UNDP	United Nations Development Programme
UPSNP	Urban Productive Safety Nets Programme
UNWTO	United Nations World Tourism Organization
WASH	water, sanitation, and hygiene
WHO	World Health Organization

Part I
Shocked Economies: New Urban Thinking and Sustainable Advancement

Urbanization Motif, COVID-19, and Economic Revival: Exploratory Research from Addis Ababa, Ethiopia

Bedane S. Gemeda, Giuseppe T. Cirella, Fekede T. Gemeda, Michael J. Rosciszewski-Dodgson, and Birhanu G. Abebe

1 Introduction

COVID-19 emerged unexpectedly at the beginning of 2020. Its global reach has been far greater when compared to other outbreaks. It is fair to say that modern modes of travel, in combination with travel speed, aided in bringing the world to a standstill. As a result, many governments from around the world limited economic activities and the movement of their people—especially within large cities [1, 2]. COVID-19 affected the cityscape by forcing people to reimagine urban space in terms of communal well-being, social development, and economic security. For densely packed cities, such as Addis Ababa, Ethiopia, this was, and it still is, a major challenge. Over the last two decades, Addis Ababa's urbanization has progressed significantly. Its urbanization rate has grown from 2.1% in 1988 to 8% in 2022. This is accompanied by a gross domestic product (GDP) per capita going up from USD 124.46 in 2000 to USD 936.34 in 2020 [3]. Addis Ababa's fast-paced cityscape urbanization process—inclusive of international travel—made it Ethiopia's most affected city in the first year of the COVID-19 pandemic. In the first quarter of 2020, the total number of verified cases was 42,765. During this time, GDP fell by 31.5%, tertiary industries dropped by 17.7%, and total retail sales were down by 25.7%. This economic shock raised two notable questions. What is the

B. S. Gemeda (✉) · B. G. Abebe
Ethiopian Institute of Architecture, Building Construction and City Development, Addis Ababa University, Addis Ababa, Ethiopia

G. T. Cirella · M. J. Rosciszewski-Dodgson
Faculty of Economics, University of Gdansk, Sopot, Poland
e-mail: gt.cirella@ug.edu.pl

F. T. Gemeda
Center for Environment and Development, College of Development Studies, Addis Ababa University, Addis Ababa, Ethiopia

G. T. Cirella (ed.), *Uncertainty Shocks in Africa*, Advances in African Economic, Social and Political Development, https://doi.org/10.1007/978-3-031-21885-9_1

connection, if any, among cityscape urbanization patterns, an outbreak (or shock event), and economic recovery? Do different levels of urbanization affect a city's ability to withstand a shock event, and, if so, what is the optimal level? Based on these uncertainties, this chapter investigates the impact of cityscape urbanization patterns on economic recovery in 2020 in terms of timing, industry categorization, and district differences in Addis Ababa. A breakdown of this chapter is as follows: (1) to examine the existing problems of Addis Ababa's cityscape urbanization patterns and attempt to offer practical ideas for economic recovery post-pandemic; (2) to address the city's experience with outbreaks and assess urbanization trends in the context of the economy; (3) to utilize empirical statistics to assess cityscape urbanization patterns and the economy of Addis Ababa's sub-city districts during the first year of the pandemic; and (4) to present an economic and policy perspective on how to improve Ethiopia's urban economic resilience and reduce future economic shocks.

2 Cityscape Urbanization Patterns and Outbreaks

As countries industrialize urbanization follows, bringing a strong sense of community and economic success. This is typified by the diversity of people—mostly coming from rural communities—that make up cities and urban centers which run the large number of businesses and services that frame an urban setting. Two factors play an important role in this process. First, there is a material growth stage which refers to the transfer of rural (i.e., countryside) people to non-agricultural businesses which help to expand built-up urban locales. Second, there is the urban development stage which refers to the implementation of advanced city infrastructure outwardly, i.e., from the city to the countryside [4–6]. In a broader sense, urbanization is an all-encompassing transformation that affects the economy, community, politics, culture, and inhabitants—following an S-shaped growth curve [7, 8].

The process of urbanization in Western industrialized countries has taken a long time. In the United States, it took 80 years for the cityscape pace to grow from 30% to 70% [9]. Japan had the fastest rise in urbanization among developed countries, despite the fact, it took approximately 50 years to reach this milestone [10, 11]. When the pace of urban development approaches 50%, it enters a crucial development point often associated with "built-up sickness," i.e., people in densely populated areas suffer from symptoms of illness or become infected as a direct result of poor water supplies, living conditions, inadequate cleanliness, and disease outbreaks [12, 13]. At the last part of the nineteenth century, 70% of the British populace resided in cities, making Britain the world's first urbanized country. However, due to Britain's rapid urbanization, housing constraints, the presence of slums, low air quality, and lack of communal hygiene services, this buildup, created informal settlements in large urban areas such as London and Manchester [14, 15]. As a result, British cities became breeding grounds for different diseases, including several flu and cholera outbreaks. To measure the range and origin of each

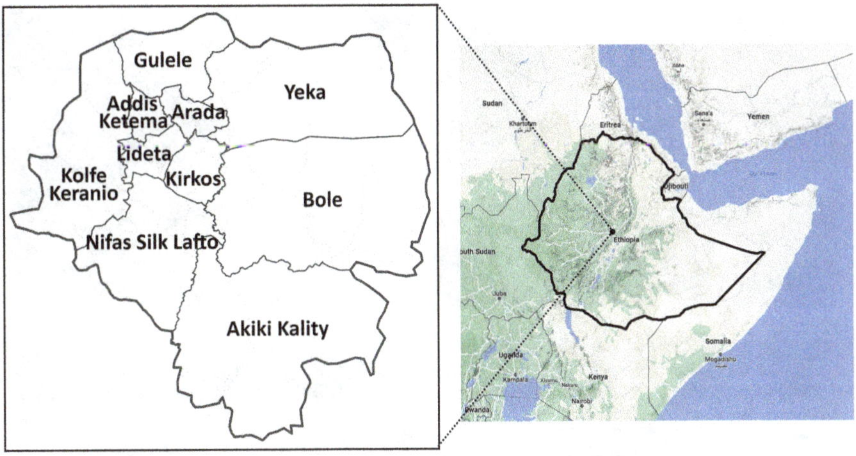

Fig. 1 Map of the ten sub-city districts of Addis Ababa, Ethiopia. Source: adapted from Wikimedia Commons [17] and Google Maps [18]

disease outbreak, a number of hypothetical approaches throughout history, such as the garden municipality, outpost metropolis, district unit, and organic transference theories, have been utilized to advance the cityscape urbanization model that mitigates against various urban-centric crises [8, 16]. This chapter utilizes the case of the ten sub-city districts of Addis Ababa to probe such patterns and examine the effect of the COVID-19 outbreak during 2020 (Fig. 1).

2.1 Ethiopia's Rural-to-Urban Transition

Ethiopia is one of the world's least urbanized countries. Only 22.2% of the country's population lives in cities; however, the percentage of people moving to the city is annually increasing by 4.7% [19]. This influx is primarily occurring due to the high rate of in-migration to towns and an increase in the number of urban centers [20, 21]. By 2050, the country's urban population is predicted to increase by 3.98% on average, with urban areas accounting for 42.1% of the overall population [21, 22]. Despite the fact that Ethiopia has over 900 urban centers, Addis Ababa, the country's capital, accounts for roughly 23% of the country's overall urban population. As a result, the city has been extending horizontally into its peri-urban districts to accommodate for the ever-increasing number of inhabitants, industries, and service-oriented businesses. The impact of urbanization in Ethiopia includes deforestation, soil degradation, decreased water availability, agricultural decline, and increased informal (i.e., squatter) settlements—all documented by Abdissa [23], Melese [24], Gete [25], and Geda [26]. As such, a considerable amount of people looking for any kind of inexpensive labor continues to drive the shift from the rural countryside to populated urban areas, resulting in a significant demographic divide

Fig. 2 Divided socioeconomic levels of Addis Ababa, Ethiopia: (*top left*) central business district and ongoing development of high-rise buildings, (*top right*) business center and triple bypass, (*bottom left*) congested and unplanned housing in Markata area of Bole sub-city district which has no waste management system, and (*bottom right*), slum area in Addis Ketema sub-city district which lacks access to portable water and has no paved or cobblestone roads. Source: (*top left*, *bottom left*, and *bottom right*) Photographs by Bedane Shata Gemeda, August 1, 2022; (*top right*) photograph by Fekede Terefe Gemeda, July 27, 2022

within the country's urban cityscape (Fig. 2). Consequently, a gap between essential public services, such as schooling and healthcare, is becoming gradually more apparent for the most vulnerable and poor. This divide is placing extreme pressure on urban poverty levels by decreasing public means of mobility and augmenting crime [27].

In essence, these types of problems demonstrate the conflict created when population growth in cities exceeds the urban development threshold. In Addis Ababa much of these distresses are evident. The fact that Addis Ababa's current infrastructure cannot properly provide sufficient goods and services, i.e., for its growing number of inhabitants, is troubling [28]. This discrepancy becomes even more pronounced in the face of a public health emergency such as the COVID-19 pandemic. Due to the fact that, the city has significant compactness and movability requirements, making it a "hotspot" for government intervention, as with most heavily infected urbanized areas throughout 2020 [29–31]. Conversely, because cities have accumulated considerably more health-related resources and public amenities than rural areas, they should be able to provide better outbreak deterrence and public direction. This begs the question, whether it was favorable to live in a highly urbanized area, like Addis Ababa, during the initial outbreak phase and, if so, what are the best areas within a city for future shocks?

2.2 *Addis Ababa and COVID-19*

The current backdrop of Addis Ababa is one of urbanization and regional integration, resulting in the extraordinary and difficult propagation the city faced during the height of the COVID-19 pandemic. The shock of the pandemic on Ethiopia's financial system, and the general public, was greater than that of previous outbreaks. At the start of the pandemic, in 2019, Addis Ababa's urbanization rate was 6.6%. Its population density and mobility had also considerably grown as a result of the rural-to-urban transition occurring throughout the country. Addis Ababa's population flow reached 6.36 million in 2019, generating a triple rise in the city's inhabitants since 2002. In terms of the city's financial system, outlay and international trade were the leading drivers of growth in 2003, but domestic spending is now the key driver. Addis Ababa's consumer spending accounted for 21.4% of GDP in 2019, up from 6.4% in 2007. Also in 2019, the tertiary sector accounted for 47.4% of GDP, up nearly 9% from 2003. With the onset of pandemic, a direct correlation between COVID-19 and resident restricted spending behavior became apparent. This relationship severely altered the economy of Addis Ababa, reducing consumer motivation and purchasing power parity, while razing the percentage of people that lived close to the poverty line [26]. Since there was a drop in consumption, i.e., mostly due to manufacturing and service business stagnation, considerable economic loss was followed by low levels of cash flow and turnover. This negatively impacted the city's consumption patterns by reducing resident income and increasing unemployment—putting pressure on residents to increase (i.e., build) precautionary savings and resource reserves [26]. This decline further caused heavy economic losses to other metropolitan regions in Ethiopia—causing much of the country's urban city centers to suffer.

During the pandemic, high rates of clustering, i.e., internal migration into cities, sparked new growth potential in various, less developed sectors. Since city populations constitute a vast marketplace, and function as the substratum for the creation and growth of the latest products and manufacturing processes, the growth of information technology and the internet became very popular [32–34]. For instance, online shopping and fresh food e-commerce grew substantially throughout the pandemic. Emerging business models were heavily promoted, comprising of online healthcare, online schooling, and isolated workplaces. COVID-19 aided in the optimization of people's purchasing psychology, needs, and arrangements (Fig. 3). The eagerness to buy insurance, entertainment, and schooling climbed dramatically, as did hygienic goods, medical equipment, and sports fitness products [35]. In Addis Ababa, much of these daily necessities, however, were not equally available throughout the city and its sub-city districts. As a result, the heavily

Fig. 3 COVID-19 lockdown measure in Addis Ababa, Ethiopia where customers weigh their own fruits, vegetable, spices, and cereals as well as maintain a 2 m distance from sellers. Source: Photographs by Bedane S. Gemeda, August 1, 2020

urbanized city center differed from the sub-city districts, resulting in space-based disparity. At present, a post-pandemic, nonhomogeneous economic recovery can be detected throughout the city. Some key factors that play a part in this disparity include the continual increase in urbanization and lack of communal services and infrastructure.

3 Defining the Methodology and Data

The allotted period of research for this chapter is from July to December 2020; the data covers all the sub-city districts in Addis Ababa and contains the sum of the day-to-day transaction variables from sixteen industries, e.g., resident services, real estate, transportation, and schooling. Also, within this period, COVID-19 case data was obtained from the Addis Ababa City Health Office, which included information on the total figure of verified cases, daily new cases, cured patients, and deaths. The total cured cases and deaths were subtracted from the total confirmed cases to arrive at the actual daily cases. This research used control variables such as compactness, GDP per capita and disposable income, and communal spending as well as the number of tertiary industries, internet users, and doctors per thousand citizens to understand how economic shocks affected the city. The Addis Ababa City Government Plan and Development Commission provided the control variables. Table 1 shows the statistical properties of the data.

Generalized method of moments (GMM) estimator and limited information maximum likelihood (LIML) estimator were used to assess the data in terms of cityscape urbanization patterns and economic development during the first year of the COVID-19 pandemic in Addis Ababa. From the viewpoint of tertiary industries and sub-city district differences, these methods attempted to illustrate if high levels of urbanization created a stagnation period. To do so, an examination of the COVID-19 response in Addis Ababa, its economy, along with the cityscape urbanization

Table 1 Statistical characteristics of the data, July 3, 2020-December 7, 2020

	Variables	Mean	Standard deviation	Least	Highest
Case variables	Whole cases	2034	7675.71	0	42,765
	Actual cascs	653	2987.34	0	28,345
	Cured cases	1987	5432.09	0	39,098
	Deaths	89	420.09	0	2176
Transaction variables	Total transaction	14,341	22,341.16	0	17,342
Control variables	Lockdown policy	0.41	0.39	0	2
	Urbanization rate	3.1	1.2	2	6.2
	Population density	330.2	190.8	20	1200
	Public expenditure	30.79	41.8	2	220
	Tertiary industries (i.e., proportion)	20	4.2	20.4	40.2
	Number of hospitals	12	7.9	4	14
	Number of doctors per thousand	4.6	1.31	3.87	7.65

Source: Addis Ababa City Healthy Office and Addis Ababa City Government Plan and Development Commission [36]

plan, i.e., as outlined by the municipal government, was performed. Next, GMM, LIML, and an ordinary least squares (OLS) regression model were used to assess relational differences. Since COVID-19 is an exogenous shock to the economy, i.e., as denoted in the model of the research, the cityscape urbanization rate is defined as an interior component that can afflict or intensify economic hardship. To assess the impact on the economy, the actual cases from the city and the cityscape urbanization rate were employed as the primary explanatory variables. The model used Eq. 1 to calculate the findings.

$$\begin{aligned} \text{Economy}_{i,t} = {} & \alpha_0 + \alpha_1 \text{Actualcases}_{i,t} + \alpha_2 \text{Lockdownpolicy}_{i,t} \\ & + \alpha_3 \text{Urbanizationrate}_{i,t} + \alpha_4 \text{Populationdensity}_{i,t} \\ & + \alpha_5 \text{Expenditure}_{i,t} + \alpha_6 \text{Industry}_{i,t} + \alpha_6 \text{Hospitals}_{i,t} \\ & + \alpha_7 \text{Doctors}_{i,t} + X_{i,t} + \gamma_i + \delta_{i,t} + \epsilon_{i,t} \end{aligned} \tag{1}$$

Where: $\alpha_1\text{Actualcases}_{i,\ t}$ = actual cases in the city, $\alpha_2\text{Lockdownpolicy}_{i,\ t}$ = dummy variables for city lockdown policies, $\alpha_3\text{Urbanizationrate}_{i,\ t}$ = cityscape urbanization rate, $\alpha_4\text{Populationdensity}_{i,\ t}$ = population density, $\alpha_5\text{Expenditure}_{i,\ t}$ = public expenditure, $\alpha_6\text{Industry}_{i,\ t}$ = proportion of tertiary industry, $\alpha_6\text{Hospitals}_{i,\ t}$ = number of hospitals, $\alpha_7\text{Doctors}_{i,\ t}$ = number of doctors per thousand, i = city, t = date, α_0 = constant term, X = control variable, γ = time fixed effect, and ϵ = error term.

4 COVID-19, Cityscape Urbanization, and the Economic Condition of Addis Ababa

4.1 COVID-19 Situation Analysis

According to the data collected from the Addis Ababa City Healthy Office, COVID-19 in Ethiopia was first announced on March 13, 2020, when the first confirmed case was found. Overall, the total number of confirmed COVID-19 cases during the allotted study period in Addis Ababa went up from 5200 in late-July 2020 to 42,765 in late-October 2020; the total number of treated cases went from 4786 to 39,098; while the total number of deaths went from 105 to 912, respectfully. After the number of daily cases peaked in October 2020, they started to decrease and reached zero in late-April 2021.

4.2 Cityscape Urbanization Pattern and Economic Situation

Figure 4 illustrates the cityscape urbanization rate of Addis Ababa from 2009 to 2022. The pace has slowly grown and is currently at 4.43%. Interestingly, GDP and secondary and tertiary industries over the same period followed suit. Also, it is worth noting that during this period, the number of hospitals and number of doctors per thousand people did not increase as profoundly, reflecting how Addis Ababa's urbanization strategy prioritized economic expansion and industrial development over basic communal needs such as health services and well-being.

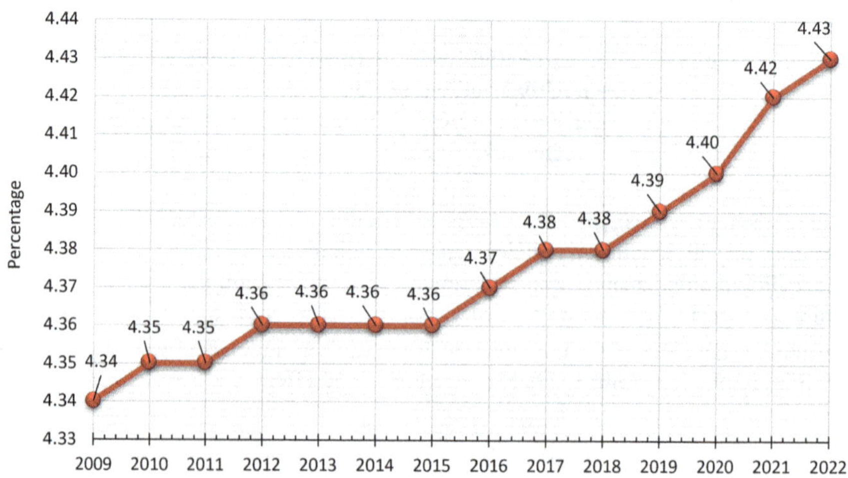

Fig. 4 Cityscape urbanization rate of Addis Ababa, 2009–2022. Source: United Nations [37]

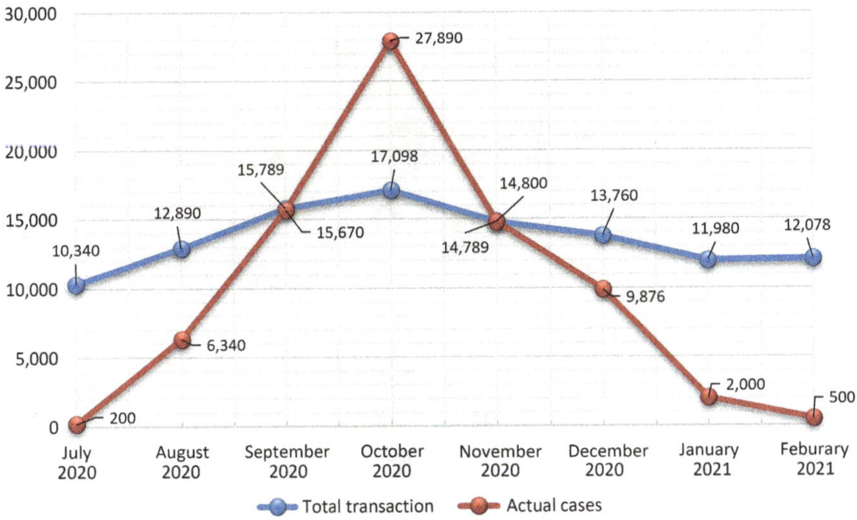

Fig. 5 COVID-19 actual cases and economic total transactions in Addis Ababa, July 2020–February 2021. Source: Addis Ababa City Healthy Office [36]

When COVID-19 is combined with the total transaction variables, it is clear that the epidemiological and economic trends have an approximate negative linkage (Fig. 5). As such, daily trading plummeted significantly when the government decided to implement its lockdown measures in August 2020. This unexpectedly resulted in a short-term increase in economic activity (i.e., most likely due to personal savings being used up) followed by a stagnation period and subsequent decrease. As the pandemic diminished and more Ethiopian cities removed their lockdown measures, the daily transaction volume returned with continued fluctuation. These irregularities throughout the country were the effects of public uncertainty towards the future that has been repeatedly documented in other countries [38–40].

According to the data on the total transactions from July to December 2020, general department retailers had the highest transaction volume—followed by clothing, bags, house building supplies, artistic supplies, entertainment, refreshments, and monetary services. Medical facilities and tourism came in third and second from the bottom of a list of sixteen categories, with schooling and tutoring coming last. The largest transaction volume, i.e., sales of general department retailers remained the most stable, since resident spending primarily was used to cover daily needs while living in lockdown. Throughout the lockdown period, i.e., with the loss of work, people stayed at home and utilized audio and visual entertainment, read, ordered takeout, and exercised at home. The Addis Ababa City Health Office showed that financial service transactions may have been linked to an increased desire for private and health insurance products. The low use of healthcare services could have also been attributed to this change in transaction activity since a drop in

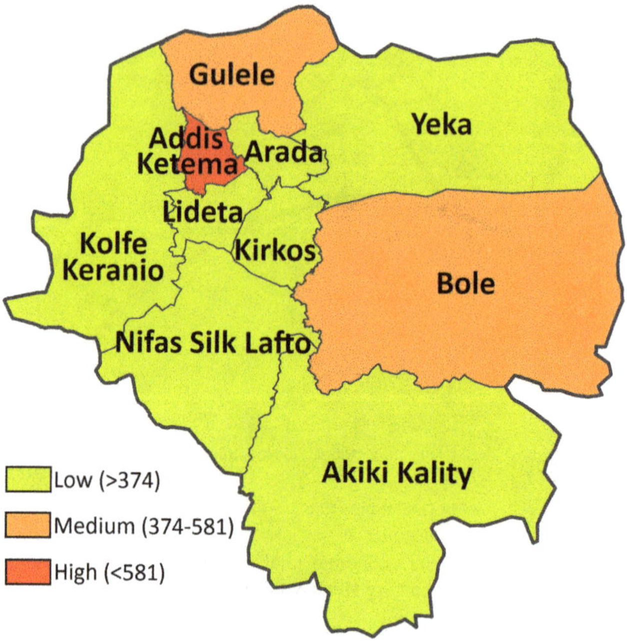

Fig. 6 Total COVID-19 cases via a space-based breakdown of the sub-city districts of Addis Ababa, July 2020. Source: compiled from Addis Ababa City Health Office and adapted from Kassahun [41]

demand for doctor care was recorded. Moreover, schooling and tutoring had the lowest transaction volume, indicating the shock for students to stay home and attend online classes generated little, if any, monetary turnover.

Evidence shows that disparities in the space-based distribution of COVID-19 and the economy had a sub-city district effect. By contrasting economic dealings and cases, a space-based distribution of transaction sizes, data from key informant interviews, and focus group discussions revealed Addis Ababa's sub-city districts were affected differently during the first year of the pandemic. For illustrative purposes, Fig. 6 shows a space-based breakdown for the month of July 2020. Furthermore, even though Addis Ababa's economic activity from July to December 2020 accounted for more than one-third of all of Ethiopia's cities, on close inspection, Kolfe Keranio, Yeka, and Akaki Kality, made a three-point vertex around the city's periphery—creating a triangle pattern around the city center districts of Addis Ketema, Arada, Lideta, and Kirkos. Addis Ketema suffered the most rigorous shock from COVID-19—both from a sub-city district and from an Ethiopia-wide perspective—with Gulale and Bole suffering medium-level shocks.

5 Analysis of the General Shock on the Urban Economy

The initial findings used OLS regression to analyze and demonstrate that actual cases had a considerable reduced influence on the transaction size of sub-city districts in Addis Ababa. This however did not prevent transactions from recovering in the subsequent years of 2021 and 2022. The cityscape urbanization rate and transaction volume show a significant negative downturn, once the city's lockdown measures were implemented (Table 2). The analysis from the control variables demonstrates that GDP per capita, average disposable income as well as the number of hospitals in use have a downbeat shock on transactions, while communal financial spending, tertiary industries, and internet users have an upbeat shock effect.

However, the outcome of the OLS model may be skewed since an endogenous association among the cityscape urbanization rate and transaction size can exist. An instrumental variable was used to adjust for skewness, that being the birthrate of people during this time. The rates of birth in Addis Abba were chosen because cities traditionally have stricter fertility rates than rural areas and the costs of bringing up children in cities is higher than in countryside communities. As a result, implementing birthrates into the model, enabled any increase in the rate of cityscape

Table 2 Results of the total shock on the urban economy

Variables	Model 1 OLS	Model 2 2OLS	Model 3 LIML	Model 4 GMM
Actual cases	−0.3150*** (0.071)	−0.3120*** (0.082)	−0.3140*** (0.082)	−0.3140*** (0.082)
Actual cases, *t*-test	0.3040*** (0.082)	0.3123*** (0.075)	0.3023*** (0.081)	0.3423*** (0.073)
Cityscape urbanization rate	−0.4201*** (0.101)	2.310*** (0.121)	2.140*** (0.141)	2.230*** (0.101)
Lockdown policy	−0.201*** (0.0351)	−0.253*** (0.0342)	−0.241*** (0.0350)	−0.292*** (0.0380)
Population density	−0.0132 (0.0154)	−0.0329** (0.0118)	−0.0219** (0.0158)	−0.0309** (0.0108)
GDP per capita and disposable income	−0.4091*** (0.2730)	−4.0731*** (0.6371)	−4.0511*** (0.6071)	−4.0701*** (0.651)
Communal spending	0.1438*** (0.0209)	0.0581*** (0.0351)	0.0565*** (0.0301)	0.0549*** (0.0371)
Number of hospitals	−0.0102*** (0.0310)	−0.1034*** (0.0201)	−0.1434*** (0.0211)	−0.1234*** (0.0251)
Constant	15.710*** (1.3401)	41.4561*** (3.1910)	41.809*** (3.2091)	41.909*** (3.259)
R-squared	0.8731	0.8721	0.8721	0.8721

Note: standard errors are shown in parentheses; ***$p < 0.01$, **$p < 0.05$

Table 3 Endogeneity test and validity of instrumental variables

Check aims	Test method	Index	Statistical result	*p*-values
If there are endogenous variables	Hausmann test	Chi-squared	197	0.00
		Robust test for heteroscedasticity	205	0.00
Association test of instrumental variables	Results of the first stage	Populace birth rate	−0.4	0.00
		College students	0.28	0.00
		F-statistics	287.80	0.00
Weak instrumental variable test	Weak instrumental variable test	Least Eigen value	201.87	
		Statistics		
		Cragg-Donald Wald F	214.75	
		Statistics		
		Kleibergen-Paap Wald *F*-statistics	455.23	
Exogenous test of instrumental variables	Critical value of Weak instrumental variable	Critical value of 10%	15.43	
		Critical value of 15%	10.12	
	Over identification test	Hansen J statistics	1.75	0.14

urbanization to have no significant change to the city's economic uptake during the study period. Moreover, the instrumental variable was interrelated with the location of higher education institutions, i.e., colleges and universities in Addis Ababa, which, correspondingly, are frequently located in the outer sub-city districts. Due to the fact that when colleges and universities are operational (i.e., in session), there is economic growth in a number of urban sectors. This could be because colleges and universities draw a large number of learners to their sub-city district which aids in increasing the permanent population and cityscape urbanization rate. Interestingly, COVID-19 emerged during the winter break of the academic calendar so many of the higher education institutions were not in session at the inception of the pandemic. Likewise, after the winter break, a considerable number of college students from outside Addis Ababa were unable to return to the city because of the lockdown measures. Hence, they had no connection to the city's transaction volume during this time. As a result, an additional instrumental variable of the cityscape urbanization rate was chosen, i.e., number of college students. The Hausmann test yielded a *p*-value of zero, showing that the cityscape urbanization rate is an endogenous variable in the model. The two instrumental variables, i.e., birthrate and number of college students, had a strong relation with the rate of cityscape urbanization even though they only weakly passed the endogeneity test and validity test (Table 3). This indicates that they are useful and rational, but the result should be observed with caution.

Table 3 shows the findings of the instrumental variable techniques in columns two through four. The consequences of the tested methods are fairly similar, demonstrating that they are reliable. The results from GMM and LIML using instrumental factors deviate, however, from the OLS findings. Firstly, the rate of cityscape urbanization had a large upbeat shock effect on transaction size, demonstrating that the rate is an imperative determinant of economic growth. The greater the transaction value, the more elevated the rate of cityscape urbanization. Secondly, internet consumers had a downward shock on transaction size, implying that the internet users in the sub-city districts are comparatively low and that online transactions are not actively promoted and not favorable to increased transaction volumes. Thirdly, the number of hospitals had an unfavorable impact on transaction volume, demonstrating that more hospitals did not equate to a higher level of economic growth. These tests augmented the accuracy of the three methods used in the research and evaluated how current conditions and future outlook for Addis Abba could be measured for future shock events.

6 Conclusion

Although Addis Ababa's rapid urbanization has recently yielded a tremendously high influx of people, the city's ability to respond to issues of well-being has fallen short. COVID-19 was a significant shock that negatively affected the city's economy and its residents. This chapter used Addis Ababa's sub-city districts as an example to undertake experimental analyses that associated cityscape urbanization rate and economic growth with the exogenous influence of the pandemic. The findings emphasize two aspects interlinking urbanization and economic outcome. First, the COVID-19 pandemic showed how as cases worsened, economic activities reduced in scale especially districts with the larger and denser populations. Second, it results reveal how, developed tertiary industries and communal spending created better circumstances for economic stability. That being said, in the less urbanized outer sub-city districts, economic activity was better during the first year of the pandemic. Subsequently, the post-pandemic economic recovery of these outer sub-districts is faster when compared to the city center districts. As stated, general department retailers, entertainment, and digital services where not as severely impacted when compared to the health services and tourism sectors. However, the inadequacy and backwardness of internet services hampered the growth of online dealings, so economic growth was mostly superficial from this sector.

From July to December 2020, the cityscape urbanization rate was hardest hit in the sub-city districts of Addis Ketema, Gulale, and Bole. Equally, these districts had the highest cityscape urbanization rate and, unfortunately, have not rebounded as quickly as the outer sub-city districts of Addis Ababa. The reason for this is that in locations with higher urbanization and higher concentrations of people, a higher level of susceptibility was found in combination with the lack of general services. This was worsened by insufficient communal spending and infrastructure along with poor basic health services that were not prepared to respond to the abrupt public health emergency. COVID-19 shed light on how urbanization can quickly become a problem in Ethiopia and around the world. Namely, in Addis Ababa the outbreak pressured authorities to better examine economic shock preparedness by scaling up and promoting economic resilience from not only a top-down perspective, but from grassroots, a bottom-up understanding that builds more effective personal resource reserves and savings to mitigate uncertainty and future shock occurrences. The empirical statistics suggest that COVID-19 had a negative shock on the more urbanized areas, revealing how cities are more vulnerable than less urban communities. Since more verified cases were found in higher urbanized and populated sub-city districts, the 2020 effects of the pandemic in Addis Ababa revealed these districts to have experienced a slower economic recovery in 2021 and 2022. To achieve faster post-pandemic recovery and resilience in the future, cityscape infrastructure needs to be well-ordered and effectively managed. Thus, economic policy should focus on preparedness and diverse mitigation strategies implemented and tailored to resident well-being—starting with the city's most vulnerable inhabitants in the most urbanized areas.

References

1. Pallett SJ, Brown CS, Mughal N et al (2021) Optimising the initial investigation of suspected cases of SARS-CoV-2 reinfection. Travel Med Infect Dis 42:102078. https://doi.org/10.1016/j.tmaid.2021.102078
2. Hoehl S, Rabenau H, Berger A et al (2020) Evidence of SARS-CoV-2 infection in returning travelers from Wuhan, China. N Engl J Med 382:1278–1280. https://doi.org/10.1056/NEJMC2001899
3. World Bank (2020) World development indicators. WDI World Bank. https://datatopics.worldbank.org/world-development-indicators/. Accessed 18 Jul 2022
4. Bell GD, Halpert MS, Kousky VE et al (1999) Climate assessment for 1998. Bull Am Meteorol Soc 80:1040–1040. https://doi.org/10.1175/1520-0477(1999)080<1040:caf>2.0.co;2
5. Kedir AM (2005) Understanding Urban chronic poverty: crossing the qualitative and quantitative divide. SSRN Electron J 30. https://doi.org/10.2139/SSRN.1753687
6. Ohno K (2009) Ethiopia: political regime and development policies. Japan Int Coop Agency, Work Pap 1–30
7. Northam RM (1979) Urban geography. Wiley, New York
8. Liu F, Sun W (2020) Impact of active "organic decentralization population" policy on future urban built-up areas: Beijing case study. Habitat Int 105:102262. https://doi.org/10.1016/J.HABITATINT.2020.102262
9. Greenberg MR (1983) Urbanization and cancer mortality: the United States experience, 1950-1975. Oxford University Press, Oxford
10. Shibata T (1979) Urbanization in Japan. Bull Concern Asian Sch 11:44–57. https://doi.org/10.1080/14672715.1979.10424036
11. Mulugeta E (2008) Urban poverty in Ethiopia: the economic and social adaptations of women. Addis Ababa University Press, Addis Ababa
12. Gans HJ (1993) People, plans, and policies: essays on poverty, racism, and other national urban problems. Columbia University Press, New York
13. Kropko J (2011) New approaches to discrete choice and time-series cross-section methodology for political research CORE view metadata, citation and similar papers at core.ac.uk provided by Carolina Digital Repository. University of North Carolina, Chapel Hill

14. Szreter S (1988) The importance of social intervention in Britain's mortality decline c. 1850–1914: a re-interpretation of the role of public health. Soc Hist Med 1:1–38. https://doi.org/10.1093/SHM/1.1.1
15. Garside PL (2007) "Unhealthy areas": town planning, eugenics and the slums, 1890–1945. Plan Perspect 3:24–46. https://doi.org/10.1080/02665438808725650
16. Wang S, Jia M, Zhou Y, Fan F (2019) Impacts of changing urban form on ecological efficiency in China: a comparison between urban agglomerations and administrative areas. J Environ Plan Manag 63:1834–1856. https://doi.org/10.1080/09640568.2019.1689932
17. Wikimedia Commons (2022) Addis Ababa district map. https://commons.wikimedia.org/wiki/File:Addis_Ababa_district_map.svg. Accessed 22 Jul 2022
18. Google Maps (2022) Google Maps. https://www.google.com/maps/. Accessed 4 Mar 2022
19. MacroTrends (2022) Ethiopia Urban Population 1960-2022. MacroTrends. https://www.macrotrends.net/countries/ETH/ethiopia/urban-population. Accessed 21 Jul 2022
20. UN-Habitat (2020) World cities report 2020: the value of sustainable urbanization. United Nations Human Settlements Programme, Nairobi
21. UN-Habitat (2018) The state of African cities 2018: the geography of African investment. United Nations Human Settlements Programme, Geneva
22. UN-Habitat (2007) State of the world's cities 2010/2011 - cities for all: bridging the urban divide. United Nations Hum. Settlements Program. https://unhabitat.org/state-of-the-worlds-cities-20102011-cities-for-all-bridging-the-urban-divide. Accessed 23 May 2022
23. Abdissa A (2005) Urban expansion and the livelihood of the peri-urban agricultural community: the case of Addis Ababa. Addis Ababa University, Addis Ababa
24. Melese M (2007) City expansion, squatter settlements and policy implications in Addis Ababa: the case of Kolfe Keranio sub-city. Ethiop J Soc Sci Humanit 2:50–79. https://doi.org/10.4314/ejossah.v2i2.29866
25. Gete Z (2007) Draft conceptual framework of RUL thematic research area of GMP. In: Proceedings of a planning workshop on thematic research area of the global mountain program. Addis Ababa University, Addis Ababa, pp 27–44
26. Geda A (2021) The macroeconomic and social impact of COVID-19 in Ethiopia in the global context. UNCTAD, Addis Ababa
27. Alwan KH, Hamden MY, Mahdi WA, Motlak JB (2020) Urban pathology in residential neighborhoods: a case study in Dahana and Qanbar Ali Areas. IOP Conf Ser Mater Sci Eng 745. https://doi.org/10.1088/1757-899X/745/1/012152
28. Simtowe FP (2010) Livelihoods diversification and gender in Malawi. African J Agric Res 5: 204–216. https://doi.org/10.5897/AJAR09.386
29. Bhardwaj G, Esch T, Lall SV et al (2020) Cities, crowding, and the coronavirus. World Bank, Washington, DC
30. Huang Q, Jackson S, Derakhshan S et al (2021) Urban-rural differences in COVID-19 exposures and outcomes in the South: a preliminary analysis of South Carolina. PLoS One 16: e0246548. https://doi.org/10.1371/JOURNAL.PONE.0246548
31. Aguilar J, Bassolas A, Ghoshal G et al (2022) Impact of urban structure on infectious disease spreading. Sci Rep 12:1–13. https://doi.org/10.1038/s41598-022-06720-8
32. Jahan I, Hosen I, Al Mamun F et al (2021) How has the COVID-19 pandemic impacted internet use behaviors and facilitated problematic internet use? A Bangladeshi study. Psychol Res Behav Manag 14:1127–1138. https://doi.org/10.2147/PRBM.S323570
33. Dahiya S, Rokanas LN, Singh S et al (2021) Lessons from internet use and performance during COVID-19. J Inf Policy 11:202–221. https://doi.org/10.5325/JINFOPOLI.11.2021.0202/292023/LESSONS-FROM-INTERNET-USE-AND-PERFORMANCE-DURING
34. De' R, Pandey N, Pal A (2020) Impact of digital surge during Covid-19 pandemic: a viewpoint on research and practice. Int J Inf Manag 55:102171. https://doi.org/10.1016/J.IJINFOMGT.2020.102171

35. Connolly C, Keil R, Ali SH (2020) Extended urbanisation and the spatialities of infectious disease: demographic change, infrastructure and governance. Urban Stud 58:245–263. https://doi.org/10.1177/0042098020910873
36. AACHO (2022) Addis Ababa Data. Addis Ababa City Healthy Office, Addis Ababa
37. UN (2022) World urbanization prospects. United Nations Population Division. https://population.un.org/wup/country-profiles/. Accessed 22 Jul 2022
38. OECD (2022) International trade during the COVID-19 pandemic: Big shifts and uncertainty. Organisation for Economic Cooperation and Development. https://www.oecd.org/coronavirus/policy-responses/international-trade-during-the-covid-19-pandemic-big-shifts-and-uncertainty-d1131663/. Accessed 24 Jul 2022
39. Szczygielski JJ, Bwanya PR, Charteris A, Brzeszczyński J (2021) The only certainty is uncertainty: an analysis of the impact of COVID-19 uncertainty on regional stock markets. Financ Res Lett 43:101945. https://doi.org/10.1016/J.FRL.2021.101945
40. Abdelkafi I, Loukil S, Ben RY (2022) Economic uncertainty during COVID-19 pandemic in Latin America and Asia. J Knowl Econ 1–20. https://doi.org/10.1007/S13132-021-00889-5/TABLES/4
41. Kassahun D (2021) A story map of COVID19 cases in Addis Ababa. Addis Ababa City Administration Health Bureau. https://storymaps.arcgis.com/stories/a7db254fbe1543a0b15164c84bfc0551. Accessed 23 May 2022

Lessons for Sub-Saharan Africa: Using the Development Model from East Asia in Nigeria, 1965–2015

Olajumoke I. Omodara, Giuseppe T. Cirella, and Andrzej Paczoski

1 East Asia and the "Miracle" Development Model

East Asia, known for tremendous growth, has been recognized to have economies that are the most economically and politically effective among the developing world. Development economics, an important component of economics, consequently, has attracted scholars to search for effective public policies to ensure development in developing countries. The field of development economics earnestly started at the close of the Second World War. Since then, economists and policymakers have debated the appropriate role of public policy in developing economies [1]. Triggered by the global integration of world markets, especially in the 1990s, e.g., with entities such as the European Union and the North American Free Trade Agreement, East Asia began to identify itself with miracle economies driven by a particular growth model. This title, however, was dismissed by Krugman [2] where he attributes East Asia's success to high educational achievement, investment in physical capital, and high population work ratio. Khan [3] states "the newly industrializing countries of Asia, like the Soviet Union of the 1950s, have achieved rapid growth in largest part through astonishing mobilization of resources." The development model of East Asia in this chapter refers to the development strategies with public investments in which some profitable economic sectors and underlying economic fundamentals guide economic policymaking. For any single development model to hold, certain conditions must be fulfilled. This chapter explores these conditions and sets the stage for extended, transference research in a sub-Saharan Africa setting.

O. I. Omodara (✉) · G. T. Cirella · A. Paczoski
Faculty of Economics, University of Gdansk, Sopot, Poland
e-mail: gt.cirella@ug.edu.pl; andrzej.paczoski@ug.edu.pl

G. T. Cirella (ed.), *Uncertainty Shocks in Africa*, Advances in African Economic, Social and Political Development, https://doi.org/10.1007/978-3-031-21885-9_2

1.1 East Asia's Development Model

Prominent development economist, Kuznets [4] argues that "any development model must have a particular attribute if it is to be a convincing and operational model." Perkins [5] submits that no single model could describe what the most successful economies in East Asia did to achieve such regional transformation. This misconception was displaced in a World Bank report emphasizing that "there is no single East Asian model of development" [6]. For East Asia, much of the region experienced similar growth features ranging from state intervention through to the creation market-friendly policies, monitoring of market performance, incentives support for domestic industries, management of the finance sector, regional and global economic integration (i.e., leading to increased accumulation of physical and human capital), better allocation of resources, and high export growth. Perkins [7], in his opinion, identifies the export models by state interventionist theory in Japan, Korea, and Taiwan; the free trade barrier and commerce models of Singapore and Hong Kong (i.e., the Hong Kong Special Administrative Region of China and here forth "Hong Kong"); and the models of natural resource endowment in Indonesia, Malaysia, and Thailand, as fundamental to these countries' economic success. Moreover, the successful capitalist ones mentioned by Berger and Hsiao [8], i.e., "Japan, [and] the so called Four Little Dragons, South Korea, Taiwan, Hong Kong, and Singapore and increasingly, at least some of the countries of ASEAN besides Singapore," have distinctive socio-cultural features that highlight entrepreneurialism and the free market system. Johnston [9], Wade [10], and Amsden [11] center on East Asia's growth in terms of regulatory economic policies adopted by governments as key to their success. For example, the important role of the Japanese government to work with its bureaucrats, especially those in the Ministry of International Trade and Industry, to limit corruption and inspire a national work ethic [9, 12]. All told, this explains the institutional model perspective in terms of East Asia's region-centric growth. Figure 1 illustrates the key East Asian countries reviewed in this chapter.

1.2 Sustained Economies, Exogenous and Endogenous Growth, and Institutional Economics

In contrast, Domar [14] and Harrod [15] in their neoclassical view identify sustained economies due to different mechanisms at different development phases. The model classified as "sustained economies" functions through factor accumulation, resulting from increased capital wedges such as physical land, natural resources, and minerals at the early phase [16] and total factor productivity growth engine at the latter phase. Solow [17] argues and classifies labor and capital, as an exogenous model needed for any economic growth which is consistent with the growth model stated by Swan [18]. Solow [19] further adds total factor productivity growth to the capital and labor

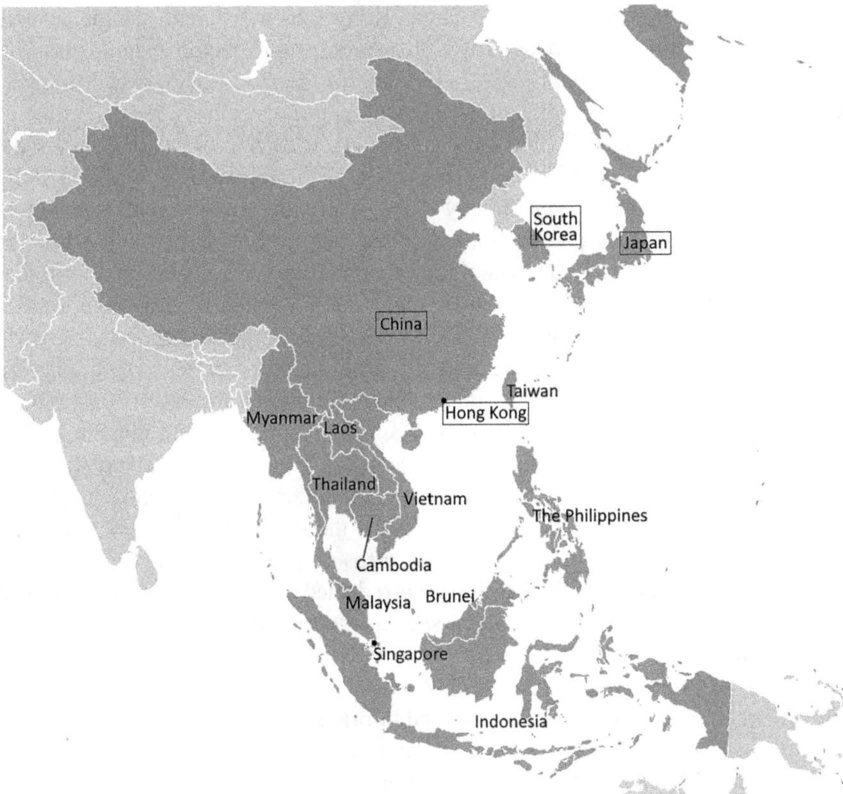

Fig. 1 Reviewed countries' development model in East Asia. Selected comparative assessment from 1965 to 2015 on countries with a box around their name. Source: adapted from Wikimedia Commons [13]

factors, suggesting that a balanced economy with a constant growth rate of capital, output, population, and consumption as the model anew. Conversely, Romar [20] and Lucas [21] suggest an endogenous growth model as improved technological progress and enhanced economic growth through investment in research and development and innovation. Krugman [2], however, argues that this growth can only be attributed to neoclassical growth theory of increases in productivity with an illustration of the Singaporean government and that of Stalin's Soviet Union in the 1950s. As such, most of East Asia's economic growth can be attributed to capital accumulation through high savings instead of technological progress. Krugman [2] points out that, in the long-run, accumulation of capital cannot be sufficient to maintain economic growth, i.e., "the rapid growth in output could be fully explained by rapid growth in inputs: expansion of employment, increases in educational levels, and above all, massive investment in physical capital." Similarly, Young [22] concludes that total factor productivity does not account for the economic growth in East Asia and attributes the rapid economic growth to a highly skilled workforce dating back to the 1960s. This, however, excludes Hong Kong which has had a high positive relationship with growth productivity. "In general, rapid factor accumulation, of both capital and labor, explains the lion's share of the East Asian growth miracle, both in the aggregate economy and in the manufacturing sector" [22].

Drysdale and Huang [23], in contrast to Krugman's labor and capital accumulation factor, attribute the rapid economic growth of the region to high productivity and technological advancement. In any event, while the growth models cannot be singularly attributed to a particular model, this chapter considers many economic growth drivers, particularly on how South Korea rapidly developed, and attributes those growth factors to regional, demographic, human resource, economic, institutional, and social factors since the 1960s. Moreover, an important economic growth trend, worth mentioning at this point, are institutional theories which play an important role in economic development. They emphasize the role of institutions in economies and the development advantage of having secure and reliable institutions that are trusted by the citizenry. Veblen [24] suggests the need to study the culture of the society through mental habits, traditions, norms, and customs to determine the shape and order of institutions of the state. Mitchell [25] and Commons [26] formalize institutional issues by measuring and studying the impact of institutions on the economy. This influence is reflected on the historical conditions of shaping the institutional order in which special attention is paid to economic transactions and related transaction costs. Based on this concept, new institutional economics was created by Coase [27], Alchian and Kessel [28] and Arrow [29] with reference made to transaction costs and information asymmetry in an economy. Williamson [30] and North [31] arrange and develop the problem of transaction costs. North [31] points out the importance of formal and nonformal regulations in shaping the institutional order of the economy, while De Soto [32] emphasizes the importance of property rights as an important factor in the level of institutional development of the economy.

1.3 Learning from East Asia and Moving Outward

Dating back to the 1960s, a leading development textbook ranked Africa's growth potential ahead of East Asia—as a whole [33]. While it is obvious that East Asian countries are experiencing rapid economic growth, sub-Saharan African countries have, regrettably, been experiencing slow, stagnate growth in comparison. Lawrence and Thirtle [34] and Easterly and Levine [33] made comparative analyses to find reasons for growth divergence between Asian and African countries despite similar income levels in the 1960s and found factors such as "ethnic diversity, low schooling, political instability, underdeveloped financial systems, distorted foreign exchange markets, high government deficits, and insufficient infrastructure" [33] as key differences. Collier and Gunning [35] in their study found internally faulty public policy as a factor for growth tragedy in sub-Saharan Africa. Frankel [36] classifies natural resources as the main cause as it often shifts the attention of the economy away from developing other sectors such as manufacturing. However, Presbitero [37] infers some lessons that sub-Saharan Africa could learn from East Asian economies by emphasizing investment in education and human capital, macroeconomic stability, increases in manufactured exports, and equitable and re distributive economic growth. Whilc it is obvious that sub-Saharan Africa, generally, could learn from the export diversification model of East Asian countries, there is still a need to address future economic sustainability through the adoption of aggressive financial policy and proper management of household debt.

This chapter evaluates the "miracle" development model of East Asia, to derive lessons for sub-Saharan Africa's regional economic growth. The idea employs a mixed qualitative and quantitative research method by combining the literature with analyses of official data from reputable databases to present an in-depth understanding of economic growth of the selected subregions. Using a mixed method has the benefit of (1) analyzing the extent of the development and divergence between the two regions and (2) employing theories from economic and social scientific fields with a clear focus on growth, economic, institutional, and social development factors. Considering the broadness of economic activities and large number of countries in the selected subregions, this chapter uses case research from South Korea and Nigeria as representative entities of East Asia and sub-Saharan Africa, respectively. An in-depth look at the economic growth of the subregions between 1965 and 2015, i.e., five decades, is the timeline of the research. This chapter also identifies initial similarities as well as major growth determinants between the two and pieces together the main challenges confronting sub-Saharan Africa's economic growth and draws out applicable lessons for sub-Saharan African countries in regard to growth resilience from East Asia. In addition, suggestions are drawn out to better understand how East Asia has been able to sustain economic growth and what sub-Saharan Africa could do in terms of transparency and innovative advantage. This refers to a proffering of solutions to further develop, promote, and sustain an inclusive economic model of growth and progress in sub-Saharan Africa that has been successfully tried and tested. A breakdown of the subsequent sections are as follows: to review the patterns of East Asia's development model and identify major economic indicators to better understand the contributing economic growth factors, to identify factors of economic growth in South Korea and Nigeria and analyze economic performance over the five-decade timeline of the research (i.e., drawing out lessons for Nigeria), and to discuss how South Korea can further sustain its economic growth in an ever-increasing competitive global market.

2 Key Economic Indicators that Boost Economic Growth in East Asia and Stagnate It in Sub-Sahara Africa

The major economic indicators that contributed to economic growth in East Asia revere around the region's development model and historical top-down decisions that went hand-in-hand with visionary socio-cultural factors. Specifically, an analysis on East Asia's development model is centered on questions that try to identify positive indicators and reasons to how they developed and to the rapidity their development. What model accounted for East Asia's rapid economic growth? Is there a unified East Asia growth model? Why has East Asia succeeded while other subregions from around the world, such as sub-Saharan Africa, have not? What factors have driven the divergence of economic performance between East Asia and other subregions from around the world, including sub-Saharan Africa? These questions date back to East Asia's post-war persistence, its year-on-year economic growth championed by Japan, South Korea, Taiwan, Singapore, Hong Kong, and China—i.e., popularly referred to as economies that transformed independence to industrialization, and the subregion's ability to incorporate and engage its population with effective public policies. Comparatively, sub-Saharan Africa is considered among those with growth potential but faces underutilization of economic growth with inappropriate public policies that attribute poor economic performance and growth.

Historically, East Asia and sub-Sahara Africa were predicted of having a high tendency of population growth prior to the Second World War. It is well documented that different trends of population growth over the last 50 years shows two different growth models. In most cases, both subregions increased in population, however, on a year-on-year basis selected East Asian countries have decreased this rate significantly, i.e., China having the highest recorded average population growth of 92.7% over the five decades, while Japan, South Korea, and Hong Kong average 28%, 75%, and 90%, respectively. Contrariwise, sub-Saharan African countries continue to boost their population at increasing rates over the same period, i.e., Nigeria—251%, Zimbabwe—261%, Malawi—322%, and Kenya—383% (Table 1).

Rent seeking, the practice of manipulating public policy or economic conditions as a strategy for increasing profit, is another important indicator that dominated the two regions' economic activities before the start of the growth in East Asia. Specifically, rent seeking enables individuals and institutions to make money from natural resources and land, neither adding value nor contributing to society. In most cases, it is neither immoral literarily or illegal, but it does hinder local productivity and economic growth. Nonetheless, in East Asia, it can be said to have overcome the rent seeking syndrome on their way to genuine industrialization, while the problem has, generally, degenerated into blackmail and social crimes such as kidnapping and terrorism in many parts of sub-Saharan Africa, particularly in Nigeria. Similarly, the state of social and economic infrastructure in the early 1960s was very poor in both East Asia and sub-Saharan Africa, respectively. For example, the Korean War of 1950–1953 led to the destruction of major roads, sea and airports, power systems,

Table 1 Historical population change of selected East Asian and sub-Saharan African countries, 1965–2015

	1965	1975	1985	1995	2005	2015
East Asia						
South Korea	28,392,722	34,713,078	40,501,917	44,652,994	47,605,863	50,293,439
	2.52	2.00	1.58	0.77	0.60	0.49
Japan	97,341,852	110,804,519	119,988,663	124,483,305	126,978,754	126,573,481
	1.03	1.33	0.69	0.36	0.20	−0.12
Hong Kong	3,801,814	4,355,301	5,414,790	6,144,498	6,842,465	7,287,983
	4.33	1.93	1.39	1.18	0.17	0.83
China	706,590,947	905,580,445	1,052,622,410	1,227,841,281	1,305,600,630	1,376,048,943
	1.86	2.29	1.48	1.24	0.55	0.52
Sub-Saharan Africa						
Nigeria	50,238,569	63,565,598	83,901,570	108,424,822	139,611,303	182,201,962
	2.13	2.52	2.63	2.55	2.59	2.71
Zimbabwe	4,422,132	6,170,284	8,862,601	11,683,136	12,984,418	15,602,751
	3.34	3.46	3.99	2.19	0.76	2.23
Malawi	4,058,680	5,292,816	7,205,635	9,822,812	12,747,846	17,215,232
	2.32	2.83	3.17	0.86	2.64	3.11
Kenya	9,504,702	13,486,241	19,660,713	27,373,035	35,349,040	46,050,302
	3.24	3.69	3.86	3.15	2.62	2.69

Note: *top* figure is population and *bottom* figure is percentage change
Source: World Bank [38]

Fig. 2 Capital cities in Nigeria and South Korea in the 1960s: (*top left*) tram and minibus in Soeul, South Korea, in 1966, (*top right*) busy street near the center of Soeul, South Korea, in 1965, (*bottom left*) start of the expressway Ikorodu Road, Lagos, Nigeria, in 1960, and (*bottom right*) Tinubu Square, Lagos, Nigeria, in 1960. Source: (*top left* and *top right*) Photographs by Stephen Dreher at Quora, Creative Commons Public Domain; (*bottom left* and *bottom right*) photographs by Slimthugchimee at Nairaland, Creative Commons Public Domain

and even schools, hospitals, and prisons in South Korea. Since then, South Korea has demonstrated an impressive record of economic performance. Much of its success stems from a commitment to infrastructure development. On the other hand, Nigeria remains in shortage of both social and economic infrastructure investment traced to the then Biafran War, persistent systemic corruption, lack of local know-how, and uncommitted government Fig. 2 illustrates a similar level of infrastructure between the capital cities of South Korea and Nigeria in the 1960s—noting the development in Lagos, as modestly, better than Seoul.

In terms of gross domestic product (GDP), differences in economic activity between East Asia and sub-Saharan Africa between 1965 and 2015 indicates several multiplier effects in East Asia not seen in sub-Saharan Africa. GDP, an indicator of how countries maximize their available potential, is a monetary measure of the market value of all the final goods and services produced over certain a period—usually per year. Economic performance in East Asia and sub-Saharan African as first glance appear to be positive in both subregions; however, the volume at which GDP productivity is multiplied, considering the available potential including population, differs between the two (Table 2). Examining change in GDP growth in combination with the decreasing percentage growth in population of East Asian countries, it is evident that their GDP continues to go up exponentially—due to an upward trend in industrialization advancement. Nominal GDP values of South Korea, Japan, and China moved from billions to trillions of dollars. In South Korea, for instance, the economy grew from USD 3 billion in 1965 to USD 1 trillion in 2015. The exponential growth in GDP in the selected East Asian countries indicates maximum efficiency compared to what happened in the selected sub-Saharan African ones despite their enormous natural and human resources. Even with similar economic and social structures from the 1960s and 1970s, sub-Saharan Africa experienced slow and stagnated economic growth thereafter. As such, until 2005, no country in the sub-Saharan Africa was able to grow GDP above a half trillion dollars, including Nigeria, i.e., the largest economy on the continent (Fig. 3).

A closer look at the nominal GDP per capita, i.e., a factor closely related to the average income, purchasing power parity, and access to money by individuals, indicates how the general welfare of a society fares in terms of economic performance. Often this indicator is related to a country's standard of living, even though, GDP per capita is not a measure of personal income. Clearly, positive effects of the huge economic growth in East Asia show as surge in GDP per capita over time and, hence, continuous improvement in standard of living. On the other hand, sub-Saharan Africa, with increasing population and stagnate economic growth, has many citizens living in poverty (Table 3).

3 Patterns of East Asia's Development Model: Case of South Korea

As one of the world economic powers, South Korea remains the twelfth largest economy globally and continues to be in the limelight as one of a handful of developing countries that have adjusted successfully to both the oil shocks of the 1970s and the debt shock of the early 1980s—partly due to its export-oriented growth model. South Korea's economic growth strategy shifted from import dominated to an export-oriented economy dating back to as early as 1960, yielding a tremendous positive impact to the growth of the country. Its economy which was categorized as one of the world's poorest at the end of Second World War, moved to become globally recognized as a developed economy after proper implementation of export promotion policy [10, 23, 39]. Between 1965 and 2015, South Korea has transformed GDP via continuous growth from expansion of industrial goods, manufacturing goods, and increased exportation of locally made goods. Prior to the country pursuing an export-oriented economic agenda, deficit trade balance was

Table 2 Record of nominal GDP (USD) (*top*) and GDP growth rate (annual %) (*bottom*) of selected East Asian and sub-Saharan African countries, 1965–2015

	1965	1975	1985	1995	2005	2015
East Asia						
South Korea	3,017,614,366	22,797,520,661	103,729,914,254	559,329,547,369	898,137,194,716	1,377,873,107,856
	5.2	7.3	7.5	8.9	3.9	2.6
Japan	90,950,278,257	512,861,437,158	1,384,532,251,034	5,449,116,304,981	4,755,410,630,912	4,383,076,298,081
	5.8	3.1	6.3	2.7	1.7	1.2
Hong Kong	2,435,078,534	10,048,022,369	35,699,543,050	144,652,912,433	181,570,082,162	309,234,500,374
	14.6	0.5	0.8	2.4	7.4	2.4
China	70,436,266,146	163,431,551,779	309,486,394,557	734,548,001,963	2,285,965,854,313	11,064,664,793,255
	17.0	8.7	13.4	10.9	11.4	6.9
Sub-Saharan Africa						
Nigeria	5,874,422,511	27,778,934,624	28,873,977,228	28,546,958,641	112,248,353,104	486,792,837,970
	4.9	−5.2	8.3	−0.3	3.4	2.7
Zimbabwe	1,311,435,800	4,371,300,700	5,637,259,300	7,111,270,700	5,755,215,200	14,419,185,900
	4.9	−1.9	6.9	0.2	−5.7	0.5
Malawi	229,460,183	613,196,872	1,131,349,992	1,397,454,122	3,655,892,941	6,403,820,949
	13.6	6.1	4.6	16.7	3.3	2.8
Kenya	997,919,319	3,259,344,935	6,135,034,338	9,046,326,059	18,737,895,401	63,398,041,540
	2.0	0.9	4.3	4.4	5.9	5.6

Source: World Bank [38]

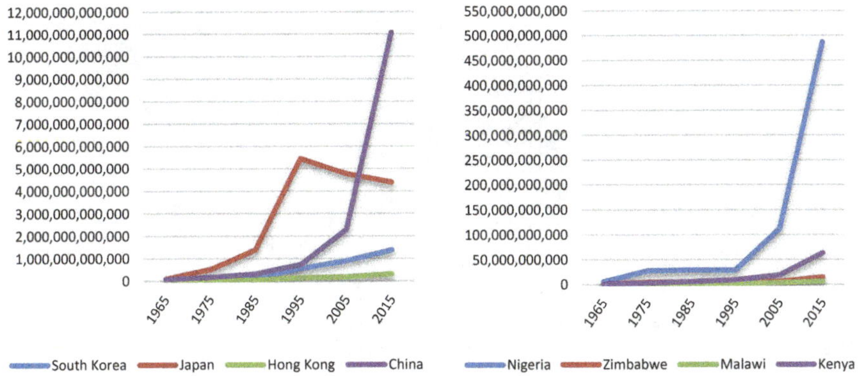

Fig. 3 GDP growth of selected East Asian and sub-Saharan African countries, 1965–2015. Source: World Bank [38]

Table 3 Record of nominal GDP per capital (USD) of selected East Asian and sub-Saharan African countries, 1965–2015

	1965	1975	1985	1995	2005	2015
East Asia						
South Korea	105.13	646.17	2542.04	12,403.91	18,657.52	27,221.52
Japan	919.78	4581.57	11,465.73	43,440.37	37,217.65	34,523.70
Hong Kong	676.81	2252.11	6542.93	23,497.49	26,649.75	42,327.84
China	98.49	178.34	294.46	609.66	1753.42	8069.21
Sub-Saharan Africa						
Nigeria	116.93	437.01	344.14	263.29	804.01	2671.72
Zimbabwe	296.56	708.44	636.07	608.68	443.24	924.14
Malawi	56.54	115.85	157.01	142.27	286.79	371.99
Kenya	104.99	241.68	312.05	330.48	530.08	1376.71

Source: World Bank [38]

noticed in foreign trade until 1985. However, the country moved to a surplus trade balance regime as a result of increased exportation of locally made goods that went up by 37%, i.e., from 8% in 1965 to 45% in 2015, while imports swelled by only 23%, i.e., from 16% to 39% [38]. Likewise, industrial and manufacturing sector contribution to nominal GDP grew from 21% to 38% and 14% to 30%, respectively. Meanwhile, contribution of the agriculture sector, i.e., the main source of country's primary goods to GDP fell drastically in the five-decade review (Table 4).

Inflation is a crucial macroeconomic indicator. South Korea maintained a positive growth, persistently achieving a reduction in the general price levels in its economy. Inflation which is simply the GDP deflators was relatively unstable until 1982. As such, inflation in South Korea reached a record high of 33% in 1964, 30% in 1974, 24% in 1975 and 1980, respectively. On the other hand, a new trend began in 1982 when the inflation suddenly dropped from a two-digit figure of 17% in 1981 to a single-digit figure of 6%. South Korea has maintained, globally, one of the relative

Table 4 South Korea economic snapshot, 1965–2015

Indicator	1965	1975	1985	1995	2005	2015
Nominal GDP (USD)	3,017,614,366	22,797,520,661	103,729,914,254	559,329,547,369	898,137,194,716	1,377,873,107,856
Inflation, GDP deflator (annual %)	6.42	24.42	4.21	7.46	1.03	2.21
Industry, value added (% of GDP)	21.31	27.39	36.10	38.38	37.50	37.98
Manufacturing, value added (% of GDP)	14.32	20.26	25.23	25.34	28.28	29.49
Agriculture, value added (% of GDP)	39.36	25.39	12.51	5.82	3.15	2.31
Trade (% of GDP)	24.22	58.64	59.01	54.32	71.18	84.84
Imports of goods and services (% of GDP)	15.92	33.33	29.23	27.66	34.37	38.94

Source: World Bank [38]

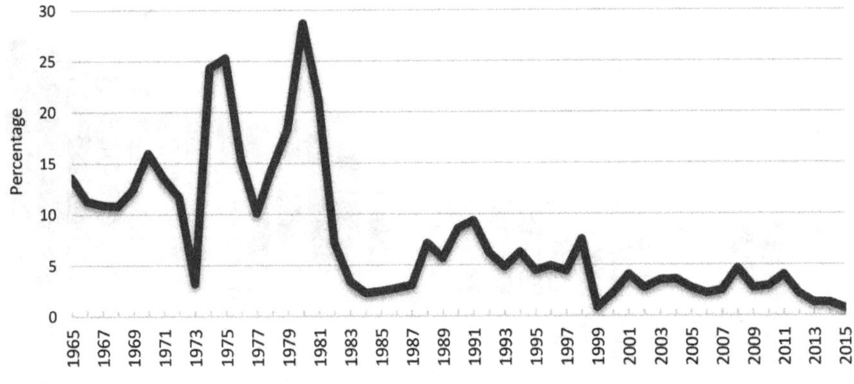

Fig. 4 South Korea inflation profile, 1965–2015. Source: World Bank [38]

lowest single-digit inflation rates for over 35 years (i.e., from 1982) with an all-time record low of −1% in 1999 (Fig. 4).

Domestic demand is the sum of household, government, and firm expenditure, i.e., respectively called consumption, public expenditure, and investment, also saw an aggregate domestic consumption in South Korea fall over the five-decade review. In 1965, approximately 92% of South Korea's GDP originated from domestic demand with household demand at 82%, while government consumption accounted for only 10%. Despite the trend of a huge increase in GDP per capita, total domestic consumption fell from 92% of GDP in 1965 to 65% in 2015. This accounted for a sharp reduction in household consumption from 82% to 49% of GDP from 1965 to 2015, respectively. As such, in 1990, South Korea's public debt represented only 13.4% of total GDP, while in 2014, the debt value jumped to approximately 35.9%, and a 1.9% rise to 37.8% in 2015. South Korea had a total debt of about USD 102.5 billion in 2002 which rose to over USD 480 billion in 2015, representing over an increase of 371% within a 12-year period. When compared with Japan, the United States, France, and the United Kingdom, where public debt to GDP was as high as 261%, 93.6%, 102%, and 103.7% in 2015 and some of the most developed economies in the world, respectively, according to the Organization for Economic Co-operation and Development (OECD) [40], with total debt less than 40% of total GDP, South Korea is still considered a financially stable country [41]. That being said, the World Bank considers any country with public debt less than 48% of GDP as a low-risk case, however, the rate of South Korea's public debt growth in the five-decade review is alarming. Nevertheless, its external debt position is still strong. Total foreign debt amounts to around 40% of GDP and around 65% of total current account receipts. Short-term foreign debt amounts to about one-third of total foreign debt (Fig. 5). As an instrument that enables South Korea to successfully divert a large portion of available resources to the leading sector [i.e., its heavy and chemical industry (HCI)], it supports the positive result of the export market which can be said to devalue the South Korean won.

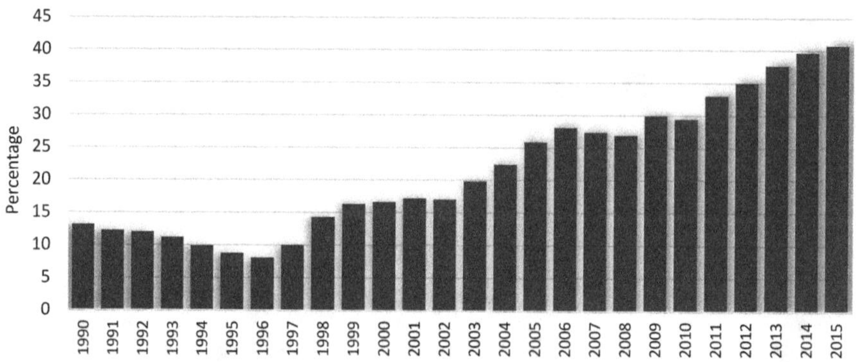

Fig. 5 South Korea total foreign debt as a percentage of GDP, 1990–2015. Source: FRED Economic Data [42]

Qualitatively, after analyzing South Korea's economic performance over the five-decade period, sound leadership, economic diversification through a shift from traditional import substitution policies to export-oriented ones (i.e., to support development of local manufacturing through various incentives), and promotion of all forms of export without distinguishing commodities from other exports are evident. The protection of the domestic market, i.e., to create competitive secondary or capital and technology-intensive manufacturing goods, is to progress to achieve a second phase that focuses on light industries and HCI as a third phase via export promotion policies. As such, South Korea adopted a number of pronounced fiscal and financial measures that pilot this change even today. Figure 6 exhibits some of the modern-day advances that highlight South Korea's prosperity and development. The export measures of South Korea comprise of tax incentives, financial incentives, establishment of free trade zones, and supporting organizations (Table 5). South Korea employs other critical complementary policies that also create investment-friendly environment and organizational measures to reinforce its export-oriented economy. Some of the major policies include free trade zones, exchange rate devaluation, and formation of organizations to further liberalized the economy in order increase the flow of foreign investment which drives export performance.

Moreover, South Korea's exports are dominated by merchandise exports and have grown from USD 173 million in value to USD 526 billion, representing 304,383% growth between 1965 and 2015. The country's exports consist of merchandise exports, commercial services, information and communication technology (ICT) services, and goods and services. Merchandise, being the leading exporting sector, comprises manufactured goods, ore and metal, food, and agricultural produce. However, manufacturing (i.e., led by high-technology goods) recorded major positive growth from 18% of merchandise to 90%. Equally, during the same period, commercial service exports which cover travel services, transport services, ICT, and insurance and financial services achieved growth of 1603%. In addition to commercial service, exports of ICT services from South Korea surged rapidly from USD

Fig. 6 Examples of modernization in Seoul, South Korea: (*top left*) integrated blue green development within the city center, (*top right*) vibrant and clean marketplace, (*middle*) perspective of the city atop Namsan Mountain exhibiting the vastness and order of the city's development, (*bottom left*) GPS bike-sharing system, and (*bottom right*) one of the many urban green-friendly parks entrenched within the city. Source: Photographs by Giuseppe T. Cirella, September 29, 2018

881 million in 1965 to USD 1.4 billion in 2015, showing approximately a 2406% increase (Fig. 7).

Increasing government expenditure on various human development incentives also accounted for the successful economic growth in South Korea. Based on World Bank data, total government investment surge from approximately USD 307 million (i.e., 3.27% of the total GDP) in 1970 to USD 60.1 billion (i.e., 4.6%) in 2013. This investment represents a total growth of 19,478% over 44 years. With a population of

Table 5 Incentives offered and supportive measures for investors in South Korea

Incentives offered for investors by the central government	
Offered	**Hi-tech businesses**
Tax reduction and exemption	• Tax reduction or exemption for 5–7 years
Land support	• Rent reduced by 50–100%
Cash grant	• Not less than 5% of the investment amount
Other support	• Employment subsidy • Education and training subsidy
Supportive measures for foreign investors taken by the Seoul Metropolitan government	
Offered	**Foreign investment company:** 1. Industry support service and high-degree technology business 2. Businesses in standalone type foreign investment zones (e.g., tourism)
Tax reduction and exemption	Income tax: • 100% for 5 years after income creation • 50% for next 2 years Acquisition and registration tax: • 100% for 10 years after income creation • 50% for next 5 years Property tax: • 100% for 5 years after income creation • 50% for next 2 years
Cash grant	• Businesses providing industrial services; hi-tech businesses; businesses building new facilities or expanding existing facilities in parts and material sectors • Employing a large number of employees (i.e., 50–300) • Employing permanent research employees (i.e., 5 or more) • Up to 50% of foreign direct investment amount
Training subsidy and employment subsidy	• Foreign investment ratio shall be over 30% • Regular worker should be over 20, USD 902 per person for 6 months, and limited to a total of USD 180,000 per company
Small and medium-sized enterprise fostering fund	• Businesses providing industrial services; hi-tech businesses; businesses engaging in knowledge-related services in manufacturing (i.e., up to 8 years and up to USD 1,739,000)
Support for fostering environment conducive to foreign investors	Business and operational expenses • Projects for the formation of foreigners' villages • Construction of infrastructure facilities designed to foster an environment suited to foreigners' everyday lives • Construction and operation of facilities related to improvement of the FDI environment
Biomedical fund	• Prestigious bio-businesses (i.e., domestic and foreign)
Research and development-related cash support	• Provision of research expenses on a selective basis for domestic university research institutes launching research institutes in Seoul jointly with world-famous counterparts

(continued)

Table 5 (continued)

	• Promotion of the Industrial Education and Industry Academic Co-operation Act

Source: Invest Soeul [43]

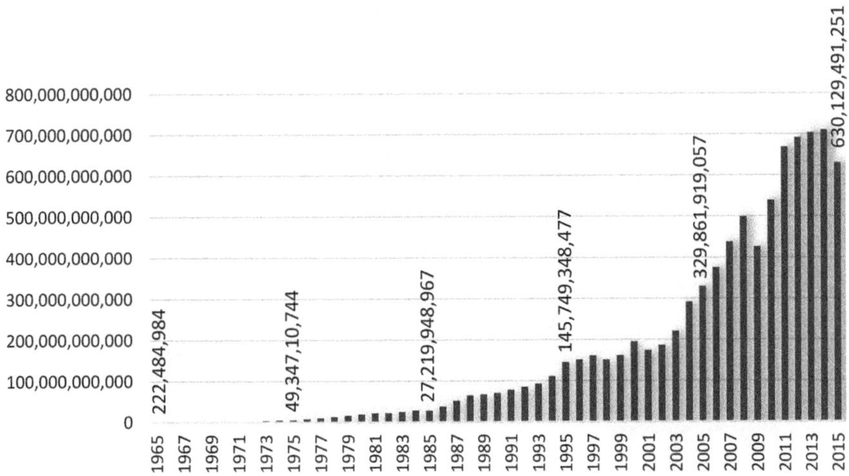

Fig. 7 South Korea export performance (USD), 1965–2015. Source: World Bank [38]

32.2 million and 50.2 million in 1970 and 2013, respectively, the surge in education investment indicates that government education expenditure was high while the population only grew by 55.76%.

4 Economy Appraisal of Nigeria and Lessons from South Korea

For a comparative analysis, GDP per capita in South Korea in 1965 was on USD 105.13 representing only 89% of that of Nigeria which was USD 116.93 per annual. Surprisingly, by 2015 South Korea GDP per capita grew to USD 27,221.52 per year, meaning 1000% above that of Nigeria that only grew to USD 2671.72 over same period. It is important to reiterate that Nigeria and South Korea shared the same socioeconomic features in the 1960s as previously narrated even with more potential for growth such as natural resources, population, and sufficient arable farmland in favor of Nigeria. However, how South Korea rapidly and consistently grew requires a critical breakdown of other developing nations at the time. An economic snapshot of Nigeria is presented in Table 6; this can be compared with South Korea's economic snapshot in Table 4.

Table 6 Nigeria economic snapshot, 1965–2015

Indicator	1965	1975	1985	1995	2005	2015
Nominal GDP (USD)	5,874,422,511	27,778,934,624	28,873,977,228	28,546,958,641	112,248,353,104	486,792,837,970
Inflation, GDP deflator (annual %)	0.86	23.50	5.54	113.08	22.02	2.86
Industry, value added (% of GDP)	–	–	29.86	46.02	43.51	20.38
Manufacturing, value added (% of GDP)	–	–	9.46	5.45	2.83	9.53
Agriculture, value added (% of GDP)	–	–	39.21	32.06	32.76	20.86
Trade (% of GDP)	26.91	41.17	25.90	59.77	50.75	21.45
Imports of goods and services (% of GDP)	16.02	22.83	8.51	24.01	19.09	10.79
Exports of goods and services (% of GDP)	10.89	18.34	17.39	35.76	31.66	10.66

Source: World Bank [38]

Table 7 Natural resources rent performance in Nigeria, 1970–2015

Indicator	1970	1975	1985	1995	2005	2015	% growth
Forest rents (% of GDP)	0.02	0.02	0.01	0.00	0.00	0.03	26.66
Oil rents (% of GDP)	1.64	1.94	2.62	8.11	2.17	1.32	(19.32)
Natural gas rents (% of GDP)	–	20.24	30.64	27.27	30.20	3.03	(85.01)
Coal rents (% of GDP)	1.64	1.94	2.62	8.11	2.17	1.32	(19.32)

Source: World Bank [38]

Despite Nigeria's huge local market and openness to regional and global markets, declining growth rate in major sectors indicates neglects and underutilization of the country's human and natural resources. Industry and agriculture value added to the percentage of GDP, i.e., as a measure of productivity, surprisingly depleted by −31.7% and −46.8% in the five-decade review. No wonder the country is ranked among the world's poorest. Nigeria's manufacturing only recorded 0.78% growth between 1965 and 2015, and the country only relies on importation of both primary and secondary goods to bridge the gap of shortages in local production. The collapse of agriculture, manufacturing, and industrial sectors forced Nigeria to depend solely on income from natural resources. Over the reviewed timeline, only forest rent recorded positive contributions to GDP. Nigeria's rents earnings from oil, natural gas, and coal which are the main stay of the economy have been deteriorating. They grew very significantly between 1970 and 2010, but dropped drastically since 2011 after persistence fall in global commodities price and advancement in energy transition to clean technology all over the world (Table 7).

Macroeconomic policy (i.e., monetary, fiscal, exchange rate, etc.) are primarily the vehicles to achieve economic growth and development within a stable and competitive market environment around the world. Various academic works attribute Nigeria's economic issues to factors such as political, security, diverse cultural, corruption, and poor infrastructural problems [44–49]. Nonetheless, for the purpose of learning specifically from South Korea's rapid economic growth, this chapter narrows the challenges. Underdevelopment and the financial market in Nigeria (i.e., with its very limited size) is unstable and continues to deepen in terms of inefficiency to mobilize savings and redirect them to the most needed. Thus, profitable investment such as domestic financing of startups of all ranges (i.e., small, medium, and large), project financing, and even government financing becomes difficult and frustrating due to increasing interest rates. For example, a critical examination of capital market valuation in Nigeria and South Korea in the 10-year period of 2004 to 2014 saw South Korea's market capitalization surge greatly from approximately USD 423 billion to USD 1.2 trillion, covering up to 56% and 89% of GDP in the respective years. Meanwhile, Nigeria market capitalization grew from USD 15.8 billion to USD 49.7 billion, representing 18% and 10% of GDP in the same period, respectively. The value of Nigeria's market capitalization stood at an average of 5% of that of South Korea annually (Table 8). Likewise, the sharp and continuous lower interest rate (i.e., lending rate) serves as another advantage of the stable financial market that encourages investment borrowing in South Korea, which is contrary to

Table 8 Market capitalization of listed domestic companies in South Korea and Nigeria, 2004–2014

	South Korea		Nigeria	
Year	Current USD	% of GDP	Current USD	% of GDP
2004	428,325,580,000	56.00	15,865,940,000	18.06
2005	718,010,710,000	79.94	22,244,000,000	19.82
2006	834,404,280,000	82.47	32,830,510,000	22.57
2007	1,122,606,330,000	99.99	84,894,570,000	51.00
2008	470,797,680,000	46.98	48,062,280,000	23.10
2009	834,596,860,000	92.53	32,223,400,000	19.01
2010	1,091,911,460,000	99.76	50,546,400,000	13.77
2011	996,139,920,000	82.84	39,028,390,000	9.55
2012	1,179,419,470,000	96.45	56,205,200,000	12.30
2013	1,234,548,550,000	94.56	80,609,900,000	15.85
2014	1,212,759,460,000	85.93	62,766,310,000	11.48
2015	1,231,199,760,000	89.36	49,973,880,000	10.27

Source: World Bank [38]

the situation in Nigeria, where the lending rate keeps going up due to scarcity of funds thereby discouraging investment.

In the case of Nigeria, political instability led to frequent change in fiscal and monetary policies resulting to the introduction of several unsuccessfully implemented policies which remain a major obstacle to economic growth in Nigeria and other sub-Saharan countries. This problem is accompanied by resource wastage, poor infrastructure, and high-country risk for businesses which impact negatively on foreign investments and real sector development (Fig. 8). That being said, the effectiveness of economic systems in these countries and the disproportions that occur in them can be related to institutional order. The regulatory order created by institutions as well as enforcement regulations can be assessed by the level of corruption and the size of the shadow economy [50–52]. The effectiveness of the institutional order is manifested in economic freedom, the rule of law, respect for private property rights, and political sovereignty (e.g., democracy) [53–55]. The high level of corruption and the size of the shadow economy usually prove to be a weakness of the economic institutions. In this case, presently Nigeria is a country with a higher degree of corruption and has a larger shadow economy as a share of its total economy. On the other hand, South Korea is not a country burdened with corruption and has a smaller shadow economy. Interestingly, data on South Korea's shadow economy over the period 1991–2015 does reveal its level of shadow economy percentage of GDP decreased from about 30% to less than 20%, respectively. In Nigeria, over the same period, the level of the shadow economy has consistently remained over 50%. Moreover, in terms of corruption, South Korea ranks much better, i.e., it has a relatively low level of corruption in comparison to Nigeria—i.e., one of the most corrupt countries in the world (Table 9). In addition, poor productivity of human resources in every sector of Nigeria's economy cannot

Fig. 8 Examples of resource wastage, poor infrastructure, and high-country risk from real sector development in Ota, Ogun, Nigeria: (*top left*) poor bridge infrastructure, (*top middle*) dilapidated electricity transformer, (*top right*) regularly flooded internal road, (*bottom left*) overflowing waste on urban road, and (*bottom right*) abandoned service station due to poor road conditions. Source: Photographs by Olajumoke I. Omodara, July 31, 2022

Table 9 Shadow economy percentage of GDP (*top*) and Corruption Index ranking (*bottom*) of South Korea and Nigeria, 1991–2015

	1991	1995	2000	2005	2010	2015
South Korea	29.13	27.48	27.50	26.03	22.97	19.83
	–	48	48	40	41	43
Nigeria	56.95	62.21	57.90	55.84	52.80	52.49
	–	90	90	152	143	136

Source: Global Economy [56] and Transparency International [57]

be separated from inadequate human capacity development. Nigeria's Human Development Index value for 2015 is 0.527—which put the country in the low human development category—positioning it at 152 out of 188 countries and territories [58] (Table 10).

The experience of a resilient economy and social transformation of South Korea serves as an encouraging model for other developing countries of the world,

Table 10 Sectors of South Korea and Nigeria, 1965 and 2015

Indicator	Country	1965	2015	% growth
Industry, value added (% of GDP)	South Korea	21.31	37.98	78.22
	Nigeria	29.86	20.38	(31.74)
Manufacturing, value added (% of GDP)	South Korea	14.32	29.49	105.88
	Nigeria	9.46	9.53	0.78
Agriculture, value added (% of GDP)	South Korea	39.36	2.31	(94.13)
	Nigeria	39.21	20.86	(46.80)
Imports of goods and services (% of GDP)	South Korea	15.92	38.94	144.64
	Nigeria	16.02	10.79	(32.63)
Exports of goods and services (% of GDP)	South Korea	8.30	36.81	343.38
	Nigeria	10.89	10.66	(2.17)

Source: World Bank [38]

particularly Nigeria. When we consider how South Korea committed its industrial upgrading from light industry to HCI, it successfully transited the country's labor force from initial subsistence sectors to advanced industrial ones. For developing subregions, like sub-Saharan Africa, an ability to uphold strong fiscal discipline, low public debt, and financial prudency and accountability as in South Korea's development model is debatable for each country's future. Developing countries, through planning and policy, must first evaluate if such a model is suitable and viable and then ascertain if aspects of such a model can be integrated and achieved within an appropriate timeframe.

5 Conclusion

The East Asian development model has no doubt been dismantled as imperfect by scholars alike [59–63]. Nonetheless, economic growth in the East Asian region has been achieved through increased labor force, investment in capital, export led growth, and technological advancement, as well as investment in research and development, an efficient market system, and proactive government implementation of various developmental and reform policies suitable to each country. Moreover, a development focus was separately determined by socioeconomic values and culture throughout the region. This chapter attributes the development model of East Asia primarily through the case of South Korea. In a general sense, this has meant supporting investment in education to enhance human capital. Education has no doubt a large effect on economic growth as it helps in innovation, new ideas, efficient productivity, and critical thinking for positive values in terms of development economics. This manner of thinking improved the region's competency, comparative advantage, and increased productivity, in turn, leading to economic growth. In addition, it can be recognized that the effective role of industrialization in South Korea aided in its economic transformation and development strategy.

Specifically, the Korean government shared in investment risk by reducing all forms of trade barriers and giving maximum support to private investors to increase market competitive performance, on a global scale, with adequate supervision of the financial sectors. As a result, the South Korean economy grew rapidly from its industrialization policies, interlinking with its OECD membership, by integrating aspects of its trade economy into its development model. Nigeria's economy, on the other hand, though recording positive economic growth from 1965 to 2015, was slow and stagnate. In 2015, South Korea's GDP per capita grew to USD 27,221.52 per year, i.e., 1000% above Nigeria's USD 2671.72, over the period of review. Overall, sectoral performance of Nigeria's economy has not been impressive despite the natural resources advantage over South Korea.

In regard to what led to the inadequate, overall, economic performance of Nigeria, this chapter points out factors such as lack of development of financial markets (i.e., with very limited size and instability), consistently boosted inefficiency of the market to mobilize savings. Also, political instability which often cause change in fiscal and monetary policies resulted in unsuccessful implementation of them, thereby altering economic growth of the country and sub-Saharan Africa at large. Moreover, poor productivity of human resources in every sector of the economy cannot be overlooked as this is chiefly caused by inadequate human capacity development. It is worth noting that the level of development of South Korea and other OECD countries is based on the foundations of efficient institutions and the regulations they create. The challenge for Nigeria should be to improve the functioning of institutions conducive to the economic and social system. The high level of corruption and the shadow economy in Nigeria requires clean-up and change in this area. As such, this chapter concludes that the experience of a resilient economy and even the social transformation of South Korea, especially its transition from being an aid receiver to aid giver, serves as hope for other developing countries. This can be achieved if countries are able to diversify their economies, improve domestic labor force skills (e.g., through enhanced research and development), innovate and advance ICT, and implement sound institutional policies capable of adequately supervising and maintaining stable financial and healthy fiscal policies. For the continued sustainable economic growth of South Korea, this work further suggests the need for further diversification of the economy to develop underperforming sectors, and to raise domestic demand and other sources of income. Developing other sectors of the economy and increasing domestic demand will serve as a security measure for the economy and protect it from potential global market shocks, e.g., the COVID-19 crisis. To end, the research work suggests strengthening budgetary control to improve fiscal solvency. Maintaining a low external debt profile will also reduce government expenditure on debt servicing and, thus, continue to boost the country's image as a stable and relatively risk-free economy, inducing further investment. The work suggests restructuring and optimization of trade through reduction in imports, and exports expansion for more efficient trade balance. Finally, as East Asia enters a new phase of Chinese dominance, sub-Saharan Africa's reliance on and support from China may offer alternate opportunities as African countries veer towards the African Union's Agenda 2063 and its blueprint and master plan to transform Africa into a future global powerhouse.

References

1. Page J (1994) The East Asian miracle: four lessons for development policy, New York
2. Krugman P (1994) The myth of Asia's miracle. Foreign Aff 73:62. https://doi.org/10.2307/20046929
3. Khan HA (2004) Interpreting East Asian growth and innovation: the future of miracles. Palgrave Macmillan
4. Kuznets PW (1988) An East Asian model of economic development: Japan, Taiwan, and South Korea. Econ Dev Cult Change 36:S11–S43. https://doi.org/10.1086/EDCC.36.S3.1566537
5. Perkins DH (2013) East Asian development: foundations and strategies. Harvard University Press, Cambridge
6. World Bank (1993) The East Asian miracle: economic growth and public policy. World Bank Group, Washington, DC
7. Perkins DH (1994) There are at least three models of East Asian development. World Dev 22: 655–661. https://doi.org/10.1016/0305-750X(94)90120-1
8. Berger PL, Hsiao H-HM (1988) In search of an East Asian development model. Transaction Books, Oxford
9. Johnston C (1982) MITI and the Japanese miracle, the growth of industrial policy, 1925–1975. Stanford University Press, Stanford
10. Wade R (1992) East Asia's economic success: conflicting perspectives, partial insights, shaky evidence. World Polit 44:270–320. https://doi.org/10.2307/2010449
11. Amsden AH (1992) Asia's next giant: South Korea and late industrialization. Oxford University Press, Oxford
12. Woo-Cummings M (1999) The developmental state. Cornell University Press, Ithaca, NY
13. Wikipedia (2007) Fichier: ECOWAS map. https://fr.wikipedia.org/wiki/Fichier:Ecowas_map.svg. Accessed 11 Aug 2022
14. Domar ED (1946) Capital expansion, rate of growth, and employment. Econometrica 14:137. https://doi.org/10.2307/1905364
15. Harrod RF (1939) An essay in dynamic theory. Econ J 49:14–33. https://doi.org/10.2307/2225181
16. Di Stefano E, Marconi D (2017) Structural transformation and allocation efficiency in China and India. SSRN Electron Journal, Bank Italy Temi di Discuss. Working Pap No 1093 1–55. doi:https://doi.org/10.2139/SSRN.2934227
17. Solow RM (1956) A contribution to the theory of economic growth. Q J Econ 70:65–94. https://doi.org/10.2307/1884513
18. Swan TW (1956) Economic growth and capital accumulation. Econ Rec 32:334–361. https://doi.org/10.1111/J.1475-4932.1956.TB00434.X
19. Solow RM (1957) Technical change and the aggregate production function. Rev Econ Stat 39: 312. https://doi.org/10.2307/1926047
20. Romer P (1990) Endogenous technological change. J Polit Econ 98:71–102
21. Lucas RE (1988) On the mechanics of economic development. J Monet Econ 22:3–42. https://doi.org/10.1016/0304-3932(88)90168-7
22. Young A (1994) Lessons from the East Asian NICS: a contrarian view. Eur Econ Rev 38:964–973. https://doi.org/10.1016/0014-2921(94)90132-5
23. Drysdale P, Huang Y (1997) Technological catch-up and economic growth in East Asia and the pacific*. Econ Rec 73:201–211. https://doi.org/10.1111/J.1475-4932.1997.TB00993.X
24. Veblen TB (1904) The theory of business enterprise. Transaction Books, New Brunswick

25. Mitchell WC (1914) Human behavior and economics: a survey of recent literature. Q J Econ 29: 1–47. https://doi.org/10.2307/1885296
26. Commons J (1934) Institutional economics: its place in political economy. The Macmillan Company, New York
27. Coase RH (1937) The nature of the firm. Economica 4:386–405. https://doi.org/10.1111/J.1468-0335.1937.TB00002.X
28. Alchian AA, Kessel RA (1959) Redistribution of wealth through inflation: contrary to the generally accepted view, business firms do not necessarily gain through inflation. Science (80-) 130:535–539. https://doi.org/10.1126/SCIENCE.130.3375.535
29. Arrow KJ (1963) Uncertainty and the welfare economics of medical care. Am Econ Rev 53: 941–973. https://doi.org/10.1215/03616878-26-5-851
30. Williamson OE (1985) The economic institutions of capitalism. Free Press, New York
31. North DC (1984) Transaction costs, institutions, and economic history. J Inst Theor Econ 140: 7–17
32. De Soto H (2000) The mystery of capital: why capitalism triumphs in the west and fails everywhere else. Basic Books, New York
33. Easterly W, Levine R (1997) Africa's growth tragedy: policies and ethnic divisions. Q J Econ 112:1203–1250
34. Lawrence P, Thirtle C (2001) Africa and Asia in comparative economic perspective. Palgrave Macmillan, London
35. Collier P, Gunning JW (1999) Explaining African economic performance. J Econ Lit 37:64–111. https://doi.org/10.1257/JEL.37.1.64
36. Frankel JA (2012) The natural resource curse: a survey of diagnoses and some prescriptions. In: HKS Faculty Research Working Paper Series. RWP12-014, John F. Kennedy School of Government of Harvard University. https://dash.harvard.edu/handle/1/8694932. Accessed 8 Jun 2022
37. Presbitero A (2014) East Asia and Africa growth experience - why divergence | PDF | Economic Growth | Gross Domestic Product. In: Working Papers. https://www.scribd.com/document/345931277/East-Asia-and-Africa-Growth-Experience-Why-Divergence. Accessed 8 Jun 2022
38. World Bank (2020) World development indicators. In: WDI World Bank. https://datatopics.worldbank.org/world-development-indicators/. Accessed 18 Jul 2022
39. Kim WS, Il LY (2007) Challenges of Korea's foreign direct investment-led globalization: multinational corporations perceptions. Asia Pacific Bus Rev 13:163–181. https://doi.org/10.1080/13602380701223001
40. OECD (2020) Korea: overview. Organisation for Economic Co-operation and Development, Paris
41. Lee J-W (2016) ADBI working paper series, The Republic of Korea's economic growth and catch-up: implications for the people's republic of China. Asian Development Bank Institute, Toyko
42. FRED (2022) General government gross debt for Korea. In: FRED Economic Data. https://fred.stlouisfed.org/series/GGGDTAKRA188N. Accessed 5 Aug 2022
43. Invest Seoul (2022) Invest Seoul: foreign investment inventives. In: Invest Seoul. https://investseoul.org/eng/mainPage.do;jsessionid=40FBB9242AB94758C70674649483A25E. Accessed 5 Aug 2022
44. Ogbeidi MM (2012) Political leadership and corruption in Nigeria since 1960: a socio-economic analysis. J Niger Stud 1:1–25
45. Suchi PM (2019) Investment in security forces and human development challenges in Africa on JSTOR. Africa Dev/Afrique Développement 44:55–76
46. Rita Ifeoma O, Purity N-O, Anagbogu T (2015) Security challenges and the implications for business activities in Nigeria: a critical review. J Policy Dev Stud 9:157–168
47. Yusuf A, Mohd S (2022) Growth and fiscal effects of insecurity on the Nigerian economy. Eur J Dev Res 1–27. doi:https://doi.org/10.1057/S41287-022-00531-3/FIGURES/1

48. Abu N, Staniewski MW (2019) Determinants of corruption in Nigeria: evidence from various estimation techniques. Con Res Istraživanja 32:3052–3076. https://doi.org/10.1080/1331677X.2019.1655467
49. Yagboyaju DA, Akinola AO (2019) Nigerian state and the crisis of governance: a critical exposition. SAGE Open 9. https://doi.org/10.1177/2158244019865810
50. Kirchgässner G (2017) On estimating the size of the shadow economy. Ger Econ Rev 18:99–111. https://doi.org/10.1111/geer.12094
51. Medina L, Schneider F (2018) Shadow economies around the world: what did we learn over the last 20 years? IMF Work Pap 18:1. https://doi.org/10.5089/9781484338636.001
52. Buehn A, Dell'Anno R, Schneider F (2018) Exploring the dark side of tax policy: an analysis of the interactions between fiscal illusion and the shadow economy. Empir Econ 54:1609–1630. https://doi.org/10.1007/s00181-017-1277-7
53. Morgan G (2009) Globalization, multinationals and institutional diversity. Econ Soc 38:580–605. https://doi.org/10.1080/03085140903190342
54. Naumann G, Barbosa P, Garrote L et al (2014) Exploring drought vulnerability in Africa: an indicator based analysis to be used in early warning systems. Hydrol Earth Syst Sci 18:1591–1604. https://doi.org/10.5194/hess-18-1591-2014
55. Markovic N, Bokonjic D, De Lepeleer G (2021) Development and implementation of internationalization in Bosnia and Herzegovina higher education. Int J Educ Manag 35:1263–1276. https://doi.org/10.1108/IJEM-01-2021-0002/FULL/XML
56. Global Economy (2022) Global economy, world economy. In: Global economics and business economics data 200 ctries. https://www.theglobaleconomy.com/. Accessed 5 Aug 2022
57. Transparency International (2022) Corruption Index. In: Transparency International. https://www.transparency.org/. Accessed 5 Aug 2022
58. UNDP (2016) Human development report 2016: human development for everyone. United Nations Development Programme, New York
59. Park JH (2016) The East Asian model of economic development and developing countries. J Dev Soc 18:330–353. https://doi.org/10.1177/0169796X0201800403
60. Klenner W (2006) The East Asian development model. Dev Model Glob Econ 90–104. doi: https://doi.org/10.1057/9780230523555_6
61. Park YC (2005) Failures of the East Asian development model: an overview. Econ Lib Integr East Asia 33–36. doi:https://doi.org/10.1093/0199276773.003.0004
62. Danju I, Maasoglu Y, Maasoglu N (2014) The East Asian model of economic development and developing countries. Procedia - Soc Behav Sci 109:1168–1173. https://doi.org/10.1016/J.SBSPRO.2013.12.606
63. Singh A (2002) Asian capitalism and the financial crisis. In: Eatwell J, Taylor L (eds) International capital market: systems in transitions. Oxford University Press, Oxford, pp 339–368

Economic Shocks from COVID-19 and the Assessment of Micro-, Small-, and Medium-Sized Enterprises Emergence of Insurance Coverage in Urban South-West, Nigeria

Adeyemi E. Ayinde-Olawale, Idowu T. Ogunyemi, and Giuseppe T. Cirella

1 Introduction

Micro-, small-, and medium-sized enterprises (MSMEs) play an important role in the economic development of many countries. The aggregate contribution of MSMEs to national development cannot be overlooked. This is because the development of MSMEs is viewed as one of the sustainable ways of reducing the levels of poverty and improving the quality of livelihoods through job and wealth creation [1]. According to the World Bank, MSMEs are defined as follows: micro enterprises: 1–9 employees, small enterprises: 10–49 employees, and medium enterprises: 50–249 employees [2]. However, the local definition of an MSME varies from country to country and is based not only on the number of employees but also by the inclusion of other variables such as turnover and assets. In the private sector, micro and small enterprises are the driving force of innovation and sustainability with about 365–445 million MSMEs in emerging markets, i.e., 25–30 million of these are formal small and medium-sized, 55–70 million are classified as formal micro, and 285–345 million are informal [3]. According to the Organization for Economic Co-operation and Development [4], MSMEs have been recognized as the "lifeblood and economic muscle" of most countries. Despite this significance, most of these MSMEs do not survive beyond a decade after being established while for others, surviving has continued to be a constant struggle [5–7]. While several factors

A. E. Ayinde-Olawale (✉) · I. T. Ogunyemi
Department of Planning, Research, and Development, Nigerian Agricultural Insurance Corporation, Abuja, Federal Capital Territory, Nigeria
e-mail: adeyemi.ayinde@naic.gov.ng; idowu.ogunyemi@naic.gov.ng

G. T. Cirella
Faculty of Economics, University of Gdansk, Sopot, Poland
e-mail: gt.cirella@ug.edu.pl

G. T. Cirella (ed.), *Uncertainty Shocks in Africa*, Advances in African Economic, Social and Political Development, https://doi.org/10.1007/978-3-031-21885-9_3

are associated with these struggles, the inability to properly manage risks can be regarded the most critical [5]. The European Commission [8] in 2015 reported that about 23 million small and medium-sized enterprises (SMEs) generated EUR 3.9 trillion in value added and employed 90 million people. Other estimates suggest that more than 95% of enterprises from around the world are SMEs, accounting for about 60% of private sector employment [9]. In industrialized countries, Japan had the largest percentage of SMEs, accounting for more than 99% of total enterprises in 2007. While the estimated data for the 27 countries in the European Union for 2012 (i.e., excluding Croatia which joined in 2013) showed that MSMEs accounted for 99.8% of enterprises and employed 67% of workers. In comparison, India had 13 million SMEs in 2008, i.e., equivalent to 80% of its country's businesses. In developing countries, the formal SME sector is competing with a large informal one. According to the World Bank [3], out of the estimated 445 million MSMEs in emerging markets, over 70% are being operated informally which can be as high as 90% in some of these countries. This brings to the forefront the need to emphasize appropriate risk management strategies such as insurance uptake so that these enterprises will be able to remain in business in the event of unforeseen catastrophes such as fire, theft, burglary, and business interruption as a result of a shock event such as the COVID-19 pandemic.

Globally, the unprecedented pandemic has had enormous economic consequences for many MSMEs. Its impact has affected the ability of markets to function normally, thereby creating an economic shock which has led to broader fiscal impacts. Economically, the pandemic is reported to have generated stress in capital markets and triggered a forceful response from central banks of most economies. This has directly caused a number of setbacks which negatively affected priority sectors such as agriculture, healthcare, defense, finance, and construction [10]. An economic shock, also known as a macroeconomic shock, is any unexpected event that has a large scale, unexpected impact on the economy. Economic shocks can be macro, supply side, demand, upward, and downward; however, the downward economic shocks are events that directly hurt the economy, causing loss in value, a slowdown in production, and, in some cases, downsizing and layoffs. Thus, the need for a robust response such as insurance cannot be overemphasized to mitigate the economic downturn caused by such a shock event. This scenario highlights the need for insurance products to safeguard and stabilize local supply chains involving MSMEs to avoid slowdown and closure. As such, the uptake of insurance coverage would mitigate shocks and protect them against future occurrences. Evidently, MSMEs have been found to be very vulnerable to exogenous hazards [11], associating them in developing countries with very low insurance uptake [12]. Bodies of literature stress the importance of MSMEs as employment generators, innovators, factors in the supply chains of larger enterprises, and (important) contributors to gross domestic product. However, few studies exist that investigate the importance of insurance on the growth of MSMEs, especially in a post-pandemic circumstance. This chapter attempts to add knowledge base to this gap in the literature and serve as reference material for future research in the post-pandemic era. It highlights why access to insurance by MSMEs can help build assets, absorb shocks, and manage risks associated with irregular and unpredictable income. Moreover, proper risk management tools can be used to reduce or eliminate the financial impact in the event that a particular insured risk crystallizes. In all, insurance can make MSMEs more resilient to shocks and financially sound.

Across the world, there are inadequate insurance products for MSMEs. In developing economies, industry players need to rethink MSME insurance as current approaches seem not to be yielding appropriate results. In sub-Saharan Africa, for example, an estimate of less than 2% of MSMEs has any form of insurance. Even those that have insurance are only covered for the personal impacts on their health expenses while their enterprises remain highly exposed to risks. Currently, commonly available insurance products are not adaptable to the needs of most MSMEs. However, while MSMEs may find some value in existing micro insurance products, as businesses grow insurance needs become more sophisticated and heterogeneous which often leaves SMEs entirely out in the cold. This calls for evidence-based research on the effect of the pandemic on MSMEs uptake of insurance coverage. Case research in Nigeria is conducted to examine this relationship using the following objectives: (1) profile the nature of MSMEs and examine the level of awareness and uptake of insurance services among them, (2) assess whether the level of production income, i.e., the willingness to take insurance coverage among MSMEs is in any way influenced by the pandemic, (3) examine the effect of the pandemic on MSMEs' uptake of insurance coverage, (4) investigate and identify the constraints to the uptake of insurance coverage among MSMEs, and (5) examine the impact of the pandemic on the uptake of insurance coverage and productivity of MSMEs.

2 Case Research Methodology

2.1 Study Area

The research is carried out in the urban areas of South-West, Nigeria, which consists of six states: Lagos, Ogun, Oyo, Osun, Ondo, and Ekiti. The region is bordered by the Gulf of Guinea to the south, Kwara and Kogi states to the north, Edo and Delta states to the east and the Republic of Benin to the west. The people of South-West are predominantly farmers, traders, and artisans. The area lies between longitude 2° 311E and 6°001E and Latitude 6°211 N and 8° 371 N with a total land area of 77,818 km^2 and an estimated population of 32.5 million [13, 14]. Key urban areas within South-West include Lagos and the surrounding sub-city districts, Abeokuta, Ibadan, Osogbo, Ado Ekiti, Ife, Ogbomosho, and Akure (Fig. 1).

Fig. 1 Major urban areas and location of South-West, Nigeria: (*top left*) aerial skyline of Lagos, (*top right*) Lagos street market, (*bottom left*) aerial view of Obanikoro Street, Somolu in Lagos, and (bottom right) adapted map of the states that makeup South-West, Nigeria. Source: (*top left*) Photograph by Nupo Deyon Daniel on Upsplash, Creative Commons Public Domain, April 19, 2021; (*top right*) photograph by Namnso Ukpanah on Upsplash, Creative Commons Public Domain, April 9, 2022; (*bottom left*) photograph by Omotayo Kofoworola on Upsplash, Creative Commons Public Domain, January 28, 2020; (*bottom right*) adapted from Wikimedia Commons [15]

2.2 *Source of Data*

The source of data for this chapter is predominantly from an online survey. Additional, secondary data was collected from journals, reports, newsletters, and books. The online survey was an investigation carried out using Google Forms throughout the year of 2021. This tool is a Google application that allows for the quick creation and distribution of forms to gather information. The respondents were communicated to via WhatsApp technology. The social media served as a catalyst in carrying out of the research, especially via the process of the survey's distribution. The data collection ensured easy access to the respondents, minimal cost of research materials and reduced expenses, and enhanced quantity and quality of data. The option of an online investigation offered flexibility for respondents to share their views concerning MSME uptake of insurance coverage and allowed respondents to participate due to the restriction in physical contact because of the pandemic. The study employed a two-stage sampling technique to select 192 MSME operators from the study area. First, the purposive selection of the urban areas throughout the South-West was performed. The purposive sampling technique is a non-probability sampling technique which relies on the judgment of the researcher in the selection of the sample for the study. This is because the study focuses on specific characteristics of a population that are of interest (i.e., MSME operators). Also, most of the MSMEs are residents in the urban centers. Second, the selection of 192 MSMEs was performed using a snowballing sampling technique. The snowballing technique is a form of non-probability sampling in which decisions concerning the individuals in the sample are based on their knowledge of the research issue. This technique is quite suitable for use where members of a population are difficult to locate and closely interconnected, e.g., a city center.

2.3 Analytical Techniques and Formulation

The study employed descriptive statistics, Pearson correlation coefficient, Cramer's V, logistic regression, and the propensity score matching (PSM) method in analyzing the collected data. The descriptive statistics were used to analyze the socioeconomic characteristics of MSMEs by measuring mean, standard deviation, and frequency distribution. Pearson correlation coefficient is a measure of linear correlation between two sets of data. It is the ratio between the covariance of two variables and the product of their standard deviation. Thus, it is essentially a normalized measurement of the covariance, such that, the result always has a value between negative one and one. This measure can only reflect a linear correlation of variables and ignores any other type of relationship or correlation. Cramer's V is similar to the Pearson correlation coefficient in that it is commonly used to calculate correlation in tables with more than two-by-two columns and rows. Cramer's V varies between zero and one. A value close to zero means that there is very little association between the variables while one indicates a very strong association. The logistic regression model was used to assess the effect of the COVID-19 pandemic on insurance uptake among MSME operators, i.e., Eqs. (1) and (2).

$$\text{Logit }(Y) = \text{natural log (odds)} = \ln\left(\frac{\pi}{1-\pi}\right) = \alpha + \beta X \tag{1}$$

$$\pi = \text{probability}\left(Y = \frac{\text{outcome of interest}}{X} = X,\ \text{a specific value of } X\right)$$

$$= \frac{e^{\alpha+\beta x}}{1+e^{\alpha+\beta x}} \tag{2}$$

Where: π = probability of the outcome of interest; α = intercept of Y; β = regression coefficient; $e = 2.71828$, i.e., the base of natural logarithms; Y_i = Do you have insurance coverage? (i.e., no = 0, yes = 1); $X_{1i}, X_{2i}, \ldots X_{ni}$ = vectors of explanatory variables; $\beta_0, \beta_1, \ldots \beta_n$ = coefficients of explanatory variables; X_1 = age of MSME operator (i.e., years); X_2 = gender of MSME operator (i.e., female = 0, male = 1); X_3 = years of business experience; X_4 = member of a cooperative society (i.e., no = 0, yes = 1); X_5 = awareness of the insurance concept (i.e., no = 0, yes = 1); X_6 = average monthly income (i.e., Nigerian Naira (NGN)); X_7 = access to credit (i.e., no = 0, yes = 1); X_8 = high cost of premium; and X_9 = business was affected by the COVID-19 pandemic (i.e., no = 0. yes = 1).

PSM was used to assess the impact of the COVID-19 pandemic on the uptake of insurance coverage among MSMEs in the study area. The propensity score is the probability of insurance uptake rather than non-uptake of insurance in a treatment group. In the treatment effect literature, this predictor, i.e., given observable variables, is an important intermediate step even though the ultimate interest lies in the outcome of that treatment [16]. Several matching methods have been developed to match treated with non-treated of similar propensity scores. Asymptotically, all matching methods yielded the same results; hence, in practice there were trade-offs in terms of bias and efficiency with each proposed method [17]—i.e., a balancing test. After matching to ascertain whether the difference in covariates (i.e., between the two groups) in the matched sample has been eliminated, the matched comparison group can be considered as a plausible counterfactual [18], i.e., there should be no systematic differences in the distribution of covariate between the treated and control groups. This result is the standardized mean difference, i.e., the pseudo-R-squared which should be lower and the joint significance of covariate should be rejected [19]. If there are unobserved variables that simultaneously affect the operators' decision and the outcome variable, a selection or hidden bias problem might arise to which matching estimators are not sufficiently robust. While this controlled for many observable results, it also checks the sensitivity of the estimated average participation effects to hidden bias, i.e., using Rosenbaum's [20] bounds sensitivity approach. The purpose of this is to investigate whether inferences about treatment effects may be changed by unobserved variables. The main parameter of interest, in this case, is the average treatment effects on the treated (ATT), as expressed in Eq. (3).

$$\mathrm{ATT} = E\left(\frac{Y_1 - Y_0}{D} = 1\right) = E\left(\frac{Y_1}{D} = 1\right) - E\left(\frac{Y_0}{D} = 1\right) \quad (3)$$

Where: ATT = average treatment effect on the treated; Y_1 = treated outcome; Y_0 = untreated outcome; and D = treatment status (i.e., one if the individual receives treatment and zero otherwise).

However, an evaluation problem arises from the fact that the untreated outcome for a treated individual, i.e., $E\left(\frac{Y_0}{D} = 1\right)$, can never be observed. Using the outcome for untreated individuals as an estimate of the counterfactual will generate an equal bias, i.e., Eq. (4).

$$B = E\left(\frac{Y_1}{D} = 1\right) - E\left(\frac{Y_0}{D} = 1\right) \quad (4)$$

If the selection is based on variables that are observable, the problem of selection bias can be solved by controlling for these variables in a regression analysis or by using PSM. However, if the selection is based on variables that are unknown other methods are applied. In the impact analysis, treatment is largely based on household characteristics and asset holding that are observable.

The advantage of using PSM compared to non-regression analysis is that it is a non-parametric approach in which the functional relationship between the dependent and independent variables is not specified, and no distributional assumptions are made for the outcome variable [21, 22]. PSM relies heavily on two assumptions that formally can be written as Assumption 1 (i.e., Eq. (5)—conditional independence) and Assumption 2 (i.e., Eq. (6)—common support).

$$Y_0 \perp \frac{D}{X} \tag{5}$$

Where: $\perp$ = stochastic independence; X = set of observable characteristics; and D = treatment status (i.e., one if the individual receives treatment and zero otherwise).

$$Pr\left(D = \frac{1}{X}\right) < 1 \tag{6}$$

Assumption 1 implies a conditional a set of observed characteristics, the untreated outcome is independent of treatment status, i.e., $E\left(\frac{Y_0}{D} = 1\right) = E\left(\frac{Y_0}{D} = 0\right)$. This implies that the untreated outcome can be used as an unbiased estimate in terms of the counterfactual outcome for the treated individuals, which solves the evaluation problem described. Rosenbaum and Rubin [22] were the first to show that matching on the probability of treatment, i.e., $p(x) = Pr\left(D = \frac{1}{X}\right)$, referred to as a valid PSM score. Assumption 2 implies no explanatory variable is allowed to perfectly predict treatment. In order to control for time invariant unobserved heterogeneity, this chapter will follow the approach suggested by Heckman et al. [21] and used changes in Y as the outcome variable.

3 Results from MSME Operators

The initial result of the data analyses is a breakdown of the socioeconomic characteristics of the sampled MSME operators in South-West (i.e., age, gender, marital status, educational status, etc.) (Table 1). Results revealed that about three-fifths of the respondents (i.e., 57.8%) were between the ages of 31 and 40 years and are considered to be in their economically active years, while only few were aged 51 years and above. The average age of the operators stood at 37.3 ± 7.2 years which implies that MSME operators are young and vibrant. This could affect their uptake of insurance since the mid-30s is a positive age bracket for insurance coverage of all sorts [23–26]. Similar findings are reported by Kamara and Makori [27] in their study on determinants of uptake of insurance services among SMEs where 80% of the respondents were aged 20 to 39 years. Moreover, the majority of

Table 1 Socioeconomic characteristics of MSME operators in South-West, $n = 192$

Socioeconomic characteristics	Frequency	Percentage
Age (i.e., years)		
≤ 30	43	22.4
31–40	111	57.8
41–50	26	13.5
≥51	12	6.3
Gender		
Male	107	55.7
Female	85	44.3
Marital status		
Single	74	38.5
Married	113	58.9
Divorce	5	2.6
Educational status		
Secondary	51	26.6
Tertiary	141	73.4
Primary occupation		
Full time business operator	50	26.0
Product marketing	21	10.6
Civil and public service	110	57.3
Produce processing	11	5.7
Categories of MSMEs		
Micro (i.e., <10 employees)	156	81.3
Small (i.e., 11–49 employees)	32	16.7
Medium (i.e., >50 employees)	4	2.0
Monthly income (i.e., NGN)[a]		
<20,000	80	41.6
20,000–55,999	83	43.2
≥56,000	29	15.2
Years of business operation		
≤5	110	57.2
6–10	48	25.0
11–15	15	7.8
>15	19	9.9
Membership of a cooperative society		
Member	52	27.1
Non-member	140	72.9
Access to credit facilities		
No	78	40.6
Yes	114	59.4
Sources of credit facilities		
None	78	40.6
Family and friends	30	15.6
Cooperative societies	44	23.0
Microfinance banks	5	2.6
Commercial banks	35	18.2

[a]USD 1.00 = NGN 415.00; Source: online survey, 2021

MSME operators (i.e., 55.7%) were males. Based on this, it can be deduced that MSME operators are dominated by men. With respect to marital status, a larger percentage of the respondents were married (i.e., 58.7%). This corroborates with the findings of Jatto [28] in the study on assessment of farmer's awareness of agricultural insurance packages in which evidence from communities with the motto "farming is our pride" were married (i.e., 89%). The educational status of MSME operators showed that over three-fifths of the respondents had secondary education (i.e., 73.4%), while 26.6% had primary education. This implies that most of the respondents had at least one form of formal education which should have a positive effect on uptake of insurance since educated people have more positive attitudes to insurance than the less educated [29, 30]. The majority of MSME operators are engaged in a low-capital business venture with less than ten employees (i.e., 81.3%). This means that a greater percentage of the respondents (i.e., 84.8%) earn less than NGN 56,000 (i.e., USD 135.00) per month—i.e., the mean monthly income of greater than NGN 35,000 (i.e., USD 85.00). This reflects that most MSME operators are generating income and are thus exposed to diverse risks which could act as a positive influencer on uptake of insurance.

Experience is the skill or knowledge acquired from a particular action carried out over time which eventually distinguishes one out from others. Results revealed that the majority of MSME operators have between 1 and 10 years of business experience (i.e., 82.2%) while only 9.9%% had more than 15 years of business experience. The mean years of business experience of MSME operators stood at 6.59 ± 5.8 years. This implies that most of the operators are highly experienced, and it is anticipated that the higher the years of business experience the higher the output and risk and, hence, the need for insurance coverage uptake. Also, most MSME operators were not members of any form of cooperative association (i.e., 72.9%) thus exposure to high risks with limited help from available cooperative societies. More than half of MSME operators (i.e., 59.4%) had access to credit facilities while 40.5% do not have access. This suggests that credit facilities were not accessible to about two-fifths of the sampled operators. Therefore, there is a need to increase access to credit facilities as this will ensure improved productivity which will give rise to an increased need for the uptake of insurance. The nature of MSMEs and level of awareness of insurance among the surveyed operators in South-West is visually broken down in terms of the businesspeople profile (Figs. 2 and 3).

Furthermore, Fig. 4 reveals that among the sampled MSMEs, only 31.8% had insurance coverage while over three-fifths (i.e., 68.2%) did not have any form of insurance. This implied that the majority of MSMEs were exposed to one form of risk or another and are more vulnerable to the effect and impact of economic disruptions such as the COVID-19 pandemic than their counterparts (i.e., that are insured). This high percentage of no insurance uptake can be related to the inadequate access to information on the availability and benefits of insurance products and services. Also, poor testimonials and image of insurance officers and companies might be responsible for the inaction of the operators towards insurance products and services. Among MSMEs that had obtained insurance, Fig. 5 illustrates only 47.5% had the intention of renewing their insurance coverage while more than half (i.e.,

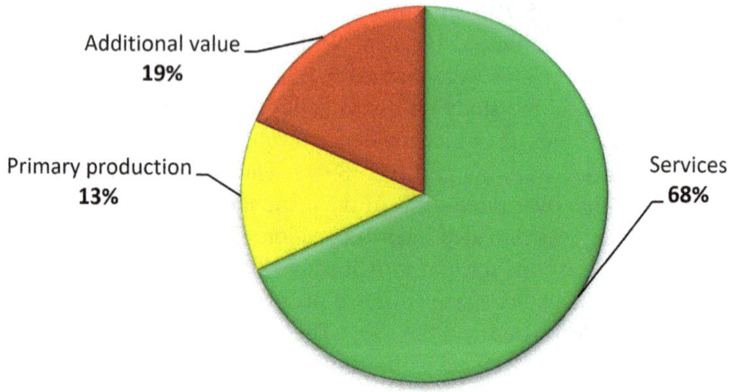

Fig. 2 Nature of MSMEs in South-West

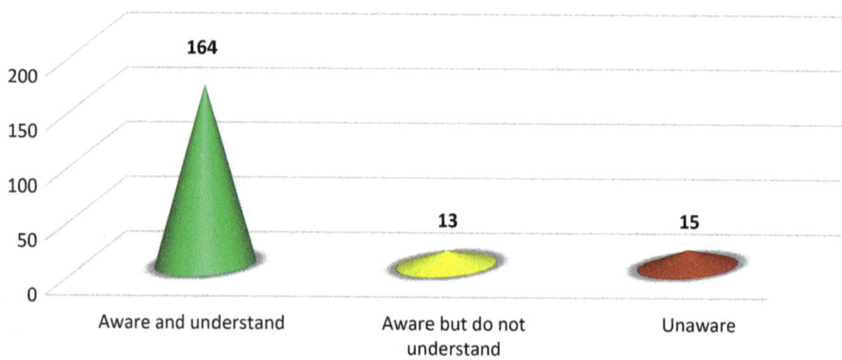

Fig. 3 Level of awareness, i.e., frequency, of the concept of insurance of MSMEs in South-West, $n = 192$

52.5%) did not intend to renew. This might be due to high cost of premiums and unsatisfactory services rendered by the insurance companies.

Regarding any hinderance to taking up insurance coverage, 61% of the operators did not believe they will need insurance coverage; hence, no uptake is planned for these operators. This, however, might be attributed to the level of understanding in terms of the benefits of insurance, the knowledge of products available, and their access to insurance officers (Fig. 6). Moreover, 11% and 16% of them complained that the high premiums and unimpressive attitude of insurance companies discouraged them from demanding insurance, respectfully. Thus, the marketing strategies and attitude of insurance companies need to be improved if an increased uptake is warranted. Correspondingly, Fig. 7 showed that 69% were willing to take insurance coverage to mitigate future risks, while 31% had no plan to obtain insurance even in the future. This might be attributed to the low level of awareness and education of the benefits of insurance especially in a post-pandemic, new-normal era.

Fig. 4 Insurance uptake among MSMEs

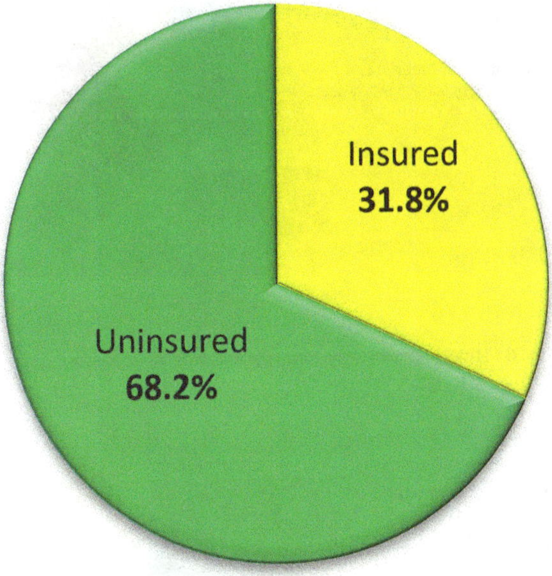

Fig. 5 Willingness to renew insurance coverage among MSMEs

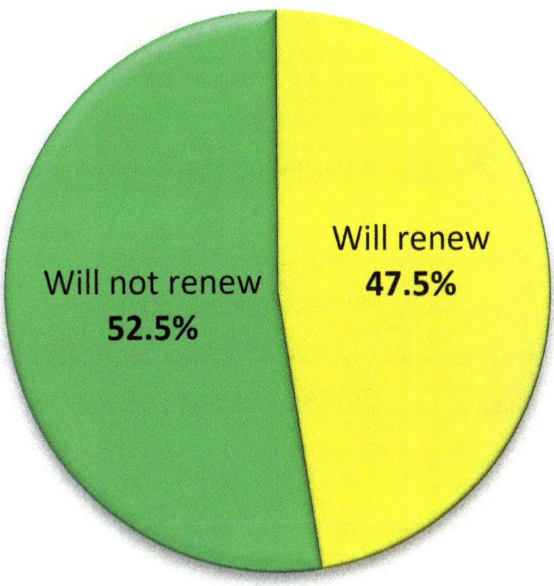

Further detailed findings revealed that 45.3% of MSME operators showed more interest in fire and special perils insurance products than any other available product (Fig. 8). Also, about 28% of the operators were interested in business interruption insurance products which reflects the proactive nature of such operators to doing business in this new-normal era. The results with respect to the effects of the

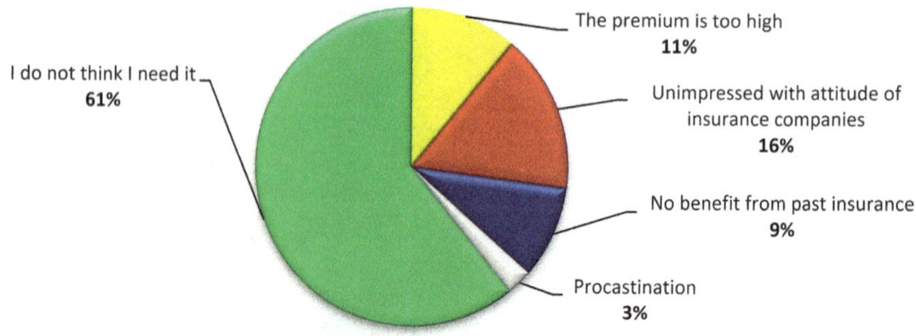

Fig. 6 Hindrances to insurance uptake among MSMEs

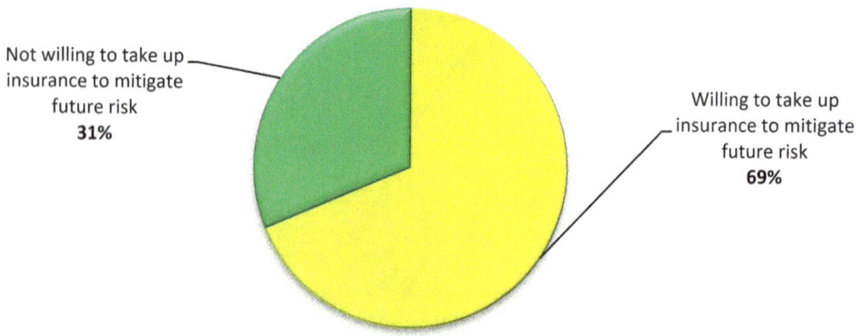

Fig. 7 Willingness of MSMEs to take insurance cover to mitigate future risk

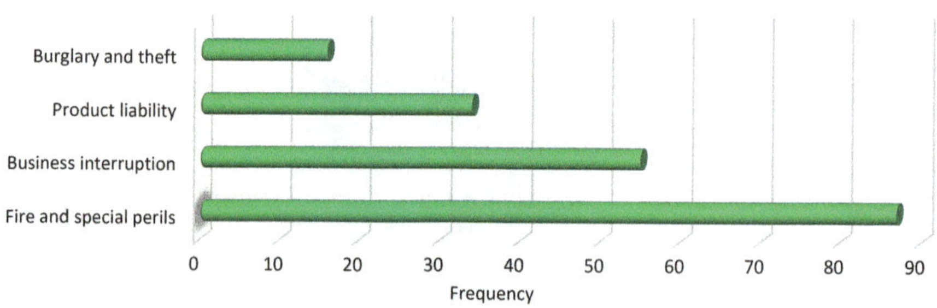

Fig. 8 Types of insurance coverage desired by MSMEs, $n = 192$

COVID-19 pandemic showed that most MSME operators (i.e., 90.7%) had reduced income and patronage in which 6.8% of them were severely affected and had to close down their business enterprise (Fig. 9). This implied that most MSME operators in South-West were exposed to greater risks, thus, an urgent need of insurance coverage to guide against future occurrences should be implemented.

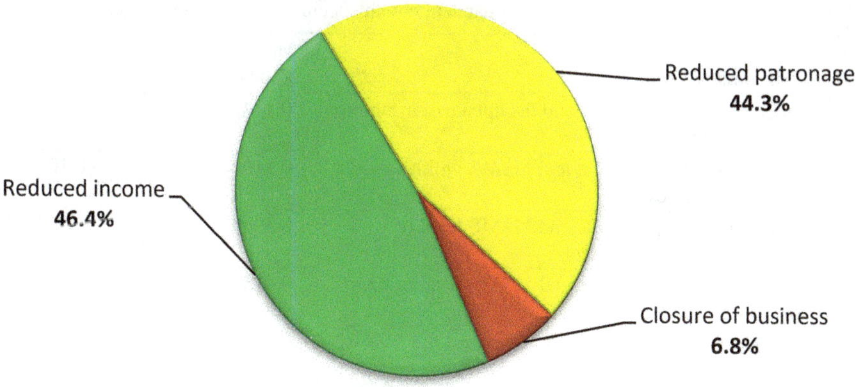

Fig. 9 Effects of the COVID-19 pandemic on MSMEs

4 Effect of the COVID-19 Pandemic on Insurance Uptake Among MSMEs in Urban South-West

In terms of a correlative analysis of MSME operators that were affected, specific variables such as uptake of insurance coverage, MSME willingness to insure, MSME level of awareness about insurance, and MSME productivity are examined. It was found that only MSME level of awareness about insurance was positively correlated at less than 1% level of significance. This was related directly to whether MSMEs were affected by the global pandemic using Pearson correlation coefficient and Cramer's V. Moreover, MSME level of productivity also showed a significant positive correlation using Pearson correlation coefficient. These results implied that a strong correlation can be made among MSMEs who were affected by the COVID-19 pandemic and their level of awareness about insurance and productivity. This also can suggest that MSMEs who were adversely affected by the pandemic now know the benefit of insurance as well as have become more aware of its effectiveness. Nonetheless, this awareness has not translated into full insurance uptake as noted by the result that showed the uptake of insurance among MSMEs using Cramer's V coefficient which is strongly correlated (Table 2).

In an attempt to better understand the data, the effect of the COVID-19 pandemic on insurance uptake among MSMEs was also assessed using a logistic model. The dependent variable, in this case, is whether or not MSMEs have insurance coverage. The result of this analysis showed that the estimated model had explanatory power as shown by the likelihood ratio which is significant at the 1% level. The result illustrated that five out of the eight variables included in the model were statistically significant (i.e., positive and negative) to MSME uptake of insurance coverage. The variables that positively influenced MSME uptake of insurance coverage were the gender of the operator, membership with a cooperative society, and whether the business was affected by the pandemic, while those that negatively influenced

Table 2 Relationship of the COVID-19 pandemic with specific insurance uptake indicators

S/N	Indicators	Pearson correlation coefficient	Cramer's V
1	Affected by the pandemic and the uptake of insurance among MSMEs	0.114	0.112
2	Affected by the pandemic and MSME willingness to insure themselves	0.110	−0.105
3	Affected by the pandemic and MSME level of awareness about insurance	0.396***	0.396***
4	Affected by the pandemic and MSME level of production income	0.413***	0.048
5	Uptake of insurance among MSMEs and the level of production income	−0.112	0.723***

***$p < 0.01$; Source: online survey, 2021

Table 3 Effect of the COVID-19 pandemic on insurance uptake among MSMEs in urban South-West

Variables	Odds ratio	Coefficient	Standard error
Gender (i.e., female = 0, male = 1)	2.85	1.05**	0.4752
Age (i.e., years)	1.04	0.04	0.0381
Nature of MSMEs	0.56	−0.58*	0.3074
Business experience (i.e., years)	0.97	−0.03	0.0423
Cooperative membership (i.e., yes = 1)	12.71	2.54***	0.5620
Access to credit (i.e., yes = 1)	1.26	0.23	0.4864
High cost of premium	5.20	−1.65***	0.5000
Affected by the COVID-19 pandemic	29.71	3.39***	0.6750
Constant	0.01	−5.40	1.7050
Log-likelihood	−65.1755		
LR (chi-squared)	−135.73***		

*$p < 0.1$, **$p < 0.5$, ***$p < 0.01$; Source: online survey, 2021

MSME uptake of insurance coverage were the nature of MSMEs and high cost of premium (Table 3).

The positive coefficient of gender implied that the male MSME operators had a higher likelihood of taking insurance coverage than female MSME operators. Also, MSME operators who were members of cooperative societies had a higher likelihood of taking insurance coverage than those who did not. This can be attributed to the fact that for most cooperative societies to have access to credit facilities, especially from the government, had to get their businesses insured. Also, cooperative societies had proved to be one of the avenues for promoting awareness and knowledge on the importance of insurance uptake. This is consistent with the findings of Rejda [31], Banerjee et al. [32], and Dayour et al. [12], where it was concluded that benefits such as easy access to loans, enhancing business image, and helping with a quick revamping of businesses after eventualities (i.e., in relation to cooperative societies) can improve uptake of insurance coverage among MSMEs. A business that was negatively affected by the pandemic had first-hand experience of the impact and, thus, did not need to be told before they took insurance coverage to mitigate future risk. This goes further to buttress the popular adage that says, "experience is the best teacher." However, it is important to stress that proactive business operators do not need to wait until they become negatively affected before they get insurance. The negative and significant coefficient of the nature of MSMEs and high cost of premiums implied that MSME operators that are into production as well as those that are into value addition were more likely to take insurance coverage than those that render services. This can be attributed to the fact that production and value addition tend to pose more risk than those that render services, hence the need to take insurance coverage to mitigate any associated risk. For the high cost of premiums, the likelihood to get insurance reduced as the cost of premium increased. For insurance coverage to be attractive for MSME operators, the cost should be affordable and payment plans should be more flexible than what is currently obtainable in the country. When this is put in place, more MSME operators will most likely get insurance. This result is in accordance with Chisala and Musawa's [33] research for the cost of insurance premiums and the empirical evidence they relate it to in terms of policymaking and insurance companies on how MSMEs can be protected.

4.1 Constraints Faced by MSME Operators Based on Severity

Several constraints were encountered by MSME operators which affected their uptake of insurance products. Some of the constraints were identified from the literature review and then proposed to the operators to indicate the level of severity. To complement this intervention, MSME operators were asked to state other constraints they encountered to better piece together the actual situation of each MSME. Responses from the operators are presented in Table 4.

According to Table 4, misunderstanding the concept of insurance was the sixth constraint based on severity—not a major constraint faced by MSMEs. This signals that the majority of the MSME respondents were educated and aware of the concept

Table 4 Constraints faced by MSME operators based on severity

Constraints	Frequency	Percentage	Rank
Inadequate access to credit facility	62	32.3	1st
Insufficient income	46	24.0	2nd
Low perceived risk	37	19.3	3rd
Inadequate asset to capital	31	16.1	4th
Unavailability of desired product	10	5.2	5th
Misunderstanding of the concept of an insurance contract	6	3.1	6th
Total	192	100	

Source: Authors' own elaboration

of insurance. Unavailability of the desired product was the fifth most severe constraint mentioned, which could mean, most of the operators have not been introduced to new products that might suite and meet their needs. Also, a low attendance of insurance officers was reported by the respondents, implying an inadequate level of customer care and information on up-to-date insurance coverage. MSMEs also reported the way they perceived risks, i.e., as the third major constraint. The reason for this can be attributed to the fact that there is still a low level of awareness from the benefits, opportunities, and solutions derived from obtaining insurance. Next, the second most severe constraint was insufficient income. The economic situation in Nigeria is alarming and most of the operators do not derive financial satisfaction from their business enterprise, especially during the pandemic lockdowns imposed by the government. Finally, the most severe constraint faced by MSMEs in South-West was inadequate access to credit facilities. This could be a result that the majority of MSME operators did not belong to any form of cooperative association where they could have access to society-assistance. This is corroborated by the result of the socioeconomic characteristics in this chapter in which 72.9% of the operators had no membership of any form in any cooperative society and 40.6% had no access to credit. Consequently, access to credit is a major limiting factor for the uptake of insurance products and services for MSMEs in South-West.

4.2 Impact of the COVID-19 Pandemic on MSME Level of Production and Willingness to Buy Insurance Coverage

A principal factor to understanding the impact of the COVID-19 pandemic on South-West's MSMEs is whether their level of production income, their willingness to buy insurance coverage, and their actual uptake of insurance coverage can be deduced. To best achieve this, the ATT formulation was applied. From Table 5, it can be inferred that the nearest neighbor and PSM methods of the treated equated to 60 while that of the control is more than the treated at 132. Table 5 illustrated that ATT both significantly impacted the level of MSME production income for the two matching methods while it only significantly impacted MSME willingness to buy insurance coverage using the nearest neighbor matching method. These results imply that the COVID-19 pandemic reduced the level of production by as much as NCN 84,642.86 (i.e., USD 205.00) for the PSM method and NCN 72,464.29 (i.e., USD 175.00) for the nearest neighbor matching method. It is important to highlight that given the result of this assay, the effect of the pandemic had not translated into the uptake of insurance coverage among MSMEs; however, it significantly impacted farmers' willingness to getting insurance.

Table 5 Impact of the pandemic on MSME level of production, willingness to buy insurance cover, and level of uptake of insurance coverage

			Production income		Willingness to buy insurance coverage		Uptake of insurance coverage	
Matching method	Treated	Control	ATT	*z*-value	ATT	*z*-value	ATT	*z*-value
Nearest neighbor	60	132	–72464.29	–5.25***	0.25	2.98***	–0.21	–1.14
PSM	60	132	–84,642.86	–3.43***	0.01	0.06	–0.12	–1.04
Balancing test satisfied	Yes	Yes						
Common support Imposed	Yes	Yes						
MSMEs on-support	41	98						
MSMEs off-support	19	34						

***$p < 0.01$; Source: online survey, 2021

5 Recommendation to Moving Forward

This chapter has shown that in as much as the global COVID-19 pandemic had a negative impact on the production income of MSMEs in South-West, it has also revealed the fact that it has created an avenue to show, in practical terms, the essence of insurance services. This chapter revealed that factors such as gender of MSME operators, nature of MSMEs, membership with cooperative societies, cost of premiums, and whether or not a business was affected by the pandemic significantly influence the likelihood of MSMEs taking insurance coverage of any form. From the ATT analysis, it also became evident that even though the pandemic has increased MSME willingness to take insurance, it has not translated into real uptake of insurance coverage to date. This can be greatly attributed to inadequate access to credit facilities, unavailability of desired products, and high cost of premiums. In-line with these findings, the following recommendations are outlined to improve MSME uptake of insurance coverage in South-West. First, there is the need for a massive and continuous awareness campaign, particularly in market centers, to boost the understanding and confidence of the people on the nature and concept of insurance. This will help erode the current mindset most people have about insurance—in general. Second, development of customized insurance products for MSMEs must meet their specific needs. Third, flexible payment platforms must be put in place so as to cater for those business operators that cannot afford to pay the insurance premium in full upfront. These recommendations will improve the level of understanding about insurance among MSMEs which will eventually result in actual uptake of insurance coverage. This increased uptake should boost the confidence of

MSME operators in venturing into other businesses with the knowledge that in the event of any insured adverse situation, they will not be worse off.

References

1. Kilonzo S (2011) Consultative forum on the proposed market for SMEs. CMA, Nairobi
2. Kushnir K, Mirmulstein ML, Ramalho R (2010) Micro, small, and medium enterprises around the world: how many are there, and what affects the count? | MFW4A - Making Finance Work for Africa. IFC, The World Bank, New York
3. World Bank (2021) World Bank SME finance: development news, research, data. World Bank. https://www.worldbank.org/en/topic/smefinance. Accessed 8 Jun 2022
4. OECD (2017) Understanding financial accounts. OECD
5. Gbireh N (2013) Use of general insurance as a tool in managing the risk of small and medium enterprises (SMES) in Ghana. University of Southampton, Southampton
6. Ngoasong MZ, Kimbu AN (2019) Why hurry? The slow process of high growth in women-owned businesses in a resource-scarce context. J Small Bus Manag 57:40–58. https://doi.org/10.1111/JSBM.12493
7. Kimbu AN, Ngoasong MZ (2016) Women as vectors of social entrepreneurship. Ann Tour Res 60:63–79. https://doi.org/10.1016/J.ANNALS.2016.06.002
8. European Commission (2016) Annual report on European SMEs 2015/2016, SME recovery continues. In: Publications Office of the European Union. https://op.europa.eu/en/publication-detail/-/publication/4872cbee-aa5a-11e6-aab7-01aa75ed71a1. Accessed 8 Jun 2022
9. European Parliament (2019) Fact sheets on the European Union. https://www.europarl.europa.eu/factsheets/en/home. Accessed 8 Jun 2022
10. Sharif A, Aloui C, Yarovaya L (2020) COVID-19 pandemic, oil prices, stock market, geopolitical risk and policy uncertainty nexus in the US economy: fresh evidence from the wavelet-based approach. Int Rev Financ Anal 70:101496. https://doi.org/10.1016/J.IRFA.2020.101496
11. Miklian J, Hoelscher K (2021) SMEs and exogenous shocks: A conceptual literature review and forward research agenda. Int Small Bus J Res Entrep 40:178–204. https://doi.org/10.1177/02662426211050796
12. Dayour F, Adongo CA, Kimbu AN (2020) Insurance uptake among small and medium-sized tourism and hospitality enterprises in a resource-scarce environment. Tour Manag Perspect 34: 100674. https://doi.org/10.1016/J.TMP.2020.100674
13. Agboola SA (1979) An agricultural atlas of Nigeria. Oxford University Press, Oxford
14. NPC (1991) National Population Commission 1991. National Population Commission, Abuja
15. Wikimedia Commons (2018) Nigeria states map. https://commons.wikimedia.org/wiki/File:Nigeria_States_map.svg. Accessed 8 Aug 2022
16. Cameron AC, Trivedi PK (2022) Microeconometrics: methods and applications, 2nd edn. Stata Press, College Station
17. Caliendo M, Kopeinig S (2008) Some practical guidance for the implementation of propensity score matching. J Econ Surv 22:31–72. https://doi.org/10.1111/J.1467-6419.2007.00527.X
18. Lee DS (2008) Randomized experiments from non-random selection in U.S. House elections. J Econom 142:675–697. https://doi.org/10.1016/J.JECONOM.2007.05.004
19. Sianesi B (2004) An evaluation of the swedish system of active labor market programs in the 1990s. Rev Econ Stat 86:133–155. https://doi.org/10.1162/003465304323023723
20. Rosenbaum PR (2002) Observational studies, 2nd edn. Springer, New York
21. Heckman JJ, Ichimura H, Todd P (1998) Matching as an econometric evaluation estimator. Rev Econ Stud 65:261–294
22. Rosenbaum PR, Rubin DB (1983) The central role of the propensity score in observational studies for causal effects. Biometrika 70:41–55. https://doi.org/10.1093/BIOMET/70.1.41

23. Yu D, Portera C (2014) Insurance companies have a big problem with millennials. In: Gall News Bus J. https://news.gallup.com/businessjournal/181829/insurance-companies-big-problem-millennials.aspx. Accessed 7 Jul 2022
24. Kwapisz A (2020) Health insurance coverage and sources of advice in entrepreneurship: gender differences. J Bus Ventur Insights 14:e00177. https://doi.org/10.1016/J.JBVI.2020.E00177
25. Wolfe MT, Patel PC (2019) To your health: health insurance, self-employment exit, and older entrepreneurs. J Small Bus Manag 57:593–615. https://doi.org/10.1111/JSBM.12412
26. Kelly M, Nielson N (2006) Age as a variable in insurance pricing and risk classification. Geneva Pap Risk Insur Issues Pract 31:212–232. https://doi.org/10.1057/PALGRAVE.GPP.2510082/TABLES/3
27. Kamara JM, Makori M (2017) Determinants of uptake of insurance services among small and medium enterprises in Nairobi City County, Kenya. Strateg J Bus Chang Manag 4:1054–1072
28. Jatto AN (2019) Assessment of farmer's awareness of agricultural insurance packages: evidence from "Farming is our pride" communities of Zamfara State, Nigeria. Agric Trop Subtrop 52:79–83. https://doi.org/10.2478/ATS-2019-0009
29. Churchill C (2007) Insuring the low-income market: challenges and solutions for commercial insurers. Geneva Pap Risk Insur Issues Pract 32:401–412. https://doi.org/10.1057/PALGRAVE.GPP.2510132/TABLES/1
30. Alesane A, Anang BT (2018) Uptake of health insurance by the rural poor in Ghana: determinants and implications for policy. Pan Afr Med J 31:124. https://doi.org/10.11604/PAMJ.2018.31.124.16265
31. Rejda GE (2015) Social insurance and economic security, 7th edn. Taylor and Francis, New York
32. Banerjee A, Duflo E, Hornbeck R (2014) Bundling health insurance and microfinance in India: there cannot be adverse selection if there is no demand. Am Econ Rev 104:291–297. https://doi.org/10.1257/AER.104.5.291
33. Chishala C, Musawa N (2018) Determination of factors influencing micro and small and medium enterprises from taking insurance as a risk management tool. Int J Multidiscip Res 695:1–11

Shocks from the COVID-19 Crisis in Ethiopia

Solomon T. Abebe and Giuseppe T. Cirella

1 Introduction

The nation state is a complex system that is vulnerable to many types of shocks and stressors. These include natural hazards such as storms and sea-level rise, but also manmade phenomena, e.g., economic transformation and rapid urbanization. These disturbances have the potential to reverse years of socioeconomic development gains by increasing poverty and inequality in rural and urban communities. Nation states that hope to grow and thrive in the future will need to take precautionary steps to address these threats. Simply put, a resilient nation state can adapt to these changing conditions and withstand such shocks while still providing essential services to its people. By doing so, those that account for these pressures can continue to thrive and meet their long-term development goals despite these challenges. The world came to a standstill when the COVID-19 pandemic sprung out of Wuhan, China, quickly bringing human misfortune and huge economic harm around the world [1, 2]. As of August 8, 2022, there have been over 584,637,073 confirmed cases of COVID-19 around the world with 6,418,203 confirmed deaths attributed to the disease [3]. Clearly, pandemics can harm economic activities [4, 5]. Given the speedy unfolding of COVID-19, countries throughout the world have adopted several public health measures, inclusive of social distancing [6]. In Ethiopia, 492,412 cases were registered with 7569 passings—August 8, 2022 [3]. Numerous scholars have noted that the COVID-19 pandemic will continue to cause widespread increases in global poverty and food insecurity. Moreover, Barrett [7] underscored how the most vulnerable segments of the population, i.e., low and middle-income countries, are

S. T. Abebe (✉)
Polo Centre of Sustainability, Imperia, Italy

G. T. Cirella
Faculty of Economics, University of Gdansk, Sopot, Poland
e-mail: gt.cirella@ug.edu.pl

G. T. Cirella (ed.), *Uncertainty Shocks in Africa*, Advances in African Economic, Social and Political Development, https://doi.org/10.1007/978-3-031-21885-9_4

most susceptible to these negative impacts. Laborde et al. [8], Swinnen and McDermott [9], and Torero [10] estimate that due to the COVID-19 pandemic over 140 million people will fall into extreme poverty and suffer from food insecurity and hunger, with many of these individuals coming from sub-Saharan Africa. As such, disruptions to food systems and changes in farming and consumer prices could turn out to be major drivers of food insecurity [11–13]. Given the importance of agricultural prices for the income of farmers and food prices and the purchasing power of consumers, changes in agricultural prices are one of the main concerns policymakers in low and middle-income countries must consider when faced with a global economic shock [7, 14]. In this chapter, the economic shock of the pandemic will be explored by examining the macroeconomy, poverty and food insecurity, and social conditions of Ethiopia from 2019 (i.e., before the COVID-19 outbreak) to the end of 2021.

2 Macroeconomic Status: Pre- to Post-pandemic

Before the impact of COVID-19, the Ethiopian macroeconomy had massive imbalances in economic outputs, unemployment, and inflation [15, 16]. This is the result of structural factors and corrupted administrations that dominated from 1991 to 2018 before the modern-day high minster, Prime Minister Abyi Ahmed, took office on April 2, 2018. Varying efforts have been made to quantify the effect of COVID-19 on the economy of Ethiopia by using various scenario-driven approaches. By calculating the severity of the pandemic with ongoing trends in the Ethiopian and world economy, Cancedda et al. [17], the United Nations [18], the International Monetary Fund (IMF) [19], Beyene et al. [20], and Goshu et al. [21], have pinpointed the initial downfall at the beginning of 2020 and the rebound at the end of 2021. The unfolding of COVID-19 brought economic activities throughout the world to a near-standstill. According to the World Bank [22], global gross domestic product (GDP) in 2020, relative to 2019, fell by 5.9%, before jumping back up by 9.1% in 2021, i.e., 3.2% higher than pre-pandemic levels (Fig. 1). According to the Organization for Economic Co-operation and Development, as countries emerged from the most acute phase of the COVID-19 pandemic, "addressing structural inequalities, accelerating the green transition, and strengthening resilience in the face of future challenges" [23] was critical to best deal with the hardship for low-income people and the world's poorest economies.

Before the start of COVID-19, Ethiopia's government predicted economic growth between 2019 and 2020 at 9%. The World Bank and IMF revised this estimate to 6% at the onset of the pandemic and later lowered it again to 3.5% in June 2020, i.e., once the macroeconomic impacts of the pandemic began to reveal themselves [24]. Furthermore, IMF projected a macroeconomic growth rate of 4.4% in the stronger economies of the developed world (e.g., the USA, Japan, Germany, and the UK). Broadly speaking, their exceptional fiscal, monetary, and regulatory response helped to maintain disposable income, defend monetary flows for

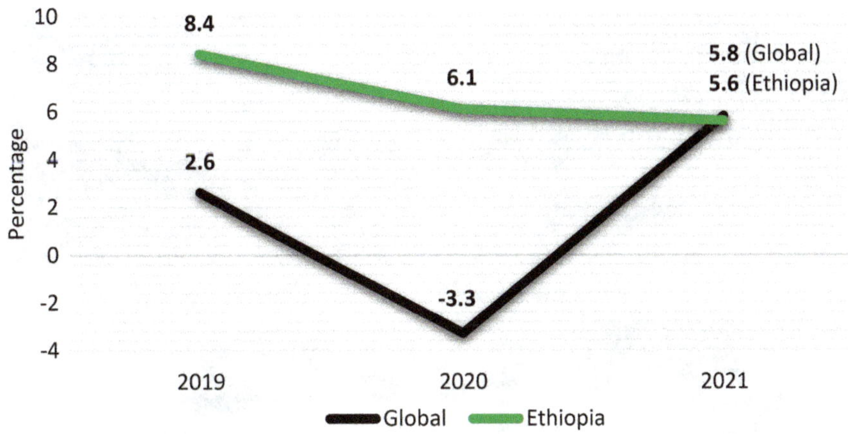

Fig. 1 Global and Ethiopia's annual GDP growth, 2019-2021. Source: World Bank [22]

enterprises, and assist in savings provisions [25]. The real issue on how a developing country with a weaker macroeconomic status such as Ethiopia has found it difficult to recover from the economic shock of COVID-19, largely, tells the story of an underdeveloped and underachieving economy. According to the United Nations Conference on Trade and Development, demand management is an important policy direction for the sustainable recovery of primary extraction industries which are tied to such commodity and mineral export revenues—a primary function of Ethiopia's developmental operability. The need for this revival is not only needed to recover from the global shock of the pandemic but it also dates back to the lingering effects of the global financial crisis of 2008 which still has a macroeconomic impact on Ethiopia's growth [26]. In terms of output gap, i.e., the percentage deviation of actual output from its potential level, Abebaw [27] pieced together important potential output and output gap research in Ethiopia from 1990 to 2018, i.e., pre-pandemic. Over the span of 29 years, key macroeconomic indicators that had an effect on the country's output gap included trade openness and lending rate (i.e., by way of a positive effect), and foreign direct investment (FDI) and inflation (i.e., by way of a negative effect). Abebaw [27] suggested that "augmenting domestic production and utilization capacity, avoiding unrestricted importation and, export diversification, lowering lending rate and increasing FDI inflow" would help reduce the overall output gap. Correspondingly, in 2017, Moller and Wacker [28] concluded that key drivers of Ethiopia's growth were "public infrastructure investment, restrained government consumption, and a conducive external environment." In this research, the macroeconomic imbalances only moderately slowed some aspects of growth, explaining why economic growth quickly rose in Ethiopia up to the beginning of the start of the pandemic. Also, it has been suggested that since Ethiopia has somewhat properly focalized infrastructure development for some decades, this has outweighed "moderate shortcoming in the macro framework at early stages of [its] development" [28]. This can be confirmed by Gemechu [29] who looked at the

Fig. 2 Urban development in Addis Ababa, Ethiopia. Source: (*top left*, *bottom left*, and *bottom right*) Photographs by Solomon T. Abebe, July 27, 2022; (*top right*) photograph by Solen Feyissa on Upsplash, Creative Commons Public Domain, January 24, 2022

macroeconomic effects of fiscal policy shocks in Ethiopia during the period 2000–2015, and found that output, inflation, interest rate, and exchange rate had a positive influence on the economy. In Ethiopia, traditionally such government spending shocks have positively affected GDP and recurrent expenditure which have bettered actual output levels. As such, these moves, empirically, supported the macro development of Ethiopia pre-pandemic even if the country's high debt burden—i.e., external debt stock at USD 27 billion or 28.1% of GDP and total debt at USD 54 billion or 56% of GDP [30]—in 2019 forced the government to restructure external debt to allow for some "breathing space" [31]. Currently, the economic recovery process has exhibited some positive signs of bouncing back from the "two-fold fiscal impact, pulling in opposite directions" [32], i.e., from the health side of the pandemic and from the economic shock side filtering through the economy. Significant urban institutional and infrastructure development have been seen as a result of the country's post-pandemic fiscal redirection, e.g., Addis Ababa's continued development of high-rises and road infrastructure in its city center [33–36] (Fig. 2). The macroeconomic big picture of Ethiopia indicates the need for investors and policymakers to mitigate the consequences of the pandemic by continuing to jumpstart GDP, employment, and inflation via a consumer price index revival [37] and constructive macroeconomic policy that will keep its people safe and secure. On that note, this chapter will now focus on the socioeconomic imbalances in Ethiopia by reevaluating how the pandemic shocked the poor and most vulnerable in society. Linkages between social and economic measures are considered, including how to best deal with the pandemic's aftereffects and mitigate future shocks.

3 Socioeconomics and Inequality Shock: Rethinking Availability

Traditionally, people who have a lower socioeconomic status are more exposed to the risks of inflation, unemployment, and other difficulties associated with economic hardships [38]. Though COVID-19 is a transitory shock, it could have lasting negative socioeconomic impacts for Ethiopian households following the lockdown measures carried out by the government. The impact for citizens has already manifested in several ways, most notably, with regards to decreased salaries and non-labor incomes, increased living costs (e.g., imported goods and carrier disruptions), and suspension of schooling and food programs [39]. Data suggests that the economic costs of the COVID-19 lockdowns were worse felt by low profit, informal workers in cities who were unable to work from home and not covered by social security or any other form of social insurance [40]. The impact on such a large demographic group will be a challenge and could set off a slowdown effect in economic growth for the poor—i.e., potentially raising the poverty rate and prolonging a post-pandemic revival [41]. The latest poverty headcount estimate for Ethiopia is 23.5% based on the national poverty line and 27% based on the international poverty line. These figures are based on an adjusted daily purchasing power of USD 1.90 per day [42, 43]. In a World Bank survey, it was confirmed that about 18% of urban respondents lost their job since the pandemic began; however, it is worth noting that around 40% of these people attributed their job loss to non-pandemic reasons, instead stating the cause to seasonal or transient work environments [43].

In repeated studies by Harris et al. [39, 44], from August 2020 to August 2021, the common month-to-month earnings of Ethiopian households were found to increase over five cycles, from ETB 2016 (i.e., USD 39.00) in the first to ETB 3045 (i.e., USD 58.00) in the fifth. The share of households that pronounced the capacity to earn identical earnings to pre-pandemic levels was also elevated from 66% to 91%, respectfully. They observed that having an equal income, or having a reduced income, during the yearlong study, was due to variations in living and job type. As such, acquiring a sufficient amount of food still remained (and remains) the most necessary undertaking for the urban poor. Income inequality among Ethiopians suggests that the decline in the purchasing strength of the Ethiopian Birr affected their capacity to pay for the fundamental costs of food, shelter, and clothing. Notably, the pandemic created food insecurity since it was unaffordable due to the large and frequent price increases. Comparably, Dasgupta and Robinson [45] indicated that higher income households in Ethiopia were less likely to suffer from food insecurity due to the pandemic. They illustrated how households that were in a position to depend on their financial savings had a decreased likelihood of suffering from meals and food insecurity. In contrast, poorer households with no savings that had suffered an income loss had a reduced livelihood resilience and where more likely to go through meals and food insecurity even post-pandemic. In spite of this, Harris et al. [39, 44] found that the share of households who had a common of three or more meals per day had gradually improved: 62.5% in August 2020, 74.4% in October 2020, 79.9% in November 2020, 83.8% in May 2021, and 85.4% for August of 2021. This revealed how in 1 year food security improved for Ethiopians by 22.9%. However, despite the gradual improvement throughout the five rounds, the result is still beneath the pre-COVID-19 period, when 94.2% of households consumed a common of three or more meals per day. To help alleviate some of this burden, the Urban Productive Safety Nets Program (UPSNP), established in 2016, covering eleven major regional cities in Ethiopia, aided in closing the socioeconomic gap by targeting the urban poor at risk and focusing on the homeless and underage. Other social protection initiatives included community-based health insurance, introduced in 375 districts between 2017-2018 covered 15% of all households—with an 80% target for 2020. Unfortunately, due to the COVID-19 pandemic, this target was not met. Thus, in 2020 temporary support of more than 550,000 additional households in 27 Ethiopian cities using UPSNP were provided by the government and the World Bank. This response initially lasted for 3 months before being topped up by the United Nations International Children's Emergency Fund for an additional 60,000 UPSNP households [46]. As a result, it is estimated that the beneficiaries of UPSNP will increase from 9 to 10–15 million people in the near future. Regrettably, this will increase the level of extreme poverty and continue to pressure vulnerable groups for a longer period post-pandemic.

4 Poverty and the Environment: Linkages to Better Understand How Ethiopia Fell Short During the Pandemic

According to the World Bank [47], with over 115 million people in 2020, Ethiopia has the second largest population in Africa after Nigeria. Despite the problems and economic slowdown from the pandemic, it still had the fastest-growing economy in the region with a 6.1% growth between 2019 and 2020. Ethiopia, however, concurrently is also one of the poorest countries in the world with a GDP per capita of USD 944.00 [48]. Over 24.2 million of its total citizens live in absolute poverty, i.e., when calculating ETB 20 (i.e., USD 0.40) per day per person as the poverty line. Moreover, when compared to the global poverty scale, over 80 million Ethiopians (i.e., 73%) are considered impoverished, living on less than USD 1.25 per day [15]. In Ethiopia, the majority of the population living in poverty are subsistent agriculturalists and farmers that live in rural areas and grow food crops to meet their (family and community) needs. Moreover, many working in the formal (and informal) sector in urban areas also live with insufficient funds. These two population groups are vulnerable to external shocks, such as droughts and outbreaks, which can push them further into life-threatening situations. The economic effect of COVID-19 in Ethiopia aggravated the challenge of poverty, especially for the urban poor [16] (Fig. 3). In any case, the focus on the rural poor should not be understated. In fact,

Fig. 3 Urban and rural poor in Ethiopia: (*top left*) dilapidated houses made up of wood, mud, and corrugated iron sheet, Arada sub-city district of Addis Ababa, (*top right*) crowded marketplace in northern Ethiopia, (*bottom left*) rural agriculture farmer plowing land, and (*bottom right*) rural woman using a donkey to collect water. Source: (*top left*) Photograph by Bedane S. Gemeda, August 1, 2022; (*top right*) Photograph by Lesly Derksen on Upsplash, Creative Commons Public Domain, October 25, 2020; (*bottom left* and *bottom right*) photographs by dMz on Pixabay, Creative Commons Public Domain, April 11, 2019

since rural communities predominately grow and produce their own food, prioritizing rural communities and getting them back on their feet as quickly as possible will allow more resources to be then focused on urban settings, i.e., by using rural resources (e.g., food grown in the countryside) as an additional internal support mechanism.

In many parts of the Global South, the impact of the pandemic is more pronounced in urban areas where a large share of the population lives in poor, unsanitary conditions without electricity and water supplies [49]. In the face of the COVID-19 crisis, there was an increasing indication that existing gender inequalities in economic opportunities worsened across the globe [50]. As stated, female employees in had an elevated chance of experiencing a damaging effect from the pandemic when compared with men. Cancedda et al. [17] found that in three of the most affected sectors in Ethiopia, women represent more than 80% of the workforce, i.e., 74% in tourism, 80% in fabric and garment industries, and 85% in floriculture. Moreover, female-headed households had an excessive poverty persistence of 45%, suggesting that post-pandemic, it will continue to have an extreme impact on the welfare of Ethiopian women living in urban areas [41]. Similarly, in terms of youth, job losses continued for both the formal and informal sector. "A monitoring survey of 3107 households, conducted by the World Bank in April and June 2020, [indicated] that 38% of casual laborers have lost income or their job" [51]. This is reported to be predominately from the services sector and secondary agriculture work such as street vendors and food processing facilities. Several studies showed that approximately one-fifth of Ethiopia still experiences a lack of food [51, 52] with affordability being the main concern. It is estimated, from pre-pandemic to the end of 2020, that food waste has increased by 11–15% and severe acute malnutrition unexpectedly increased by 10–15% [53]. This alone has cause for concern as severe interlinkage disconnects, i.e., on how Ethiopia has fallen short over that last 2 years, will make socio-ecological development and social protection harder to achieve and continue to create cyclic impoverishment at the human nature relations level [54].

4.1 Socio-Ecological Development and Environmental Degradation

Environmental concerns plague Ethiopia in terms of its ability to development in a sound and socio-ecologically manner. Keeping the country's development in-line with a sustainable, best practices approach will be challenging but crucial to people's well-being and the environment. In terms of the pandemic, the world lockdown slowed global travel, subsequently reducing the emissions of CO_2 and other pollutants. This predictively had a net positive impact on the environment [55, 56]. For example, in China, He et al. [57] illustrated how lockdown measures led to a bettering in air quality. They supported their argument by showing how the Air Quality Index and the satisfactory particulate count concentrations fell by 25% within a few weeks of the lockdown in China's colder, richer, and largest industrialized cities [57]. Similarly, Almond et al. [55] monitored air pollution and greenhouse gases in China in 2020 and discovered that, while NO_2 emissions fell precipitously, SO_2 emissions did not significantly decline. Also, for China as a whole, $PM_{2.5}$ emissions fell by 22%, while O_3 concentrations improved by 40%. These variations exhibit that there is not always an unambiguous enhancement in air pollution due to a financial slowdown. In any case, the reduction could be attributed to less mobility options (e.g., fewer non-public vehicles in use) causing a decrease in harmful pollutants and emission levels [55]. In most cases, however, travel restrictions have significantly reduced NO_2 and CO_2 which are pollutants directly associated with the transportation sector [58–60]. In this same manner, as the pandemic swept across Ethiopia many people abandoned public transit, fearful of catching the disease on crowded buses and trains. The Ethiopian government, as a result, started a program to encourage its citizens to cycle and walk (Fig. 4). Officially known as the Non-Motorized Transport Strategy 2020–2029, the idea was launched by Dagmawit Moges, Ethiopia's Minister of Transport in 2020 [61]. Accordingly, Ethiopian cities have started planning streets to accommodate non-motorized transport which, if successful, should reduce the socioeconomic gap by aiding the urban poor with better mobility options and a cleaner, sounder urban lifestyle.

Fig. 4 Well-developed pedestrian walkways and road crossings in the Addis Ababa, Ethiopia. Source: Photographs by Solomon T. Abebe, August 1, 2022

Relatedly, since a clean environment is an essential part of human survival, it makes up the fundamental part for healthy living. Reducing environmental pollution, e.g., air, water, and soil polluted with contaminants and toxins harmful to human health, can reduce disease and cancer, among other problems. Water pollution, for instance, can lead to typhoid and diarrheal diseases, which can be harmful to a person's mental and physical well-being [62–64]. Unfortunately, Ethiopia's insufficient water supply can affect everything from personal hygiene to the country's wastewater systems—in effect, suppressing the ability to adequately survive. Based on Harris et al.'s [39, 44] work from 2020 and 2021, the proportion of households that reported an incident of water shortage increased across Ethiopia—by 34% in August 2020, 32% in October 2020, 36% in November 2020, 50% in May 2021, and 39% in August 2021—compared to the average level from 2019. Though their study has some limitations, many impoverished Ethiopians were noted as unable to explore other non-COVID-19 related factors that may have influenced their livelihood and ability to better cope with the pandemic during this period. As such, important factors of well-being play an important part of environmental degradation in Ethiopia. Apart from the serious impacts of agriculture and farming which have been severe over the past 2 years, the increased vulnerability of many people to food and water insecurity, soil erosion, and land degradation combined with "population growth, intensive agricultural and pastoral use, the cultivation of marginal land, commercial timber-getting, high natural vulnerability to soil erosion, and inadequate soil conservation practices" [65], has become ever-increasingly challenging during the post-pandemic era. Key environmental issues for Ethiopians—that interlink with social and community well-being—need to consider the environmental costs of sound, clean transport; profitable and sustainable heavy and light industries; water and energy, i.e., via dam construction for electricity, to promote economic development and facilitate flood control; and agriculture development-led industrialization that can support how the majority of Ethiopians live [65]. Since Ethiopia is endowed with abundant natural resources and abundant land, many of its resources are still not properly "identified, well managed, and fully exploited" [66]. Natural resources under the influence of various connected factors, e.g., "population pressure, agricultural expansion, migration, rapid urbanization, resettlement, climate change, and environmental pollution" [66], must better amplify the connection between development and environmental consequences [67]. In doing so, the country will better manage "diverse socioeconomic problems, political instability, marginalization, poverty, and recurrent natural hazards" [66]. To date, several steps to address these problems have been introduced with limited success [66, 68]. Since an innate relationship between environmental degradation and poverty exists, Ethiopian authorities are stressed to engage in environmental education to create a sort of "poverty alleviation strategy" [68] and social protection system as part of an eco-friendly resolve to its larger COVID-19 rebound plan.

5 Social Protection and Safety Net Structures

The greatest intervention to compensate people and households for income loss related to the COVID-19 measures were direct money transfers. To aid with the devastating effects on people's ability to work, Fig. 5 illustrates the empty streets in Addis Ababa during the lockdown and the busy ones after the measures were lifted. According to the 151-country study by Gentilini et al. [42], social assistance in Africa accounted for 86% in which 50% of recipients received cash transfers. In Ethiopia, responses to COVID-19 accelerated towards humanitarian and social safety programs, i.e., from hard to reach urban areas to countrywide social protection [69]. The Ethiopian government developed the COVID-19 Multi-Sectoral Preparedness and Response Plan (MSPRP) in response to the pandemic [70]. A "vertical expansion" was applied in May 2020 in which money top-ups were presented by UPSNP direct support beneficiaries. The top-ups were, first, employed as meal plans for citizens struggling from the crisis and then used to cover electricity bills up to a maximum of 2100 watts per individual per day for 6 months. At the same time, a "horizontal expansion" by UPSNP was introduced to help, specifically, the urban population. The horizonal expansion focused on poor city households not previously registered in the eleven UPSNP cities and included 3 months of unconditional

Fig. 5 Street busyness in Addis Abada: (*left*) during the COVID-19 lockdown measures—December 19, 2020, and (*right*) no lockdown measures—July 27, 2022. Source: Photographs by Solomon T. Abebe

money transfers [53]. As part of MSPRP, a total of USD 635 million was allotted for emergency meals distribution to 15 million people in Ethiopia in which most of it was donor financed by other countries and associated humanitarian support [71]. Authorities in some Ethiopian cities such as Addis Ababa opened 1200 food banks—mobilized by the volunteers, community representatives, and non-governmental organizations—to help deliver the food and help combat hunger. As a result, COVID-19 showed the effectiveness of comprehensive, coordinated, and inclusive social safety structures of humanitarian interventions against such a shock. There is hope that the Ethiopian government will invest in constructing these systems permanently, i.e., to help empower residents, especially lower bracket earners and informal citizens protect their social safety rights and limit future shocks [69]. By enhancing the social protection system, individuals and their families will be better able to cope with crises and shocks by helping them find work, improve productivity, and invest in the health and education of their children.

In terms of personal health, previous research indicated that infectious outbreaks result in psychological problems consisting of anxiety, depression, and insomnia [72–74]. Mental health and psychological problems are most common in Ethiopia's poor due to prolonged poverty, misery, and lack of resources. During the height of the pandemic, these problems increased in many countries from around the world. For instance, a significant wave of spiked depression cases was recorded from 2019 to 2020 in China from 20.1% to 48.3% [75–77], the USA from 8.5% to 27.8% [78], India from 14.1 to 41.9% [79, 80], and Egypt from 27.9 to 67.1% [81]. In an Addis Ababa study, the prevalence of depression among the urban community was reported to be 12.4% in 2020 [82]. This figure is lower compared to other countries mentioned, most probably, due to low reporting in medical centers. Consequently, depression most likely was higher as other research by Lemma et al. [83] reported unrecognized depression in Ethiopia at 15.9% from March to April 2019—right at the start of the COVID-19 outbreak. Since this touches on the core of one's well-being, it is recommended that a future shock strategy determine the prevalence and associated factors on varying socioeconomic groups to include early depression screening carried out by health professionals [83, 84]. This will strengthen the social protection strategy and narrow the socioeconomic gap in the country. Furthermore, in the study by Kassaw [82], it was further outlined that gender, monthly income, educational status, number of family members, contact with COVID-19, and other health-related issues were significantly associated with depression. However, according to Harris et al. [39, 44], the share of respondents reporting a feeling of burden or fear with regards to COVID-19 diminished from 72% in August 2020 to 50% in August 2021. This alone could equate to an overall societal resilience and need to survive (i.e., move forward) regardless of the pandemic.

6 Rebounding from COVID-19: Recommendations

In all, Ethiopia's societal rebound must consider that nearly two-thirds of the losses from the services sector occurred because of the pandemic. Recovery scenarios by Aragie et al. [85] point out that resources can only help "if targeted in an efficient way towards sectors most affected by COVID-19, and further resources are mobilized to support strategic sectors—those with the highest economywide multiplier effects—and vulnerable communities." Utilizing a dual channel system of domestic and international impact to aid and better facilitate how direct, indirect, and economywide impacts affected Ethiopia and how the country might manage a recovery strategy is outline in Fig. 6.

Workable and precise policy recommendations in Ethiopia should first be prioritization for short-term relief measures. This should be via direct transfers to the most affected and vulnerable in which price subsidies on key consumption and intermediate commodities should be accommodated. Key targeted sectors should facilitate job creation and food security as well as severe budget constraints earmarked in an efficient way towards "sectors with the highest economywide multiplier effects and those most affected by COVID-19 related response measures" [85]. Recommendations to develop policy initiatives should allow an employment-led economic recovery to be intertwined with social partnerships for job creation, job quality, and job access in the short and long term. In terms of secondary responses, *r*esources, intensified surveillance, and capacity building should be considered. A coordinated effort to mobilize domestic and international resources that support key macroeconomic variables is needed. Economics recovery policies should be divided into two branches. First, fiscal policies should focus on supporting the household level, unemployed, businesses and small and medium enterprises, and the health sector. Second, monetary policies should be collectively arranged to aid exchange rate and capital account management, interest rate cuts, liquidity reserve requirement ratio

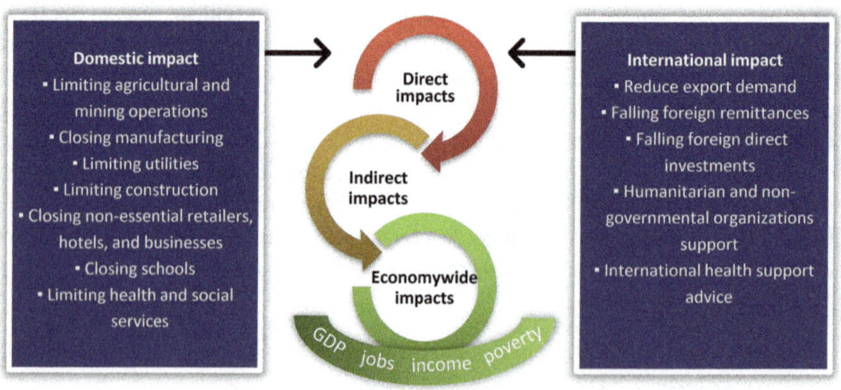

Fig. 6 Dual channel system of domestic and international impact to move forward from the COVID-19 pandemic in Ethiopia. Source: adapted from Aragie et al. [85]

cuts, and direct liquidity provision [86]. Also, on February 9, 2022, world leaders put together funding for the Access to COVID-19 Tools (ACT) accelerator to end the COVID-19 pandemic [87]. ACT should be considered as a partnership initiative for low and middle-income countries, like Ethiopia, for relief purposes. Finally, to accelerate structural change, in terms of agriculture transformation, industrialization, and digitalization [88], these sectors should be given a long-term ecologically-friendly priority as they can, consequentially, impact poverty reduction and improve human development and well-being.

References

1. Verschuur J, Koks EE, Hall JW (2021) Observed impacts of the COVID-19 pandemic on global trade. Nat Hum Behav 5:305–307. https://doi.org/10.1038/s41562-021-01060-5
2. McKee M, Stuckler D (2020) If the world fails to protect the economy, COVID-19 will damage health not just now but also in the future. Nat Med 26:640–642. https://doi.org/10.1038/s41591-020-0863-y
3. JHU (2022) Johns Hopkins Coronavirus Resource Center. https://coronavirus.jhu.edu/. Accessed 6 Jul 2022
4. Ambrocio G (2020) The impact of COVID-19 on European household expectations. VOX, CEPR Policy Portal. https://voxeu.org/article/impact-covid-19-european-household-expectations. Accessed 10 Jun 2022
5. OECD (2020) Global economy faces a tightrope walk to recovery. Organisation for Economic Cooperation and Development, Paris
6. Fong MW, Gao H, Wong JY et al (2020) Nonpharmaceutical measures for pandemic influenza in nonhealthcare settings—social distancing measures. Emerg Infect Dis 26:976. https://doi.org/10.3201/EID2605.190995
7. Barrett CB (2020) Actions now can curb food systems fallout from COVID-19. Nat Food 1: 319–320. https://doi.org/10.1038/s43016-020-0085-y
8. Laborde D, Martin W, Swinnen J, Vos R (2020) COVID-19 risks to global food security. Science (80-) 369:500–502. https://doi.org/10.1126/SCIENCE.ABC4765
9. Swinnen J, McDermott J (2020) COVID-19 and global food security. IFPRI, Washington, DC
10. Torero M (2020) Without food, there can be no exit from the pandemic. Nature 580:588–589. https://doi.org/10.1038/d41586-020-01181-3
11. Endris Mekonnen E, Kassegn Amede A (2022) Food insecurity and unemployment crisis under COVID-19: evidence from sub-Saharan Africa. http://www.editorialmanager.com/cogentsocsci 8. doi:https://doi.org/10.1080/23311886.2022.2045721
12. Tabe-Ojong MP, Gebrekidan BH, Nshakira-Rukundo E et al (2022) COVID-19 in rural Africa: food access disruptions, food insecurity and coping strategies in Kenya, Namibia, and Tanzania. Agric Econ. https://doi.org/10.1111/AGEC.12709
13. Mohamed EMA, Abdallah SMA, Ahmadi A, Lucero-Prisno DE (2021) Food security and COVID-19 in Africa: implications and recommendations. Am J Trop Med Hyg 104:1613. https://doi.org/10.4269/AJTMH.20-1590
14. Bellemare MF (2015) Rising food prices, food price volatility, and social unrest. Am J Agric Econ 97:1–21. https://doi.org/10.1093/AJAE/AAU038
15. Geda A, Yimer A (2016) Capital flight and its determinants: the case of Ethiopia. African Dev Rev 28:39–49. https://doi.org/10.1111/1467-8268.12180
16. Geda A (2021) The macroeconomic and social impact of COVID-19 in Ethiopia in the global context. UNCTAD, Addis Ababa

17. Cancedda A, Hurnik J, Minardi C et al (2020) Mitigating the socio-economic impacts of COVID-19 in Ethiopia, with a focus on vulnerable groups: annex I-vulnerability impact fiches. United Nations International Children's Emergency Fund, New York
18. UN (2020) Socio-economic impact of COVID-19 in Ethiopia. United Nations International Children's Emergency Fund, New York
19. IMF (2022) Regional economic outlook for Sub-Saharan Africa. International Monetary Fund, Washington, DC
20. Mitik Beyene L, Ferede T, Diriba G (2020) The economywide impact of the COVID-19 in Ethiopia: policy and recovery options. Addis Ababa
21. Goshu D, Ferede T, Diriba G, Ketema M (2020) Economic and welfare effects of COVID-19 and responses in Ethiopia: initial insights. Addis Ababa
22. World Bank (2022) GDP growth (annual %) | Data. https://data.worldbank.org/indicator/NY.GDP.MKTP.KD.ZG. Accessed 6 Jul 2022
23. OECD (2022) OECD COVID-19 recovery dashboard. The Organization for Economic Co-operation and Development. https://www.oecd.org/coronavirus/en/recovery-dashboard. Accessed 6 Jul 2022
24. NBE (2021) Annual report. National Bank of Ethiopia. https://nbebank.com/annual-report/. Accessed 6 Jul 2022
25. IMF (2021) World economic outlook, April 2021: managing divergent recoveries. International Monetary Fund
26. WHO (2021) TDR annual report 2020. World Health Organization, Geneva
27. Abebaw A (2021) Output gap determinants in Ethiopia. Cogent Econ Financ 9. https://doi.org/10.1080/23322039.2021.1887550
28. Moller LC, Wacker KM (2017) Explaining Ethiopia's growth acceleration—the role of infrastructure and macroeconomic policy. World Dev 96:198–215. https://doi.org/10.1016/J.WORLDDEV.2017.03.007
29. Gemechu KT (2018) The macroeconomic effects of fiscal policy shock in Ethiopia: evidence from a Bayesian VAR approach. Ethiop J Econ 26:31–66. https://doi.org/10.4314/eje.v26i1
30. Tesso G (2020) Review of the impact of COVID-19 on economic growth, unemployment and progress out of poverty in Ethiopia. Ambo University, Addis Ababa
31. IMF (2019) IMF country reports: the federal democratic Republic of Ethiopia. International Monetary Fund. https://www.imf.org/en/Publications/CR/Issues/2020/05/06/The-Federal-Democratic-Republic-of-Ethiopia-Requests-for-Purchasing-under-the-Rapid-49396. Accessed 23 Jul 2022
32. Ababulgu Abasimel N, Wana Fufa H (2022) The horrors of COVID-19 and the recent macroeconomy in Ethiopia. J Knowl Econ 13:305–320. https://doi.org/10.1007/S13132-020-00713-6/FIGURES/1
33. Beyer E, Elsner LA, Hagemann A, Misselwitz P (2021) Industrial infrastructure: translocal planning for global production in Ethiopia and Argentina. Urban Plan 6:444–463. https://doi.org/10.17645/UP.V6I3.4211
34. Gelan E, Girma Y (2021) Sustainable urban green infrastructure development and management system in rapidly urbanized cities of Ethiopia. Technologies 9:66. https://doi.org/10.3390/TECHNOLOGIES9030066
35. Horvat T, Bendix H, Bobek V, Skoko H (2020) Impacts of investments in infrastructure projects on emerging markets' growth: the case of East African countries. Econ Res Istraživanja 34:2135–2161. https://doi.org/10.1080/1331677X.2020.1860799
36. Cirolia LR, Hailu T, King J et al (2021) Infrastructure governance in the post-networked city: state-led, high-tech sanitation in Addis Ababa's condominium housing. Environ Plan C Polit Sp 39:1606–1624. https://doi.org/10.1177/23996544211037063
37. Redi SA, Novák P (2022) A review on macro-economic view in Ethiopia's entrepreneurship under COVID-19. Mod Manag Rev 27:69–79
38. Wade L (2020) An unequal blow. Science (80-) 368:700–703. https://doi.org/10.1126/SCIENCE.368.6492.700

39. Harris D, Tadesse B, Mitiku I et al (2020) The effect of COVID-19 and government response measures on poor and vulnerable groups in urban areas in Ethiopia in 2020. BRE, Addis Ababa
40. Amdeselassie T, Emirie G, Gezahegne K et al (2020) Experiences of vulnerable urban youth under COVID-19: the case of domestic workers. United Nations Population Fund, New York
41. Mekasha TJ, Tarp F (2021) Understanding poverty dynamics in Ethiopia: implications for the likely impact of COVID-19. Rev Dev Econ 25:1838–1868. https://doi.org/10.1111/RODE.12841
42. Gentilini U, Almenfi M, Orton I, Dale P (2020) Social protection and jobs responses to COVID-19: a real-time review of country measures. World Bank, Washington, DC
43. Wieser C, Marcela L, Sosa C et al (2021) Monitoring COVID-19 impacts on households in Ethiopia: results from a high-frequency phone survey of households. World Bank, Washington, DC
44. Harris D, Tadesse B, Mitiku I et al (2021) The effect of COVID-19 and government response measures on poor and vulnerable groups in urban areas in Ethiopia in 2021. BRE, Addis Ababa
45. Dasgupta S, Robinson EJZ (2021) Food insecurity, safety nets, and coping strategies during the COVID-19 pandemic: multi-country evidence from Sub-Saharan Africa. Int J Environ Res Public Health 18:9997. https://doi.org/10.3390/IJERPH18199997
46. Ethiopia UNICEF (2020) Socio-economic impacts of COVID-19. United Nations International Children's Emergency Fund, New York
47. World Bank (2022) Ethiopia overview: development news, research, data. https://www.worldbank.org/en/country/ethiopia/overview#1. Accessed 6 Jul 2022
48. World Bank (2022) GDP per capita (current US$): Ethiopia. In: World Bank Data. https://data.worldbank.org/indicator/NY.GDP.PCAP.CD?locations=ET. Accessed 26 Jul 2022
49. Biswas P (2020) Skewed urbanisation and the contagion. Econ Polit Wkly 55
50. Georgieva K, Fabrizio S, Lim CH, Tavares MM (2020) The COVID-19 gender gap. IMF Blog. https://blogs.imf.org/2020/07/21/the-covid-19-gender-gap/. Accessed 8 Jun 2022
51. de Roo N, de Boe W (2020) Rapid country assessment: Ethiopia. Wageningen University and Research, Wageningen
52. Van Berkum S, Dengerink J, Ruben R (2018) The food systems approach: Sustainable solutions for a sufficient supply of healthy food. Wageningen, Wageningen Economic Research
53. UN (2020) UN socio-economic impact assessment of COVID-19 in Ethiopia. United Nations Ethiopia, Addis Ababa
54. Cirella GT (2020) Sustainable human–nature relations: environmental scholarship, economic evaluation, urban strategies. Springer, Singapore
55. Almond D, Du X, Zhang S (2020) Ambiguous pollution response to COVID-19 in China. NBER Work Pap No 27086. doi:https://doi.org/10.3386/W27086
56. Cicala S, Holland SP, Mansur ET, et al (2020) Expected health effects of reduced air pollution from COVID-19 social distancing. NBER Work Pap No 27135. doi:https://doi.org/10.3386/W27135
57. He G, Pan Y, Tanaka T (2020) The short-term impacts of COVID-19 lockdown on urban air pollution in China. Nat Sustain 3:1005–1011. https://doi.org/10.1038/s41893-020-0581-y
58. Dantas G, Siciliano B, França BB et al (2020) The impact of COVID-19 partial lockdown on the air quality of the city of Rio de Janeiro, Brazil. Sci Total Environ 729:139085. https://doi.org/10.1016/J.SCITOTENV.2020.139085
59. Baldasano JM (2020) COVID-19 lockdown effects on air quality by NO2 in the cities of Barcelona and Madrid (Spain). Sci Total Environ 741:140353. https://doi.org/10.1016/J.SCITOTENV.2020.140353
60. Muntasir M, Syed YS (2018) Effects of urbanization on climate change: evidence From Bangladesh. J Nat Sci Res 8:1–8
61. UNEP (2020) Amid pandemic, Ethiopia launches national policy to encourage walking and cycling. In: United Nations Environ. Program. https://www.unep.org/news-and-stories/story/amid-pandemic-ethiopia-launches-national-policy-encourage-walking-and. Accessed 23 Jul 2022

62. Osiemo MM, Morara Ogendi G, M'erimba C (2019) Microbial quality of drinking water and prevalence of water-related diseases in Marigat Urban Centre, Kenya. Environ Health Insights 13:1–7. https://doi.org/10.1177/1178630219836988
63. Gauld JS, Olgemoeller F, Nkhata R et al (2020) Domestic river water use and risk of typhoid fever: results from a case-control study in Blantyre, Malawi. Clin Infect Dis 70:1278–1284. https://doi.org/10.1093/CID/CIZ405
64. Farooqui A, Khan A, Kazmi SU (2009) Investigation of a community outbreak of typhoid fever associated with drinking water. BMC Public Health 9:476. https://doi.org/10.1186/1471-2458-9-476
65. Daley B (2015) Environmental issues in Ethiopia and links to the Ethiopian economy. Evidence on Demand, London
66. Wassie SB (2020) Natural resource degradation tendencies in Ethiopia: a review. Environ Syst Res 9:1–29. https://doi.org/10.1186/S40068-020-00194-1
67. Cirella GT, Mwangi S, Streltsova K et al (2021) Human settlements: urban challenges and future development. In: Cirella GT (ed) Human settlements: urbanization, smart sector development, and future outlook. Springer, Singapore
68. Bekalo S, Bangay C (2002) Towards effective environmental education in Ethiopia: problems and prospects in responding to the environment—poverty challenge. Int J Educ Dev 22:35–46. https://doi.org/10.1016/S0738-0593(00)00076-6
69. Devereux S (2021) Social protection responses to COVID-19 in Africa: Glob. Soc Policy 21: 421–447. https://doi.org/10.1177/14680181211021260
70. FDRE (2020) COVID-19: national emergency response plan. Federal Democratic Republic of Ethiopia, Addis Ababa
71. IMF (2020) Policy responses to COVID19. International Monetary Fund. https://www.imf.org/en/Topics/imf-and-covid19/Policy-Responses-to-COVID-19. Accessed 10 Jun 2022
72. Lehmann M, Bruenahl CA, Löwe B et al (2015) Ebola and psychological stress of health care professionals. Emerg Infect Dis 21:913–914. https://doi.org/10.3201/EID2105.141988
73. Cénat JM, Blais-Rochette C, Kokou-Kpolou CK et al (2021) Prevalence of symptoms of depression, anxiety, insomnia, posttraumatic stress disorder, and psychological distress among populations affected by the COVID-19 pandemic: A systematic review and meta-analysis. Psychiatry Res 295:113599. https://doi.org/10.1016/J.PSYCHRES.2020.113599
74. Keita MM, Taverne B, Sy Savané S et al (2017) Depressive symptoms among survivors of Ebola virus disease in Conakry (Guinea): preliminary results of the PostEboGui cohort. BMC Psychiatry 17:1–9. https://doi.org/10.1186/S12888-017-1280-8/TABLES/3
75. Huang Y, Zhao N (2020) Generalized anxiety disorder, depressive symptoms and sleep quality during COVID-19 outbreak in China: a web-based cross-sectional survey. Psychiatry Res 288. https://doi.org/10.1016/J.PSYCHRES.2020.112954
76. Shadmi E, Chen Y, Dourado I et al (2020) Health equity and COVID-19: global perspectives. Int J Equity Health 19:104. https://doi.org/10.1186/s12939-020-01218-z
77. Gao J, Zheng P, Jia Y et al (2020) Mental health problems and social media exposure during COVID-19 outbreak. PLoS One 15:e0231924. https://doi.org/10.1371/JOURNAL.PONE.0231924
78. Ettman CK, Abdalla SM, Cohen GH et al (2020) Prevalence of depression symptoms in US adults before and during the COVID-19 pandemic. JAMA Netw Open 3:e2019686–e2019686. https://doi.org/10.1001/JAMANETWORKOPEN.2020.19686
79. Abdulla EK, Velladath SU, Varghese A, Anju M (2021) Depression and anxiety associated with COVID-19 pandemic among healthcare professionals in India - a systematic review and meta-analysis. Clin Epidemiol Glob Heal 12:100888. https://doi.org/10.1016/J.CEGH.2021.100888
80. Singh SP, Khokhar A (2021) Prevalence of posttraumatic stress disorder and depression in general population in India during COVID-19 pandemic home quarantine. Asia-Pacific J Public Heal 33:154–156. https://doi.org/10.1177/1010539520968455

81. Arafa A, Mohamed A, Saleh L, Senosy S (2021) Psychological impacts of the COVID-19 pandemic on the public in Egypt. Community Ment Health J 57:1. https://doi.org/10.1007/S10597-020-00701-9
82. Kassaw C (2020) The magnitude of psychological problem and associated factor in response to COVID-19 pandemic among communities living in Addis Ababa, Ethiopia, March 2020: a cross-sectional study design. Psychol Res Behav Manag 13:631–640. https://doi.org/10.2147/PRBM.S256551
83. Lemma A, Mulat H, Nigussie K, Getinet W (2021) Prevalence of unrecognized depression and associated factors among medical outpatient department attendees; a cross sectional study. PLoS One 16:e0261064. https://doi.org/10.1371/JOURNAL.PONE.0261064
84. Molla GL, Sebhat HM, Hussen ZN et al (2016) Depression among Ethiopian adults: cross-sectional study. Psychiatry J 2016:1–5. https://doi.org/10.1155/2016/1468120
85. Aragie E, Taffesse AS, Thurlow J (2021) The short-term economywide impacts of COVID-19 in Africa: insights from Ethiopia. African Dev Rev 33:S152. https://doi.org/10.1111/1467-8268.12519
86. Mwamadzingo M, Akuupa MU, Kazembe LN (2021) Macroeconomic policies for jobs-led growth and recovery following the COVID-19 pandemic, with emphasis on sub-Saharan Africa. Int J Labour Res 10:66–80
87. Adepoju P (2022) Africa prepares for endemic COVID-19. Nat Med 28:876–878. https://doi.org/10.1038/D41591-022-00040-0
88. Anyanwu JC, Salami AO (2021) The impact of COVID-19 on African economies: an introduction. African Dev Rev 33:S1. https://doi.org/10.1111/1467-8268.12531

Green Buildings and Green City Strategies for the COVID-19 Pandemic Affected Tourism Industry in Rwanda

Ilija Gubić, Dheeraj Arrabothu, Richard Ndicunguye, and Giuseppe T. Cirella

1 Background to Green Buildings and Green City Strategies in Rwanda

Implementing green buildings and green city strategies offers several environmental, social, and economic benefits, that includes prevention of climate change, minimizing CO_2 emissions and other pollutants, protecting the ecosystem, use of renewable natural resources, improving health, comfort, and well-being, alleviating poverty, improving economic growth, raising rental income, and decreasing healthcare costs [1–6]. With the beginning of the new millennium, Rwanda's urbanization was triggered [7]. The urbanization process was followed by Vision 2020, Vision 2050, Economic Development and Poverty Reduction Strategy (I and II), National Strategy for Transformation (I), National Roadmap for Green Secondary Cities Development, several master plans, and other new plans and policies related to green cities and green building design [8, 9]. Enhancing the role of policy and green development strategies, with sound liability rules will continue to make Rwanda's cities and economy sustainable [10]. Designing high-density cities is one of the key strategic recommendations for Rwanda to mitigate climate change and achieve low carbon development [11]. As it stands, Rwanda's contribution to the reduction of greenhouse gas (GHG) emissions, if well planned, can build resilience in terms of

I. Gubić (✉)
Faculty of Architecture, University of Belgrade, Belgrade, Serbia
e-mail: 2020_41012@edu.arh.bg.ac.rs

D. Arrabothu · R. Ndicunguye
Global Green Growth Institute, Kigali, Rwanda
e-mail: arrabothu.dheeraj@gggi.org; richard.ndicunguye@gggi.org

G. T. Cirella
Faculty of Economics, University of Gdansk, Sopot, Poland
e-mail: gt.cirella@ug.edu.pl

G. T. Cirella (ed.), *Uncertainty Shocks in Africa*, Advances in African Economic, Social and Political Development, https://doi.org/10.1007/978-3-031-21885-9_5

climate action and city preparedness [12]. The Rwanda Urbanization Policy promotes four pillars of sustainable urbanization, where efficient use of land and resources and compact urban development are key to achieving compact, integrated, connected, and climate-resilient urban settlements [13, 14]. Correspondingly, this is one of the major strategic objectives for the Urbanization and Rural Settlement Sector Strategic Plan 2018–2024 [15]. The need to implement green cities and green infrastructure is emphasized in the National Land Use and Development Master Plan 2020–2050 (NLUDMP), as a pathway towards achieving sustainable urbanization [16]; in conjunction with the developed city master plans for Rwanda's secondary cities, this has been the key consideration where strategic green city dimensions such as planning for compact, integrated, inclusive, connected, vibrant, resilient, and convenient cities are imperative and will guide Rwanda's urban development in the coming decades [17]. Green city indicators in Rwanda's policies are elaborated around the consideration of environmental and ecological impact such as the optimal and efficient use of natural resources that can lead to climate change. As a result, it should be inclusive to enhance the well-being of citizens and society in a way that harnesses the benefits of ecological systems while protecting and nurturing them for future generations [12]. The revised master plans for Kigali city and newly developed master plans for six secondary cities emphasize the inclusive nature of the participatory approach of developing polycentric cities. The revised Kigali City Master Plan Zoning Regulations mandate minimum green building requirements for new development or existing developments undergoing major renovations by encouraging site management and neighborhood planning, building placement and orientation to allow for natural ventilation, daylighting and minimizing direct exposure to solar radiation, storm water drainage and retention during and after construction, and the use of local construction materials. It also provides developers with incentives that permit certain additional gross floor area if a project demonstrates a sustainable building design technology and sustainable construction methods as par the green building minimum compliance system (GBMCS) [18]. In addition, District Development Strategies 2018–2024 recommend cities and other settlements within the district to use sustainable construction materials.

In 2019, the Rwanda Housing Authority in collaboration with the Building Construction Authority of Singapore, the Global Green Growth Institute, the Rwanda Green Building Organization, and other stakeholders developed GBMCS [19]. This system was approved by Rwanda's cabinet through a ministerial order determining the Urban Planning and Building Regulations and is an Annex 3 to the Rwanda Building Code 2019 [18, 20]. In addition, implementing the green building rating system contributed to buildings' performance in terms of environmental aspects [21–23]. The green building indicators in Rwanda address the basic green features that any building should have, such as appropriate orientation for daylighting, natural ventilation, rainwater harvesting, efficient plumbing fixtures, low-impact refrigerants, greenery protection, and paints not harmful to occupants. These features are applicable for new Category 4 and 5 public buildings, such as health facilities, commercial buildings, educational buildings, and cultural buildings [18]. Buildings contribute a quarter of the global CO_2 emissions that arise from energy demand during construction and operation, and hence, considerable effort has gone into reducing energy consumption in buildings since it is responsible for a third of the world's consumption [24, 25]. The third National Communication Report on Climate Change of the Rwanda Ministry of Environment estimates that CO_2 from buildings will approximately increase by 574% by 2050 compared to 2012 levels in a business-as-usual scenario [8, 18, 26]. Transition to green buildings comes with specific costs [27–31]. Thus, the Government of Rwanda and other stakeholders are pursuing sustainability in the building and construction sector by recommending the use of energy-efficient practices and sustainably produced local construction materials. The use of locally sourced raw materials for building material production reduces dependence on conventional materials such as concrete and steel, potentially relieving pressure on the material supply chain, avoiding increased construction costs while reducing transport-related GHG emissions, and providing opportunities for local economic development [32]. The Made in Rwanda policy of 2017 by the Rwanda Ministry of Trade and Industry promotes the development of local construction materials, in collaboration with the private sector, to reduce the trade deficit in construction materials [33]. Moreover, the Government of Rwanda and stakeholders organized additional outreach events to help promote green cities and green buildings, including "Urban Walk" and "Urban Cinema" [8, 34]. In addition, awareness and capacity-building programs on GBMCS were organized for government officials, the Rwanda Institute of Architects, the Institution of Engineers Rwanda, and other professionals, where the usage of green building strategies has been stressed [18, 20]. Among those that attended the learning events and capacity development events, including training, are those working for or managing the tourism sector.

2 Rwanda and Its Tourism Sector Before and During COVID-19

Tourism has been identified as one of the key economic transformation opportunities in the revised master plans in Rwanda's secondary cities. Tourism is recognized as the main catalyst in city development and Rwanda's city zoning plan provides a dedicated zones for promoting tourism and aligned activities [17]. In addition, the zoning regulations also emphasize the need for tourism buildings to be compliant with GBMCS [17]. The zoning regulations also advocate for the promotion of tourism for enhanced economic growth by encouraging a tourism promotion overlay zone that provides more flexibility to the city authorities to encourage tourism and discourage certain types of development that may affect the ambience of a certain place (e.g., lakefront areas). Further, the recently updated NLUDMP to support the country, to meet its long-term Vision 2050, provides a national spatial plan structured around several thematic areas with tourism and conservation being one among them [16]. Namely, before the COVID-19 pandemic, tourism was the biggest and

Fig. 1 Implemented lockdown measures in Kigali, Rwanda: (*left*) empty bus stop and (*right*) streetside hand washing station. Source: Photographs by Ilija Gubić, April 30, 2020

fastest-growing economic sector globally. The United Nations World Tourism Organization estimates reveal that in 2020, international tourist arrivals declined by 73% in comparison to 2019, translating into USD 1.2 trillion in international receipts (exports) [35, 36]. This was due to border closures and restrictions in passengers air travel that most countries introduced in order to deal with the pandemic. As such, East Africa generates USD 6.1 billion annually from the tourism sector [37]. Towards the end of March 2020, all East African countries initiated COVID-19 mitigation and control measures such as banning flights in and out of their countries and imposed lockdowns, which greatly affected the tourism and hospitality sector. Despite the fact that measures were differently applied through the sub-region, the East African countries lost around USD 4.2 billion in international tourist receipts and two million jobs. In Tanzania, however, the impact on jobs was slightly less compared to other partner states [37]. Rwanda closed its borders for passenger flights on March 20, 2020, and ordered closure of businesses other than those that serve essential needs. The tourism sector, in essence, saw a 76% decline in income generation in 2020 [38] (Fig. 1).

This chapter will explore that implementing green building and green city strategies in Rwanda's cities, especially those characterized as secondary, such as Musanze, Huye, Rusizi, and Rubavu, that largely depend on tourism, will be able to build back better and faster. After analyzing green buildings and green city policies in Rwanda, and the impact of the COVID-19 measures on the tourism industry, it can be argued that regardless of incremental investment for implementing green features, the tourism sector in Rwanda can reduce operations costs and provide more green jobs in the long-term if set standards are met. At length, this chapter also provides a set of economic justifications for investing in green aspects for the tourism sector in Rwanda.

3 Case Study of Musanze District

3.1 Geography

Rwanda, with its population of 12,600,000, growing 2.8% annually, and significant investments in infrastructure and construction in its capital Kigali and six secondary cities identified as poles of economic growth, aims to achieve a 35% urbanization rate by 2024 [8, 20]. Rwanda is a landlocked country divided into five administrative provinces, 30 districts, and 416 sectors [39]. The country has a density of 500 inhabitants per km^2 [16] and 18.4% urbanization rate [15]. Specifically, an exploratory look into national level and secondary city policies, regarding the impact on the tourism sector through case study research on Musanze District, i.e., one of the six secondary cities and one of the 30 districts of Rwanda, is applied. Musanze District is located in Northern Province with an area of 530.2 km^2 hosting a population of 368,267 inhabitants [40]. A total of 44,000 people work in the tourism industry of which generates 40% of the local revenue [17]. Known as the Excellence Center of Tourism Industry, Musanze's strategic location in the foothills of the Virunga Massif, at an altitude of 1850 m makes it convenient and attractive to tourism, hospitality services, and business [41]. The District is well known for its famous gorilla tracking activities in the Volcanoes National Park and other natural attractions such as underground caves, Buhanga Eco-Park, and the lakes of Karago, Burera, and Ruhondo [42]. By 2020, Musanze District had 87 hotels and 1331 rooms, i.e., second to Kigali city—Rwanda's capital city [42].

3.2 Methods

The research methods utilized for this chapter combined information from several learning events, workshops, and training sessions, including (1) ten workshops organized as part of the various GBMCS programs conducted in 2019, 2020, and 2021, which targeted multiple building industry stakeholders. This helped with understanding the policies in Rwanda as well as the willingness of the private sector to implement such policies. (2) Support for the development of the District Development Strategies for six of Rwanda's secondary cities in 2018 and 2019, including Musanze District, where green buildings and green city concepts with the local government and stakeholders were discussed in ten sessions. (3) Active participation in the development of the master plans for secondary cities, including Musanze District, and outcomes from two discussion sessions where the tourism industry was

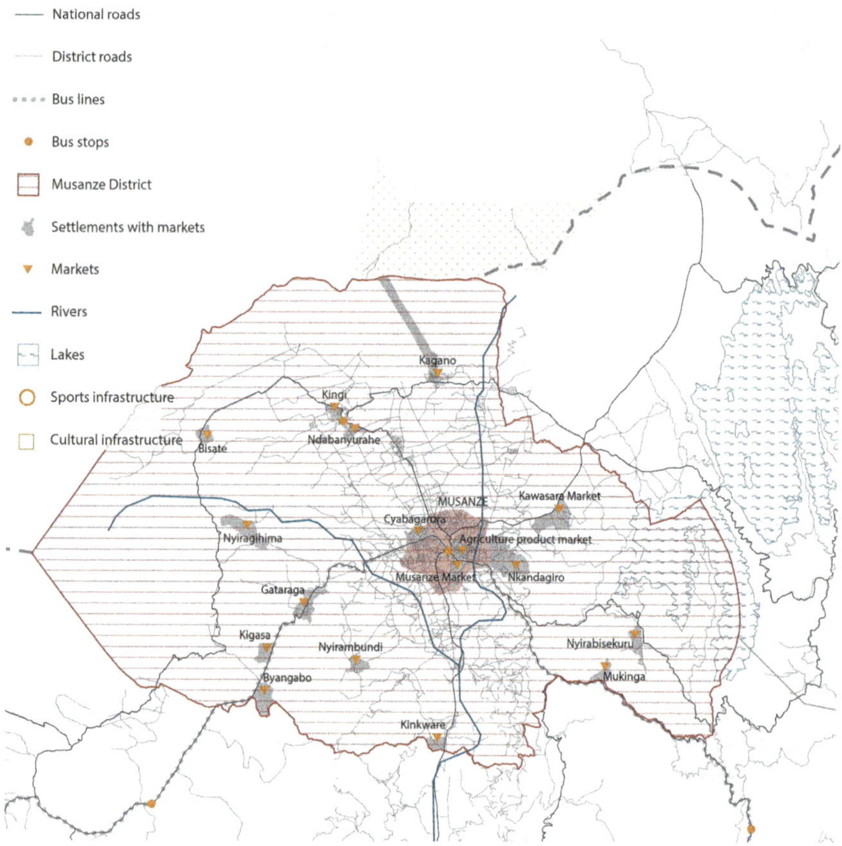

Fig. 2 Map of Musanze District with 16 mapped markets centered around Musanze's city center. Hotels and other tourism facilities are being supplied with food items from markets. Source: Gubić and Kabera [43]

discussed with the government and hotel managers. (4) To better understand the impact of COVID-19 on the livelihoods of those that depend on the tourism industry, a survey conducted in 2020 with small-scale farmers and market workers in Musanze District was administered (Fig. 2).

An additional step was to examine the origin and global spread of COVID-19 in the context of measures implemented by various governments through a review of news, blogs, Twitter posts, and other online material from around the world, as well as the World Health Organization Health Emergency Dashboard [44]. This was conducted in order to better understand how the progression of the COVID-19 pandemic was linked to government decisions to ban or restrict the movement, and hence, influence the tourism sector. A document review covering 2020 and 2021 was utilized to understand recent developments in the policy measures introduced to restrict the movement in cities worldwide during the COVID-19 pandemic.

This focused on tracking the emerging patterns in day-to-day policy formulation and implementation. The reviewed documents included: (1) academic papers and articles published on the subject matter and (2) documents and reports prepared by the United Nations agencies and international organizations.

4 Rwanda's COVID-19 Tourism Challenges

In Rwanda, tourism is one of the key sectors of economic development, and was the country's largest foreign exchange earner, contributing to 14.9% of gross domestic product (GDP), and has generated over 90,000 jobs, representing about 13% of total employment [38]. Rwanda's tourism is founded on its four major national parks, and its capital Kigali is known for hosting multiple international events. Due to its effort in leveraging economic development opportunities, in 2018 Rwanda was ranked as the second easiest place to do business in Africa by the World Bank and has been awarded for its leadership in tourism and economic competitiveness by the World Travel and Tourism Council and the World Economic Forum [42]. With a vibrant aviation sector through Rwandair in addition to other airlines serving Kigali, coupled with "Visit Rwanda" partnership deals with football clubs, Rwanda had over 1.5 million visitors in 2018 [41, 45]. This is around 24% of the total foreign visitors in East Africa which accounts for about USD 7.1 million from international arrivals each year [37]. Tourism has remained an attractive destination for foreign investment complemented by the government and investment in tourism infrastructure prior to the COVID-19 pandemic [46, 47]. Local communities benefited from the tourism sector directly and indirectly through jobs in hospitality, small businesses in food, agriculture, transportation, culture, and crafts as well as conservation and anti-poaching initiatives where about 89,000 jobs were created, with an estimated gross fixed capital of over USD 215 million and a tourism collective consumption of over USD 7.4 million in 2019 [48]. According to the Rwanda Development Board (RDB) report, Rwanda tourism sector experienced huge losses estimated at about USD 7.6 million in the tourism and hospitality industry, while approximately 4000 employees in the sector have been temporally laid off. Some of the measures being taken by the Rwandan government to build back the tourism sector after the COVID-19 crisis include the promotion of domestic tourism, establishment of heavy promotions to attract international tourists, and negotiation for credit incentives for the private sector [49]. Operations in the tourism sector will be supported through special funds to support affected businesses to access affordable loans with good terms for working capital and other needs [50]. This will serve as a recovery fund, to help businesses, especially micro, small, and medium-sized enterprises, entrepreneurs, and workers to adapt and thrive in a new post-crisis era—e.g., by fostering innovation and digital technologies that enable sustainable practices and seamless travel. Sustainable tourism aspires to be more energy efficient and climate sound, consume less water, minimize waste, conserve biodiversity, generate local income, and integrate local communities with a view to improving livelihoods and reducing poverty, amongst others. Seemingly to different countries worldwide, the tourism sector in Rwanda considerably contributes to the emission of GHGs (i.e., the tourism sector contributes about 5% of GHG emissions worldwide) [51] and if measures are not taken post-COVID-19, tourism might grow unsustainably under a business-as-usual scenario. The rapid growth of the tourism sector potentially links energy-intensive transportation preferences, high dependency on nonrenewable energy for lighting, cooking, heating and cooling, and cleaning. Other challenges include excessive water consumption, discharge of untreated water, solid and liquid waste generation, and local biodiversity degradation.

Rwanda recorded its first case of COVID-19 on March 14, 2020, when the government decided to close its international borders and put into place additional restrictions on people's movement, including restricted use of public open spaces when the total number of positive cases reached 17 on March 21, 2020. As part of the measures, all employees of public and private businesses worked from home with restriction on unnecessary movements and visits outside the home, travel between cities and districts were suspended, public events and private gatherings (e.g., weddings) were not permitted, and places of worship, tourism, and recreation were closed. Rwanda's borders were also closed for more than 2 months and, for the significant time, traveling within different districts in Rwanda was also prohibited. All these measures had a major impact on districts of Musanze and Rubavu, as prior to the COVID-19 pandemic, the districts had significant revenue from international and local tourism as well as agriculture markets that were the main source of fresh food for hotels and other hospitality-related facilities (Fig. 3). Similar issues are also reported in other countries [52–55]. All of the measures that were introduced due to the pandemic, affected movement of people and goods across cities, towns, and villages, and disrupted urban-rural linkages, heavily affecting the livelihood of those depending on functioning markets. In light of this, an overview on how the disruption in Musanze District, due to the lockdown measures put in place, affected the livelihood of small-scale farmers and market vendors that previously supplied hotels is detailed.

4.1 COVID-19's Impact on Small-Scale Farmers Supplying the Tourism Industry

The market vendors that participated in the interviews in January 2020 from markets in Musanze were involved in selling agricultural products and fish (Fig. 1). These fresh agricultural products were found to be brought to Kariyeri market early in the morning by small-scale farmers to supply the market vendors in Kariyeri while in Karwasa market, the vendors sometimes transport the agriculture products from farmer pickup points to markets by bicycle or by foot and then resell them at a slightly higher price. In terms of income, an average earning per day was UDS 14.50 and USD 11.30 for Kariyeri and Karwasa, respectively, with the highest reported at

Fig. 3 Before and during the implemented lockdown measures in Musanze District: (*top left*) local market before the lockdown, (*top right*) nonessential shops closed during the lockdown, and (*bottom*) people lining-up and social distancing to enter an essential shop during the lockdown. Source: (*top left*) Photograph by Ilija Gubić, August 30, 2019; (*top right* and *bottom*) photographs by Andrew Kabera, March 27, 2020

USD 52.70 and lowest at USD 1.05 based on factors of time and season. This makes the vendor's livelihoods unstable and long-term planning extremely challenging—especially since they predominately do not have any other alternative source of income. In July 2020, fruits sellers at the market in Byangabo were interviewed who stated that before the COVID-19 pandemic, they could generate as high as USD 105.50 per month after paying taxes and other expenses related to their business. As selling fruits, which is considered an essential good during the nationwide quarantine, it was allowed to continue to operate. Yet, during the lockdown, sales drastically decreased, which vendors managed to only generate USD 3.20 in the first 2 weeks of the lockdown. In addition to fewer people visiting the market, fruits, and other food items sold had eventually perished which made business unsustainable. After the lockdown was lifted and the government set measures for markets to open, essential vendors did not exceed 50% of the registered traders. Musanze, known for its considerable number of hotels, restaurants, and lodges are supplied mostly from local markets. The main potato suppliers from Kariyeri market noted that they could generate more than USD 527.40 per month prior to the pandemic. During the lockdown, they were allowed to operate but did not manage to sell their products as hotels, restaurants, and lodges were closed. Evidently, their income was reduced by 35%. Although hotels and restaurants were allowed to operate from June 16, 2020, the suppliers noted that things were not yet returning to normal as tourism facilities did not have guests to accommodate.

4.2 COVID-19 and Tourism-Related Infrastructure

The Rwandan hotel investment market has progressed strongly over the past 8 years, according to the African Hotel Report 2017 published by Hotel Partners Africa. For the first time, Rwanda has entered into the "top ten" of most valuable countries in Africa for hotels. In addition, with an average growth in hotel values of 8.8% over the last 8 years, Rwanda experienced the sixth-highest growth on the continent over that period. That value increased in 2017 despite the large influx of new supply in the prior 2 years is testament to the confidence that investors have in the stability of the government and the overall investment climate. Rwanda is held out by many as a beacon across Africa for property investment. With an ease of doing business rating of 67 (i.e., out of 189) and property rights protection rating ranked at 28 (i.e., out of 145), investors have found the climate conducive to property deals. The tourism sector is highly vulnerable to climate change and at the same time contributes to GHG emission levels and air pollution. Accelerating climate action in tourism is therefore of utmost importance for the resilience of the sector [35]. According to the United Nations World Tourism Organization, the hotel sector is one of the tourism industry's largest drivers of employment and economic revenue, but at the same time it is one of the most energy intensive. In fact, hotels and other types of accommodation account for 2% of the 5% global CO_2 emitted by the tourism sector. The United Nations Environment Program has predicted that at the current consumption rate of the tourism and hospitality industry, GHG emissions will have increased by 131% in 2050, waste generation will have grown by 152%, energy consumption will have risen by 154%, and solid waste generation will have soared by 251%. The increased consumption of natural resources will greatly impact the global environment, especially in destinations renowned for their natural ecosystems [56].

Effectively, numerous public policies have been implemented globally and in the region in the last 10 years to promote green buildings in the private sector [57, 58]

Fig. 4 Green building designs in Rwanda: (*top left*) bank in Kigali, (*top right*) construction in 2019 of The Retreat hotel in Kigali, (*bottom left*) Bisate Eco Lodge in Musanze, and (*bottom right*) One & Only Gorilla's Nest Hotel in Kinigi. Source: (*top left*) Photograph by Ilija Gubić, August 30, 2020; (*top right*) photograph by Dheeraj Arrabothu, December 11, 2019; (*bottom left*) photograph by Nicholas Plewman, September 1, 2017; (*bottom right*) photograph by Andrew Kabera, August 1, 2022

regardless of the implementation drivers [4, 59–61]. The concept of green buildings and its definition is constantly updated as the construction industry develops [62, 63]. Findings on recently constructed buildings in Rwanda that serve the tourism industry and represent good examples on how such facilities could move forward have been on the rise. Some of these buildings were constructed before the government published GBMCS and before initiatives of SKAT Consulting Ltd. (i.e., promoting locally produced, low carbon bricks) such as the newly built hotels in Musanze (i.e., Bisate Eco Lodge and the One & Only resorts) and Kigali (e.g., The Retreat) (Fig. 4). By using locally sourced materials, buildings fulfill their intended sustainability objectives, serve as inspirations for industry stakeholders to emulate contemporary architecture practices, and contribute to the overall sustainability of Rwanda [64]. The Government of Rwanda initiated the Economic Recovery Fund (ERF) to enable businesses affected by COVID-19 to resume and sustain operations and preserve jobs. The USD 100 million ERF was established to refinance options for hotels with existing performing loans pre-COVID-19. As of December 18, 2020, 139 hotel loans worth USD 41.6 million had been refinanced [46]. RDB with support from development partners and commercial and development banks can potentially enhance ERF by adding a component of green retrofitting to hotels and accommodation facilities that cater to the tourism sector. Insight into how green buildings could adopt and implement such practice could take the lead from the tourism development currently ongoing in Qatar, i.e., a country with modern green city initiatives focused on tourism and mass events. Since the highly affected tourism sector of Rwanda could bounce back better and faster if green building and green city concepts were fully implemented, a brief look at the Qatar tourism industry is merited.

4.3 *Learning from Qatar*

Qatar is aiming to reduce its economic reliance on natural resources and has identified the tourism sector as one of the drivers of the economy. The Qatar National Tourism Sector Strategy 2030 aims to boost the tourism sector's contribution to its GDP by 5.2% by 2030 and increase the employment rate from 1.8% to 5.3%. Qatar has an extremely hot arid climate, low annual rainfall (i.e., 80 mm per year), high humidity, and no freshwater bodies, in addition to climate change concerns and rapidly increasing CO_2 emissions. The growth of the hospitality industry is set to rise as the country prepares for the FIFA World Cup 2022. The FIFA World Cup is expected to attract over 1.5 million tourists over the span of 28 days which will further increase the pressure on natural resources. Many of these visitors will stay in hotels, apartments, and other accommodation facilities. To reduce the environmental burden especially on the accommodation facilities, Qatar has developed the FIFA World Cup Qatar 2022 Sustainability Strategy that targets five areas of environmental focus for the accommodation sector: carbon emissions, waste management, green buildings, water, and air quality [65]. The Cornell Hotel Sustainability Benchmarking database of CO_2 emissions lists hotels in Qatar as some of the most CO_2 intensive in the world, with the average measuring 235 kg CO_2 per occupied room per night. These present significant opportunities to reduce the carbon footprint of accommodation in Qatar. By applying green building standards, the accommodation industry aims to strive for efficiency and operational improvement which would reduce their operating costs while enhancing visitor experience. The green building standards assist the facilities, including stadiums, in improving energy and water efficiency, avoiding and recycling waste, and increasing indoor air quality and occupant comfort. Many accommodation facilities have started using third-party verification programs to gain certification and to demonstrate leadership such as the Green Key Certificate [66]. The Green Key ecolabel drives high sustainability standards, efficient operations, and awareness across diverse services while offering a remarkable experience to the guests with a reduced footprint on the environment. Some of the best practices observed in Qatar's Green Key hotels in their day-to-day operations include 75% energy-efficient lighting and energy-efficient appliances, standard operational procedure to set guest room temperature between 21 and 24 °C. To further drive down the operating costs water saving fixtures, faucets, showerheads, dual flush toilets, and sensor urinals will reduce water consumption and reduce operational expenses. The use of green cleaning products for daily use to maintain healthy indoor air quality and reduce negative impact of toxic material on the environment will also be introduced. To maximize the hotel's environmental footprint, regular training and awareness programs for hotel staff have been implemented.

5 Moving Forward: Post-COVID-19

To manage the economic shocks that arose as a result of the COVID-19 lockdown, the Government of Rwanda initiated a program to cater for the well-being of the citizens, i.e., mostly the vulnerable, through provision of basic needs. The government used a poverty mapping and profiling database which categorizes households according to their economic status, supporting firstly those that reported to have lost jobs among the marginalized groups and casual workers, and then using the decentralized system for the distribution of the support in food and other needed items. This helped small-scale farmers that were relying on the tourism industry that got affected. In-line with the Rwandan government to support affected tourism businesses and livelihoods of those unemployed people, there is a need for more innovative and sustainable solutions that would help build back and allow those businesses to recover, create green jobs, and, at the same time, facilitate and achieve sustainable and green economic development. Thus, schemes to engage workers in the tourism sector and support industries through capacity building, re-purposing skills development, and provide income to sustain people and economies can help reduce COVID-19 impacts in Rwanda. Moreover, responses to the COVID-19 health crisis are also an opportunity to put Rwanda on a new path of sustainable and inclusive growth by boosting resilience, clean energy transition, and circular economy-based and creation of green jobs. Such a response would support Rwanda's tourism industry and enhance its capacity to embark on an eco-tourism path by using green growth facilities which would reduce operating costs for tourism businesses and create green jobs for those people that were vulnerable to the COVID-19 pandemic.

The overall aim is to build synergies with Rwanda Tourism operators, particularly the private sector by identifying missed opportunities for clean energy (e.g., solar PV panels and solar hot water systems), sustainable water consumption (e.g., rainwater harvesting systems), wastewater management, and biodiversity conservation (e.g., landscape restoration, development of green, and public spaces). Therefore, producing quick-wins and affordable solutions will help address challenges in eco-tourism and the COVID-19 effects to their businesses and employment. These approaches would also support the implementation of the District Development Strategies 2018–2024, where tourism is seen as a trigger towards employment creation and poverty alleviation. It would also implement master plans for secondary cities where, again, eco-tourism is seen as one of the main factors of green economic growth. The implementation of Rwanda's GBMCS, in addition to other green buildings and green city policies, is also supporting the government in its bid to promote green building by adopting sustainable construction practices along with increasing the operational efficiency of buildings to mitigate the emissions from the building sector thereby meeting the nationally determined contributions targets [45]. The government with the support from partners is encouraging the implementation of GBMCS through awareness, outreach, and capacity-building programs to ensure the environment, social, and economic benefits of green buildings trickle down along the construction value chain. The usage of locally produced construction materials supports local economic development that has the potential to not only meet the growing construction material demand but also create significant off-farm employment opportunities for Rwandans.

Hotels in Rwanda are classified under non-industrial customer category, and according to the Rwanda Energy Group, they pay an electricity tariff of RWF 157 per kWh (i.e., equivalent to USD 0.15 per kWh) [67]. Increasing operational efficiency of the hotel becomes essential given the nature of the tariff. Green hotel guidelines and third-party verification systems, as in Qatar, can be developed to guide hotel retrofitting. The guidelines can be built and standardized using GBMCS. The guidelines could emphasize the role of energy efficiency, water efficiency, waste management, and awareness for staff in promoting resource efficiency thereby reducing operating costs of these facilities. Energy-efficient features such as 100% LED lighting, solar hot water systems for meeting hot water requirements, solar PV systems for meeting a portion of electricity requirements should be emphasized. In terms of water efficiency, the guidelines could encourage the installation of rainwater harvesting systems to meet the potable water needs of the hotels, adoption of water-efficient fittings for faucets, showerheads, water-efficient urinals, and dual flush water closets to reduce dependence on the utility thereby saving costs and promoting resource efficiency. Reducing, reusing, and recycling of waste where possible can be encouraged within the hotel premises to avoid the recyclable waste being sent to landfills. The hotel staff shall be regularly trained through awareness programs to sustain and enhance the green operations of the facilities. These green retrofitting measures can be implemented through green credit lines with the government providing the guarantee for hotels seeking financial assistance from commercial or development banks. ERF can be enhanced and can provide guarantees to reduce the risk and make it potentially attractive for commercial and development banks to provide financing for retrofitting of hotels. New and upcoming hotels can also seek assistance from RDB through a guarantee facility for implementing the incremental cost of green building features. As such, hotels can payback their loans through the savings achieved from retrofitting measures. Additionally, a third-party verified certification program can be added to ensure the implementation and compliance of green retrofitting measures are at par with required standards. The buildings for tourism in Rwanda can demonstrate several green building principles that projects can adopt not just within the country but across the region to meet and potentially exceed the Rwanda GBMCS standard, and ultimately contribute towards the triple bottom line of people, planet, and prosperity.

References

1. Ali HH, Al Nsairat SF (2009) Developing a green building assessment tool for developing countries – case of Jordan. Build Environ 44:1053–1064. https://doi.org/10.1016/J.BUILDENV.2008.07.015
2. Ahn YH, Pearce AR, Wang Y, Wang G (2013) Drivers and barriers of sustainable design and construction: the perception of green building experience. Int J Sustain Build Technol Urban Dev 4:35–45. https://doi.org/10.1080/2093761X.2012.759887
3. Chan APC, Darko A, Ameyaw EE (2017) Strategies for promoting green building technologies adoption in the construction industry—an international study. Sustainability 9:969. https://doi.org/10.3390/SU9060969
4. Darko A, Chan APC, Gyamfi S et al (2017) Driving forces for green building technologies adoption in the construction industry: Ghanaian perspective. Build Environ 125:206–215. https://doi.org/10.1016/J.BUILDENV.2017.08.053
5. Zhang Y, Kang J, Jin H (2018) A review of green building development in China from the perspective of energy saving. Energies 11:334. https://doi.org/10.3390/EN11020334
6. Wang Z, Danish ZB, Wang B (2018) Renewable energy consumption, economic growth and human development index in Pakistan: evidence form simultaneous equation model. J Clean Prod 184:1081–1090. https://doi.org/10.1016/j.jclepro.2018.02.260
7. Nduwayezu G, Manirakiza V, Mugabe L, Malonza JM (2021) Urban growth and land use/land cover changes in the post-genocide period, Kigali, Rwanda. Environ Urban ASIA 12:S127–S146. https://doi.org/10.1177/0975425321997971
8. Gubić I, Baloi O (2020) Public open space initiatives for healthier cities in Rwanda. J Public Space 5(2):129–146. https://doi.org/10.32891/jps.v5i2.1287
9. Baffoe G, Malonza J, Manirakiza V, Mugabe L (2020) Understanding the concept of neighbourhood in Kigali City, Rwanda. Sustainability 12:1555. https://doi.org/10.3390/SU12041555
10. Niyonzima T (2010) Urbanization trends and green development policies in rwanda: a descriptive analysis. Int J Curr Res 12:12533–12540
11. Republic of Rwanda (2011) Green growth and climate resilience. National Strategy for Climate Change and Low Carbon DevelopmentEnhanced Reader. Republic of Rwanda, Kigali
12. Government of Rwanda, GGGI (2015) Republic of Rwanda National Roadmap for Green Secondary City Development. Global Green Growth Institute, Seoul
13. Republic of Rwanda (2015) National urbanization policy. Ministry of Infrastructure, Kigali
14. Republic of Rwanda (2017) Rwanda national land use planning guidelines. Ministry of Natural Resources, Kigali
15. Republic of Rwanda (2018) Urbanization and rural settlement sector strategic plan for national strategy for transformation 2018-2024. Ministry of Infrastructure, Kigali
16. Republic of Rwanda (2020) National land use and development master plan 2020-2050. NLUDMP, Kigali
17. RHA, GGGI (2021) Revision of master plans and development of new green conceptual detailed city development plans for six secondary cities of Rwand. Musanze Master Plan, Global Green Growth Institute, Seoul
18. Gubić I, Arrabothu D, Bugirimfura J, Hasabamagara HL, Isingizwe I, Kagina A, Karigirwa A, Mugema J, Mukiza A, Nishimwe R, Nshimiyimana W, Yuhi A (2021) Advocating for green building minimum compliance system in Rwanda: using bricks to achieve sustainability. Facta Universitatis Ser Architecture Civil Eng 19(1):67–80. https://doi.org/10.2298/FUACE210922006G
19. Republic of Rwanda (2019) Annex 3, Rwanda green building minimum compliance system. Government of Rwanda, Kigali. https://www.rha.gov.rw/fileadmin/user_upload/documents/General_documents/Laws_of_construction/Green_Building_Minimum_Compliance_System-Official_Gazette.pdf. Accessed 10 Jun 2022

20. Gubić I, Baloi O (2019) Implementing the New Urban Agenda in Rwanda: nation-wide public space initiatives. Urban Plan 4:223–236. https://doi.org/10.17645/UP.V4I2.2005
21. Shad R, Khorrami M, Ghaemi M (2017) Developing an Iranian green building assessment tool using decision making methods and geographical information system: Case study in Mashhad city. Renew Sust Energ Rev 67:324–340. https://doi.org/10.1016/J.RSER.2016.09.004
22. Khan MA, Wang CC, Lee CL (2021) A framework for developing green building rating tools based on Pakistan's local context. Buildings 11:202. https://doi.org/10.3390/BUILDINGS11050202
23. Remizov A, Tukaziban A, Yelzhanova Z et al (2021) Adoption of green building assessment systems to existing buildings under kazakhstani conditions. Buildings 11:325. https://doi.org/10.3390/BUILDINGS11080325
24. Kuo CFJ, Lin CH, Hsu MW (2016) Analysis of intelligent green building policy and developing status in Taiwan. Energy Policy 95:291–303. https://doi.org/10.1016/J.ENPOL.2016.04.046
25. Zepeda-Gil C, Natarajan S (2020) A review of "green building" regulations, laws, and standards in Latin America. Buildings 10:188. https://doi.org/10.3390/BUILDINGS10100188
26. Government of Rwanda (2018) Third National Communication Under the United Nations Framework Convention on Climate Change. Ministry of Environment, Rwanda Environment Management Authority, Kigali
27. Chan EHW, Qian QK, Lam PTI (2009) The market for green building in developed Asian cities—the perspectives of building designers. Energy Policy 37:3061–3070. https://doi.org/10.1016/J.ENPOL.2009.03.057
28. Häkkinen T, Belloni K (2011) Barriers and drivers for sustainable building. Build Res Inf 39: 239–255. https://doi.org/10.1080/09613218.2011.561948
29. Qian QK, Chan EHW, Khalid AG (2015) Challenges in delivering green building projects: unearthing the transaction costs (TCs). Sustainability 7:3615–3636. https://doi.org/10.3390/SU7043615
30. Chan APC, Darko A, Olanipekun AO, Ameyaw EE (2018) Critical barriers to green building technologies adoption in developing countries: the case of Ghana. J Clean Prod 172:1067–1079. https://doi.org/10.1016/J.JCLEPRO.2017.10.235
31. Fan K, Chan EHW, Chau CK (2018) Costs and benefits of implementing green building economic incentives: case study of a gross floor area concession scheme in Hong Kong. Sustainability 10:2814. https://doi.org/10.3390/SU10082814
32. Gardner D, Lockwood K, Pienaar J (2019) Assessing Rwanda's affordable housing sector. Centre for Affordable Housing Finance in Africa
33. Republic of Rwanda (2017) Ministry of Trade and Industry, Made in Rwanda Policy
34. Gubić I, Birungi P (2019) Rwanda kicks off annual Urban October celebrations with Urban Walk in Huye District. Global Green Grwoth Institute, Seoul
35. UNWTO (2022) International tourism and Covid-19: tourism dashboard. United Nations World Tourism Organization. https://www.unwto.org/tourism-data/international-tourism-and-covid-19. Accessed 8 Jul 2022
36. Richter F (2021) How the COVID-19 crisis has affected international tourism | World Economic Forum. https://www.weforum.org/agenda/2021/12/covid-crisis-drags-on-for-international-tourism. Accessed 8 Jul 2022
37. East African Business Council (2021) Impact of COVID-19 on tourism & hospitality industry in the East African Community (EAC) and post recovery strategy. East African Business Council https://eabc-online.com/download/impact-of-covid-19-on-tourism-hospitality-industry-in-the-east-african-community-eac-and-post-recovery-strategy/. Accessed 10 Jun 2022
38. RDB (2020) Annual report: documenting Rwanda's resilience to COVID-19. Rwanda Development Board, Kigali
39. Republic of Rwanda, Ministry of Trade and Industry (2009) Rwanda Tourism Policy. Ministry of Trade and Industry, Kigali
40. Musanze District (2022) Menya Musanze. In: Akarere ka Musanze. https://www.musanze.gov.rw/about/menya-akarere-1. Accessed 10 Jun 2022

41. Visit Rwanda (2022) Towns. Visit Rwanda. https://www.visitrwanda.com/tourism/destinations/towns/. Accessed 10 Jun 2022
42. Visit Rwanda (2020) Musanze. Visit Rwanda. https://www.visitrwanda.com/destinations/musanze/. Accessed 10 Jun 2022
43. Gubić I, Kabera A (2020) Urban-rural linkages in times of coronavirus pandemic: lessons from Musanze District in Rwanda. Global Green Growth Institute, Seoul
44. WHO (2021) WHO Coronavirus (COVID-19) Dashboard. World Health Organization. https://covid19.who.int/. Accessed 13 Mar 2021
45. Republic of Rwanda (2020) Updated nationally determined contribution
46. RDB (2021) Annual report: documenting Rwanda's resilience to COVID-19. Rwanda Development Bank, Kigali
47. RDB (2021) Tourism and hospitality sector brief. Rwanda Development Board, Kigali
48. Odunga PO, Manyara G, Yobesia M (2019) Estimating the direct contribution of tourism to Rwanda's economy: Tourism satellite account methodology. Tour Hosp Res 20:259–271. https://doi.org/10.1177/1467358419857786
49. Arrabothu D, Birungi P (2020) Engineers from IER trained on Rwanda green building minimum compliance system and templates at the continuous professional development workshop. Global Green Growth Institute, Seoul
50. Mwai C (2020) Government commits to supporting local tourism's recovery post COVID-19. New Times. https://www.newtimes.co.rw/business/government-commits-supporting-local-tourisms-recovery-post-covid-19. Accessed 10 Jun 2022
51. UNEP (2011) Towards a green economy pathways to sustainable development and poverty eradication. UN Environment Programme. https://www.unep.org/resources/report/towards-green-economy-pathways-sustainable-development-and-poverty-eradication-10. Accessed 10 Jun 2022
52. Boughton D, Goeb J, Lambrecht I et al (2021) Impacts of COVID-19 on agricultural production and food systems in late transforming Southeast Asia: the case of Myanmar. Agric Syst 188: 103026. https://doi.org/10.1016/J.AGSY.2020.103026
53. Thapa Magar DB, Pun S, Pandit R, Rola-Rubzen MF (2021) Pathways for building resilience to COVID-19 pandemic and revitalizing the Nepalese agriculture sector. Agric Syst 187. https://doi.org/10.1016/j.agsy.2020.103022
54. Rathnayake S, Gray D, Reid J, Ramilan T (2022) The impacts of the COVID-19 shock on sustainability and farmer livelihoods in Sri Lanka. Curr Res Environ Sustain 4. https://doi.org/10.1016/j.crsust.2022.100131
55. Vittuari M, Bazzocchi G, Blasioli S et al (2021) Envisioning the future of European food systems: approaches and research priorities after COVID-19. Front Sustain Food Syst 5:58. https://doi.org/10.3389/FSUFS.2021.642787/BIBTEX
56. Qatar Green Building Council (2021) Sustainable hospitality: case studies from green key hotels in Qatar. Qatar Green Building Council. https://www.usgbc.org/education/sessions/sustainable-hospitality-case-studies-green-key-hotels-qatar-12848506. Accessed 10 Jun 2022
57. Chen W, Li L (2020) Incentive contracts for green building production with asymmetric information. Int J Prod Res 59:1860–1874. https://doi.org/10.1080/00207543.2020.1727047
58. Windapo AO (2014) Examination of green building drivers in the South African construction industry: economics versus ecology. Sustainability 6:6088–6106. https://doi.org/10.3390/SU6096088
59. Darko A, Zhang C, Chan APC (2017) Drivers for green building: a review of empirical studies. Habitat Int 60:34–49. https://doi.org/10.1016/J.HABITATINT.2016.12.007
60. Darko A, Chan APC, Ameyaw EE et al (2017) Examining issues influencing green building technologies adoption: the United States green building experts' perspectives. Energ Buildings 144:320–332. https://doi.org/10.1016/J.ENBUILD.2017.03.060
61. Giesekam J, Barrett JR, Taylor P (2016) Construction sector views on low carbon building materials. Build Res Inf 44:423–444. https://doi.org/10.1080/09613218.2016.1086872/SUPPL_FILE/RBRI_A_1086872_SM7219.PDF

62. Zhang Y, Wang H, Gao W et al (2019) A survey of the status and challenges of green building development in various countries. Sustainability 11:5385. https://doi.org/10.3390/SU11195385
63. Zuo J, Zhao ZY (2014) Green building research–current status and future agenda: a review. Renew Sust Energ Rev 30:271–281. https://doi.org/10.1016/J.RSER.2013.10.021
64. Wang W, Zhang S, Su Y, Deng X (2018) Key factors to green building technologies adoption in developing countries: the perspective of chinese designers. Sustainability 10:4135. https://doi.org/10.3390/SU10114135
65. FIFA (2022) FIFA World Cup Qatar 2022 sustainability strategy. Fédération Internationale de Football Association, Zurich
66. Qatar Green Building Council (2021) Green key – Green Hotels in Qatar share their challenges, recommendations and pathways for a greener sector. https://www.greenkey.global/stories-news-1/2021/11/26/green-hotels-in-qatar-challenges-and-pathways. Accessed 8 Jul 2022
67. REG (2022) Tariffs. Rwanda Energy Group. https://www.reg.rw/customer-service/tariffs/. Accessed 10 Jun 2022

The African Union's Agenda 2063 and Africa's Tourism Industry

Gakwaya P. Isingizwe and Giuseppe T. Cirella

1 Background Knowledge of the Tourism Sector in Africa

The potential of the tourism industry has been acknowledged by policymakers at the national and international level and is, increasingly, reflected in national and international policy frameworks. It has been recognized for its capacity to stimulate economic growth and development through the creation of jobs and by attracting foreign direct investment (FDI) and promoting entrepreneurship, while also contributing, when properly adopted, to the preservation of ecosystems and biodiversity, the protection of cultural heritage, and the promotion of empowerment of local communities. Through the African Union's Agenda 2063, the continent is building its productive capacities, strengthening regional integration, and embracing economic diversification. On this note, tourism in Africa continues to develop and strongly contribute to the continent's gross domestic product (GDP). At the global level, the United Nations Sustainable Development Goals (SDGs) 8, 12, and 14 highlight the central role of tourism in creating jobs, promoting local culture, and advancing economic development. In effect, the developing tourism sector has an impact on many SDGs such as poverty, decent work, gender, and infrastructure. At the continental level, the African Union's Agenda 2063 and the Tourism Action Plan (TAP) under the New Partnership for Africa's Development acknowledge tourism's role in driving Africa's socioeconomic development and structural transformation through job creation and in inducing growth in other productive sectors such as promoting inclusiveness through the participation of youth and women in the sector's projects. At the national level, most African countries have national development plans that outline each country's vision for its future and identifies planned policies and sectoral priorities, which point out the importance of the tourism sector

G. P. Isingizwe (✉) · G. T. Cirella
Faculty of Economics, University of Gdansk, Sopot, Poland
e-mail: gt.cirella@ug.edu.pl

G. T. Cirella (ed.), *Uncertainty Shocks in Africa*, Advances in African Economic, Social and Political Development, https://doi.org/10.1007/978-3-031-21885-9_6

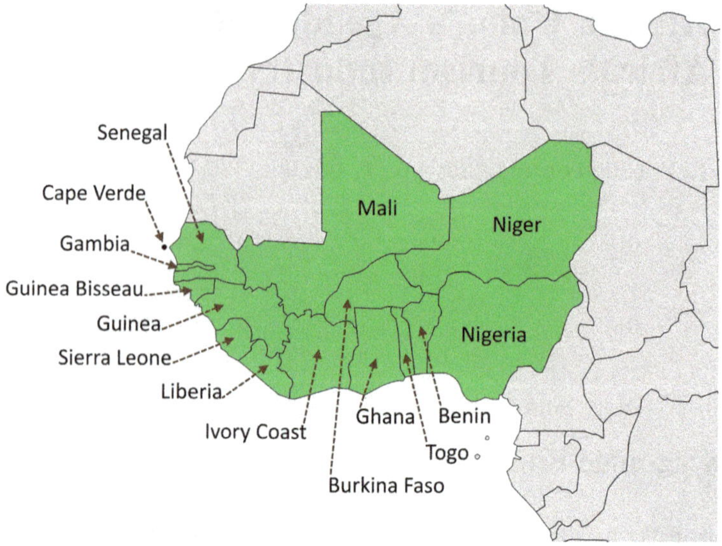

Fig. 1 Member states of ECOWAS. Source: adapted from Wikipedia [3]

[1]. The Economic Development in Africa Report 2017: Tourism for Transformative and Inclusive Growth [2] assessed the role that tourism can play in Africa's development process. It states that tourism can be an engine for inclusive growth and economic development and that it can complement other development strategies aimed at promoting economic diversification and structural transformation. At the same time, tourism has also been associated with working in isolation from other parts of the economy, enduring high financial leakage, generating socio-cultural tensions and environmental damage. History and different findings suggest that countries cannot rely on tourism as the only pathway out of poverty or to sustainable economic development. Multiple investment programs were introduced in countries with well-developed infrastructure sectors, tourism-friendly and flexible travel policies, and a hospitable business environment. There is great potential to increase tourism-related investment to the continent, after the fifteen member states of the Economic Community of West African States (ECOWAS), introduced a visa policy that allows the free movement of people among its member states and encourages people to travel more and increase the potential of investing in tourism-related businesses in those countries (Fig. 1).

Ever since Africa's emerging economies shift from highly relying on goods and agricultural products towards boosting the service economy, the tourism sector plays a big role as a service-based industry and, as a result, has become a major focus of economic growth and development strategies. The main comparative advantage of the tourism sector over other sectors is that tourism expenditure spills over into other sectors often labeled the "tourism industry." This catalytic or "flow-through" character can cut across the entire economy in terms of investment, production, and consumption which leads to employment creation in different sectors. For example, during the construction phase of infrastructure improvement or enlargement (e.g., tourism accommodation) as well as other tourism-related services, jobs are created in those sectors as a result of tourism growth and development. Tourism industry spillover effects also generate huge income for the hospitality, travel, transport, telecommunications, and financial sectors. Sectors such as farming and agriculture, fisheries, food processing, light product manufacturing, handicrafts, and the clothing industry, as well as the goods and services produced by the informal sector benefit from the tourism sector through local product consumption by tourists in hotels and other types of accommodations, local restaurants, and food markets as well as other local markets (e.g., souvenir markets). Though it is difficult to estimate the exact value of such expenditures since it can vary according to the local circumstances, generally, it can range from half to double of a tourist's accommodation expenses [4–6]. As the tourism industry grows, it provides an economic growth base for emerging economies, i.e., by investing in small businesses, this can lead to overall economic growth and development even for countries whose only development options are its cultural heritage and natural resources such as the coast, mountains, national parks, and wildlife game reserves, or a combination of some or all of them. The tourism industry is one of the sectors that energizes economies significantly when managed sustainably as it requires prudent management by addressing different tourism sector constraints environmentally, socially, and economically. Several entities both public and private, are responsible for the success of the tourism sector. The government's political support should be at its highest level since it is one of the main key players, i.e., through different strategic growth and development blueprints for the sector and coordinating stakeholders, including different public sector agencies, the private sector, and non-profit entities, as well as local communities.

In many countries, the tourism industry's contribution to the economy is officially recognized as a direct, measurable economic activity, allowing the availability of more explicit analysis and more efficient and effective strategies and policies for the sector's sustainability. Previously in the balance of payment, the tourism sector mostly depended on approximations made from other related sectors, however today a range of instruments are available to determine and trace all its high-yielding activities and determine the activities that meet tourism consumers' expectations, e.g., defining both tourists and excursionists' choices and preferences. As many countries came to the realization of how the tourism sector was impacting other countries' economies, there has been an increase in the numbers of countries that made tourism a key driver of socioeconomic progress by investing in tourism growth and development and creating a conducive and friendly business environment as well as opening up doors for private investors willing to invest in tourism industry activities. The tourism industry, as a globally traded service touches multiple sectors and the economy through export revenues, jobs, and enterprise creation, and infrastructure development; it has become one of the major trade categories for many countries' economy both developing and developed (Fig. 2).

According to Dieke [7], about 1.323 billion tourists traveled globally in 2017, approximately 84 million more than the previous year. This demand level indicates that global tourism is a huge industry. The growth in tourist arrivals led to a strong

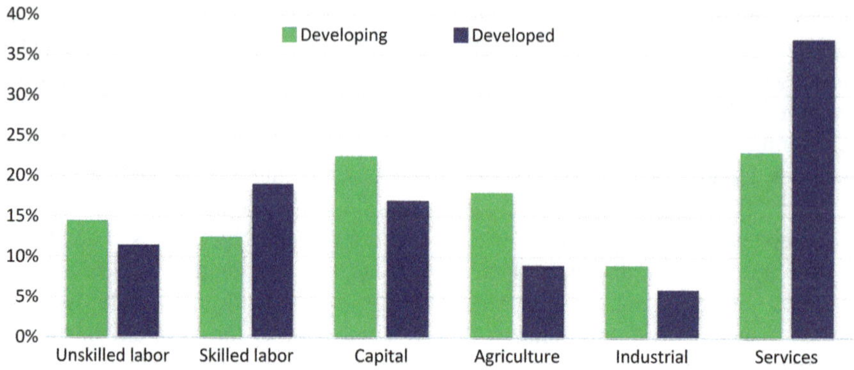

Fig. 2 Inputs into the tourism sector, developing and developed countries. Source: UNCTAD [2] derived from GTAP data

increase in exports generated by the tourism industry, which reached USD 1.6 trillion in 2017, making tourism the world's third-largest export sector. The United Nations World Tourism Organization (UNWTO) expects this number to rise further to a staggering 1.8 billion by 2030. Today, nearly half of the 1 billion international tourist arrivals in the world are traveling to emerging and developing economies. Tourism has been growing faster in sub-Saharan Africa and in many other developing regions compared to the rest of the world. It was estimated that there were 63 million international tourist arrivals in sub-Saharan Africa in 2017, however, this is only 5% of global international tourist arrivals with the receipts share for sub-Saharan Africa at 3% [8]. UNWTO expects tourist arrivals in emerging economies to grow at double the pace of advanced ones over the coming 20 years (i.e., 4.4% versus 2.2%) and foresees a higher average growth of 5% for Africa. Africa's tourism industry contributed 8.5% (i.e., USD 194.2 billion) to the continent's GDP in 2018. In that same year, domestic tourism in Africa contributed 56% with international tourism contributing 46%, and 71% being leisure-driven tourism, while 29% was business-driven [9]. Africa's tourism potential is acknowledged to be significant but underdeveloped and underexploited. Discussions on multilateral trade negotiations in services, specifically regarding tourism industry in developing countries, given historical, geographical, and other unique features, shows that developing countries can obtain a competitive advantage in the tourism part of the services sector. In fact, tourism is considered as the world's largest industry and one of the fastest-growing sectors, reckoning for over one-third of the value of total worldwide services trade [10].

A deficiency in foreign exchange earnings from exports of goods in developing countries has often put off imports of capital goods for investment purposes, but the potential foreign exchange earnings from tourism and tourism-related activities are setting up a new pattern of production and trade. Findings have shown that tourism is the leading source of foreign exchange in at least one in three developing countries that have made it a priority sector [10]. Tourism has made a crucial contribution to the socioeconomic development of several countries that have chosen it as a growth and development strategy as it is a highly labor-intensive sector due to spillover effects on other sectors of the economy. Moreover, spillover effects between countries show that there is higher tourism flows between neighboring countries. For instance, South Africa, having the second largest tourism industry in Africa, for many neighboring countries, is an important shopping destination. Many South Africans also work in neighboring states (i.e., Namibia, Botswana, Zimbabwe, and Mozambique) and many people from these countries work in South Africa as well as visit family and friends which makes for an intraregional form of tourism. This chapter expands on these interlinkages by considering four dimensions of Africa's tourism industry, namely, socio-cultural, economic, political, and environmental. The socio-cultural dimension examines positive social impacts of the tourism industry as well as its negative impacts on society. The economic dimension aims to analyze the tourism economic pros and cons. The political dimension looks at how the African Union's Agenda 2063 and other ongoing projects enhance sustainable development of the tourism industry through its member states. Finally, the environment dimension takes a deep look at protecting the natural environment, wildlife, and natural resources when developing and managing tourism activities, and cross-references this with the negative environmental impacts of tourism. Descriptive research is used to piece together the current state of the art of the tourism industry in Africa and strategize the continent's economy in conjunction with the African Union's Agenda 2063 perspective in order to achieve the desired goals specific its development.

2 The African Union and Agenda 2063: Moving Towards a Common Tourism Industry

In 2013, the Heads of State of African countries launched the African Union and the accompanying Agenda 2063, i.e., the blueprint and master plan for the next 50 years. The idea is to steer Africa's sustainable development and transform the continent into the global powerhouse of the future. The African Union is made up of 55 member states with seven Agenda 2063 aspirations envisioning "an integrated, prosperous, and peaceful Africa," driven by its own citizens and representing a dynamic force in the global arena [11–13]. Agenda 2063 aims to make Africa, a continent with seamless borders, where the free movement of people, capital, goods, and services will significantly increase trade and investment among African countries and boost Africa's performance in global trade. Also, it envisions to have a dynamic and mutually beneficial partnership with the signing of the African Continental Free Trade Area (AfCFTA) by promoting critical areas of Africa's economy, such as digital trade and investment protection, amongst other areas [14]. The seven aspirations of Agenda 2063 are: (1) a prosperous Africa based on inclusive growth and sustainable development, (2) an integrated continent politically united and based on the ideals of Pan-Africanism and the vision of an African Renaissance, (3) an Africa of good governance, democracy, respect for human rights, justice, and the rule of law, (4) a peaceful and secure Africa, (5) an Africa with a strong cultural identity, common heritage, values, and ethics, (6) an Africa whose development is people-driven, relying on the potential offered by the African people, especially its women and youth, and caring for children, and (7) an Africa as a strong, united, resilient, and influential global player and partner. These aspirations are all connected to the tourism industry either directly or indirectly, via the potential growth of tourism in Africa, as demonstrated by UNWTO. The African Union Department for Transport and Tourism aims to build a well-interconnected and integrated network of transport by pursuing a formulation and implementation of a continental tourism policy and a strategic framework in the context of Agenda 2063 [15]. By 2030, consumer expenditure on Africa's tourism and hospitality industry is forecasted to increase up to USD 261.77 billion [2, 16, 17], even though the continent's tourism sector is still at an early stage of growth. Studies and reports show that the tourism industry in Africa has only recently started to grow and remains relatively underdeveloped and only concentrated in a few key destinations. Some of the African Union member states have developed their own strategic frameworks to improve the tourism industry. Countries such as Gambia, Kenya, South Africa, and Tanzania have put significant efforts into boosting travel and tourism growth, and some other countries such as Botswana, Mauritius, Nigeria, and Rwanda are already attracting more tourism investors along with tourists [8, 9, 18].

The African Union has used various methods to develop and publicize Agenda 2063 in the interest of tourism, together with its Regional Economic Communities (RECs), the Union's approved continent's TAP, flagship projects such as the proposal of the "Pan-African passport" to ease movement within the continent, and the Single African Air Transport Market (SAATM), i.e., to protect African airlines and improve air connectivity within the continent. SAATM supplies up to fifteen carriers, which account for more than 70% of intra-African air travel, including Ethiopian Airlines, Kenya Airways, South African Express, and Egypt Air [9]. Irrespective of Agenda 2063's support for sustainable tourism and development, there are issues that are still hindering the industry's progress, e.g., visa policies and geopolitical insecurity. As a matter of concern, due to political instability, terrorism attacks, conflicts, and violence, many African countries are still considered insecure and unsafe. That being said, even more successful African destinations such as Kenya, Algeria, Morocco, South Africa, Tunisia, and Botswana are still facing security and safety issues. Nonetheless, according to the African Union, Agenda 2063 is the pathway to explore new opportunities to ensure positive socioeconomic transformation within the next 50 years as it aims to grow intra-African trade from less than 12% in 2013 to approach 50% by 2045 and fulfil this by 2063. The Agenda aspires to build integrative world-class infrastructures traversing the continent such as the Pan-African high-speed train network, high-quality roads, sea shipping lines, air transport, pipelines, information and communication super-highways, and a digitalized economy shift from a visa-free and borderless Africa to a self-reliant continental economy [12].

To date, tourism has proven to be a huge potential in Africa, a continent that is growing as a great tourism destination but still receives the lowest share of tourist arrivals in the world. Tourist spending has served as another form of export, contributing to an enhanced balance of payments through foreign exchange earnings in many countries. Notwithstanding the continuous endeavors of developing countries to increase their exports, this approach often generates little foreign exchange to their balance of payments. Tourism shows an enormous potential as a promising source of foreign exchange in Africa. Sustaining tourism in Africa requires a great awareness of its negative externalities by balancing different aspects to contribute to SDGs. UNWTO defines sustainable tourism as tourism that meets the needs of present tourists and host regions while protecting and enhancing opportunities for the future. Sustainable tourism development in Africa is about ensuring a promising and long-term future of African tourism based on environmental conservation, partnerships, and sharing the benefits with the community. It is committed to keeping negative impact on the environment and local culture as low as possible, while creating future opportunities. For Africa to realize its full potential in different sectors—sustainably—there is a need to reinforce the cooperation and integration among African states to drive economic growth and development. Different findings have strongly suggested that political stability, tourism infrastructure, marketing and availability of information, healthcare system, and the overall level of development at the destination are key determinants of travel in Africa. Poor infrastructure such as unsafe roads, inadequate water supply and sanitation, connectivity problems, access to hospitals, and inferior technology are some of the main challenges to the tourism industry. Typical developed country determinants of tourism demand, such as the level of income in the origin country, the relative prices and the cost of travel, are not as significant in terms of demand for Africa as a tourism destination [19]. Christie and Crompton [20] describe Africa's potential for tourism as exceptional, acknowledging that it has a lot to offer that can no longer be found elsewhere. Africa is perceived as the continent of explorers and adventurers. There are unique places, some of the greatest views in the world and natural attractions that few other regions can match, not only for its natural resources, but also for its culture, traditions, and customs [19] (Fig. 3).

3 Contribution of the Tourism Industry to Africa's Economic Growth and Development

Tourism in terms of its contribution to the continent's GDP, employment, and trade, is a crucial sector in many African economies, and its growth is also increasingly driven by domestic tourists doing intracontinental travels for both business and leisure. Tourism is one of the key sectors steering the economic change in so many countries and it could be an important tool for economic growth and development for developing countries. The tourism industry is complex because of its

Fig. 3 Some key tourist attractions in Africa: (*top left*) Lions Head, Cape Town, South Africa, (*top right*) Victoria Falls, Zambia-Zimbabwe, (*middle left*) Amboseli National Park, Kenya and Mount Kilimanjaro, Tanzania, (*middle right*) Virunga National Park, DR Congo, (*bottom left*) Giza Necropolis, Egypt, and (*bottom right*) Okavango Delta, Botswana. Source: (*top left*) Photograph by Tobias Fischer on Upsplash, Creative Commons Public Domain, November 26, 2018; (*top right*) photograph by Diego Delso on Wikipedia, Creative Commons Public Domain, July 27, 2018; (*middle left*) photograph by Sergey Pesterev on Upsplash, Creative Commons Public Domain, March 13, 2017; (*middle right*) photograph by Fanny Schertzer on Wikipedia, Creative Commons Public Domain, October 3, 2015; (*bottom left*) photograph by sheilapic76 on Flickr, Creative Commons Public Domain, January 28, 2020; (*bottom right*) photograph by Wynand Uys on Upsplash, Creative Commons Public Domain, July 10, 2018

multisectoral nature and spillover catalytic effect on the economy. Tourism success depends on several actors in the industry, both public and private, domestic, and international, but mainly international visitors. Tourism industry actors, in most cases, have different interests in the sector, depending on their roles in the industry and what they expect from the industry. A decade ago, in 2012, sub-Saharan Africa attracted 33.8 million visitors compared to 6.7 million visitors in 1990. At the time, the tourism industry generated over USD 36 billion, amounting to a 2.8% direct contribution to the region's GDP and a total contribution (including direct, indirect, and induced) of 7.3% to GDP. Since the 1990s, tourism has increasingly contributed to Africa's growth, employment, and trade. From 1995 to 2014, international tourist arrivals to Africa grew by an average of 6% per year and tourism export revenues, grew by 9% per year. The average total contribution of tourism to GDP increased from USD 69 billion in 1995–1998 to USD 166 billion in 2011–2014, i.e., from 6.8% to 8.5% of GDP in Africa, respectively. Moreover, tourism created more than 21 million jobs on average in 2011–2014, which equals 7.1% of all jobs on the continent. This indicates that over the period 2011–2014, one out of every fourteen jobs was supported by the tourism [16].

The tourism industry is a crucial sector for a country's economic development for several reasons. First, tourism can significantly contribute to employment, export earnings, and GDP. Second, travel and tourism have proved to provide women with more empowerment opportunities compared to other industries, which gives the sector more responsibility for women advancement. As a job-rich sector and which comparatively employs high shares of women and youth, globally, women make up between 60-70% of the tourism labor force, and half of its workers are aged 25 or younger. Thus, it has the potential to promote more inclusive growth and it can also be a compelling case for prioritization for socioeconomic development in Africa. According to United Nations Global Report on Women and Tourism [21] and UN Women [22], tourism provides better opportunities for women's participation in the workforce, women's leadership, and women's entrepreneurship than other economic sectors. Third, the tourism forecast is positive. Given the rising income level, more resources available for travel and leisure, as well as globalization which fosters business travel, international tourist arrivals to Africa are expected to continue growing strongly to 134 million arrivals by 2030 [8]. Fourth, globally, most international travel occurs within a traveler's origin region, and given that the African middle class is rising, continental disposable personal incomes are expected to increase, making the possibility to boost intraregional and continental travel in Africa easier. Fifth, tourism has strong spillover effects which contribute to poverty reduction both at the local and national level. This has the capacity to generate and spread over income through strong linkages with other sectors that catalyze a multiplier effect that can generate broad-based economic benefits and employment opportunities to a country's economy. However, in many African countries, tourism linkages remain underexploited and weak, and, as a consequent, most of the value added in the tourism sector remains with international tour operators, foreign investors, and foreign airline companies, with only a few benefits remaining within the destination country—flowing to the local citizens. Sixth, to achieve any economic development goal, promotion of peace, justice, and strong institutions are prerequisites, this applies also to SDGs related to the development of the tourism industry as a whole.

The impact of tourism expenditure in emerging economies is as important as private and public sector investments as well as development aid and assistance from foreign and developed governments. Statistically in 2015, FDI in the African continent economy added up to USD 54 billion, development assistance projects generated USD 51.04 billion [23], while tourism revenue added up to USD 39.2 billion and approximately 9.1 million direct jobs were created within the tourism sector [24]. This shows the contribution of the tourism industry to GDP, service exports, employment creation, and other sectors of development leads to global economic growth and development and, thus, poverty reduction. Many African countries have started capitalizing on different opportunities offered by the tourism industry. The World Bank noted in a study that African countries are classified into four performance categories: "pre-emergent," "potential," "emerging," and "consolidating" tourism destinations [25]. Different indicators were taken into consideration to determine the performance of countries. To mention a few, the business flexibility and ease; the tourism regulation competitiveness, infrastructure accessibility and development, and resources availability; the international arrival per head of a country's population; the tourism earnings per long-haul arrivals; and the prediction of the increase in the number of tourist arrivals. In the category of pre-emerging countries, there are countries such as Somalia and Sudan, which have been facing significant political insecurity and public governance challenges that hindered the growth and development of tourism sector under such conditions. Countries such as Ethiopia, Gabon, and Madagascar have shown some potential initiatives for tourism sector growth and sustainable development, but they are still facing political insecurities and governance challenges which hinder the implementation process. There are also some potential emerging countries, such as the Seychelles and Rwanda (Fig. 4), that are becoming more competitive as potential tourism destinations on the continent, while countries such as Morocco, South Africa, and Mauritius, are among the top leading countries with a relatively developed tourism sector. Tourism has since become integral to economic development policies. Several countries such as the Gambia, Kenya, South Africa, and Tanzania, have recently increased their commitments and efforts to improve their travel and tourism sectors.

Over two decades ago, in the 1990s, when Africa's tourism reached a 300% increase in international arrivals which eventually led to approximately 26.2 million arrivals in 2000, the African Union introduced TAP as a blueprint to bring visibility to tourism growth and development on the continent. Most African countries, still face significant challenges and constraints in exploiting the potential of tourism services in international trade and countries' economic development. The Economic Development in Africa Report 2017 [26] identified key barriers and hindrances to unlocking the potential of tourism industry in Africa to help improve and transform the continent's structural policies in countries' economy, as well as to provide strategic policy recommendations on how those barriers and hindrances could be solved. The focus was put on the following main challenges: enhancing the capacity of tourism to foster more inclusive growth, strengthening intersectoral linkages, harnessing peace and stability for tourism, and tapping the potential of intraregional tourism through deepening regional integration. In 2018, travel and tourism remained one of the key growth drivers of Africa's economy, contributing 8.5% of the GDP—equivalent to USD 194.2 billion. According to Jumia Hospitality Report Africa 2019 [27], this growth record placed the continent as the second

Fig. 4 Emerging tourism-oriented sectors in Africa: (*top left*) on route to Lalibela, Ethiopia, (*top right*) Plage de Malibé, Gabon, (*middle left*) Morondava, Madagascar, (*middle right*) giant tortoise on Alphonse Island in the Seychelles, and (*bottom*) Akagera National Park, Kayonza, Rwanda. Source: (*top left*) Photograph by Erik Hathaway on Upsplash, Creative Commons Public Domain, November 4, 2019; (*top right*) photograph by Ralph Messi on Upsplash, Creative Commons Public Domain, October 14, 2019; (*middle left*) photograph by Graphic Node on Upsplash, Creative Commons Public Domain, May 24, 2019; (*middle right*) photograph by Dan Maisey on Upsplash, Creative Commons Public Domain, June 29, 2020; photograph by Simbi Yvan on Upsplash, Creative Commons Public Domain, November 10, 2019

fastest-growing tourism region in the world, with a growth rate of 5.6% after Asia Pacific and against a 3.9% global average growth rate. This gradual increase is attributed to the affordability and ease of travel, especially within the continent. In addition, leisure travel remained an important component of Africa's tourism industry, taking up a majority of 71% of the tourist expenditure in 2018 [8].

3.1 African Continental Free Trade Area and Business Tourism

With the creation of AfCFTA in 2018, which started operations in January 2021, it is one of the largest trading blocs in the world with the majority of African countries now operating under its preferential trade structure. AfCFTA is expected to boost the continent's tourism industry as it will allow more intracontinental movement and business operations. AfCFTA trading started under a liberalized trade regime that will eventually lead to an integrated continental market within 10–13 years the through phasing out of tariffs. Both goods and services are covered by AfCFTA, and applicably, provides RECs and individual countries with a platform to participate in intra-African trade, through different tariff concession offers and service commitments with requited most-favored-nation treatment. On the continent, there is already a certain degree of liberalized trade and economic integration under the eight RECs acknowledged by the African Union, and other customs and monetary unions. Approximately 41 countries and RECs, including the Southern African Customs Union, the East African Community (EAC), the Economic and Monetary Community of Central Africa, and ECOWAS, were reported that they had submitted their tariff offers and service commitments, but the process of implementation has been slower than predicted, as the tariff books are still being reformed and administrative procedures continually unfolding. AfCFTA has five prioritized sectors for liberalization which as follows business services, communication, financial services, transport, and tourism. With the continual negotiations on how to open up the service sector, the second phase of liberalization of services is expected to cover the other remaining sectors. Approximately 60% of total intra-African trade is made up by trade in services, which is essential for the continent's overall GDP of nearly USD 3 trillion. The tourism sector is anticipated to benefit from AFCTA's trade liberalization, increasing trade movement on the continent. With Africa's emerging technological capabilities and limited legacy infrastructure to phase out, digitally delivered services seem to be the most logical large-scale expansion opportunity. This would, however, largely depend on successful negotiations that keep restrictions on cross-border services to a minimum.

Intra-African trade in services has been expanding continuously and AfCFTA would straightforwardly speed up the growth by removing the trade barriers on the continent that limit African economies. This should make basic service necessities more accessible and affordable to the average consumer by opening doors for different goods and service suppliers to reach their target market more conveniently and allow different payment options including the use of local currencies. Also, with AfCFTA multinational companies seeking growth markets may find potential opportunities to establish as well as increase their footmark in Africa's economy. In effect, the proper implementation of AfCFTA is anticipated to boost intracontinental travel, however, in order to see the full potential benefits all industry stakeholders will need to cooperate. African governments should be willing to remove visa requirements for African nationals traveling to their countries as it is one of the main travel barriers on the continent. Different government institutions and other stakeholders should introduce campaigns to promote and advertise the top travel destinations in their home countries and different tourism packages to allure more regional and global travelers to explore what the continent has to offer.

3.2 Highlights from the Travel and Aviation Industry

In 2018, Africa's passenger traffic increased from 88.5 million in 2017 to 92 million (i.e., +5.5%), but its world share was only 2.1% (i.e., a fall of 2.2% in 2017). This is mainly attributed to high competition from other uprising tourism destination such as Asia Pacific. However, Africa's aviation share is forecasted to increase by 4.9% annually over the next 20 years. The majority of African countries with a developed tourism sector, enhanced visa facilitation remains a major uplift to both the aviation and tourism industries. Countries such as Ethiopia, the visa relaxation policies combined with improved flight connectivity, placed the country as a regional transport hub as well as Africa's fastest-growing travel country, i.e., with 48.6% growth in 2018 and USD 7.4 billion worth. Most of African government leaders are currently committed to making travel between African countries more flexible and affordable for both Africans and international travelers. For example, the creation of the East Africa Visa program that allows travelers to apply for a single visa online allowing them to visit Uganda, Rwanda, and Kenya. Such cooperation is insightful and forward thinking. Regarding the top airlines earning the most revenue in African airspace, Emirates was ranked on the top of the list, generating over USD 837 million with the most popular flights to and from Johannesburg, Cairo, Cape Town, and Mauritius. For example, the air route between April 2018 and March 2019 from Johannesburg to Dubai generated USD 315.6 million in revenue, while only two African airlines made it to the top ten of Africa's highest revenue air routes, i.e., the state-owned Angola Airlines and South African Airways generating USD 231.6 million flying from Luanda to Lisbon and USD 185 million flying between Cape Town and Johannesburg, respectively.

Moreover, for instance in Morocco, since 2017, the Ministry of Tourism also features the aviation sector to supervise airport management, civil aviation, and other missions related to civil aviation. Air connectivity between Morocco and other world cities increased from 48 in 2004 to 121 in 2018 and as of October 2019, Morocco's airports amounted to 21 million passenger arrivals. A larger diversification of air connections serves as a support to achieving Morocco's tourism goal of market expansion by way of the number of tourists visiting Morocco as well as penetrating new markets and countries. In 2020, the flag carrier Royal Air Maroc launched a direct link between Casablanca and Beijing which targeted and encouraged more business and leisure travelers from China, i.e., the government's target to attract more visitors from high-growth and non-traditional markets. In 2019, a direct link between Casablanca and Boston was also inaugurated, with additional direct links between Casablanca and New York, Miami, and Washington. Directly connecting

Morocco with the US market. As such, Morocco and some other African countries have zealously opted for the tourism industry as a development tool, with hope to increase the annual number of tourists received as well as tourism receipts, to reinforce the country's economic growth and advancement. Ever since the Moroccan government instituted deliberately prioritizing the tourism sector, the country emerged as a "new starring market among overseas real estate developers" [24]. Countries such as South Africa, Egypt, Morocco, and Kenya, i.e., some of Africa's most popular tourism destinations in terms of number of tourist arrivals and the total value of tourism receipts, are some vivid tourism success stories. These African countries generate billions of dollars each year from the tourism industry. In the World Economic Forum's Travel and Tourism Competitiveness Index Ranking [28], countries such as Tunisia, Cape Verde, Botswana, and Namibia were ranked close to Kenya, which shows that there is a tourism growth and development potential throughout the continent which is a huge opportunity for other countries to grow along with the leading tourism countries in Africa.

4 COVID-19 and Tourism in Africa

The tourism industry has been one of the main sources of revenue and foreign exchange business in Africa for the last 20 years. COVID-19 has, however, created an unprecedented crisis for the tourism sector in Africa and around the world. In July 2020, the African Union estimated that the continent lost nearly USD 55 billion in travel and tourism revenue and two million jobs in the first 3 months of the pandemic. The COVID-19 pandemic has not only affected the tourism industry, but also the supporting food industry, service, and manufacturing industries that depend on tourism for income and employment. The World Health Organization declared COVID-19 a global pandemic on March 11, 2020. It has been both a health and economic crisis, with developing countries being the most affected economically. Travel restrictions such as travel bans, visa controls, and quarantines, heavily affected travel and tourism industry worldwide as well as the sectors that depend on travel and tourism revenue. Tourist arrivals dropped by 80–90% in 2020 (Fig. 5) and an average of 88% in the beginning of 2021, compared to 2019 statistics in many developing countries [30]. According to UNWTO [29], the decline in international tourist arrivals in 2020, took the tourist arrivals numbers back 30 years. Before the COVID-19 pandemic, tourism was contributing a remarkable share to many countries "[...] around the world, in countries at all development levels, i.e., many millions of jobs and businesses that are dependent on a strong and thriving tourism sector. Tourism has also been a driving force in protecting natural and cultural heritage, preserving them for future generations to enjoy"—stated Mr. Zurab Pololikashvili, Secretary-General of UNWTO [31].

The decline in tourism earnings in Africa as a direct result of the COVID-19 pandemic amounted to USD 250 billion in 2021. UNTWO's past damage assessment statistics, predicted that the industry could endure a loss in tourism receipts

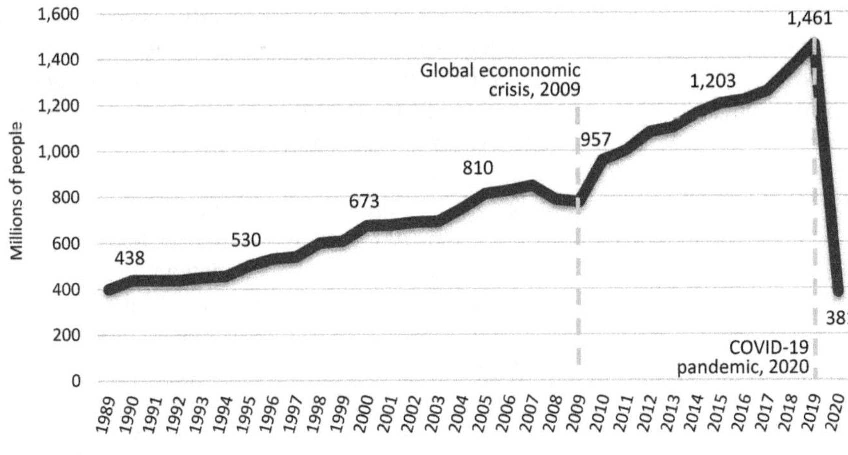

Fig. 5 International tourist arrivals, 1989–2020. Source: UNWTO [29]

between 170 billion and 253 billion US dollars in 2022—due to a slow start this year. The prediction showed a decline of 78% in tourist expenditures visiting North Africa, and 69% in the other continent's regions, resulting in a decrease in GDP of 7.5% and 5% according to the pessimistic and optimistic scenarios, respectively. In terms of jobs market, the less qualified workforce in North Africa was predicted to fall by 10% and a huge decline of 11.8% in East Africa for the most qualified workforce. According to UNCTAD, as a result of the COVID-19 almost-total shutdown for tourism sector in 2020, many African countries endured a huge drop in terms of international tourist arrivals, as follows: 79% for Tunisia and Morocco, 78% for Mauritius, 72% for Kenya, 70% for South Africa, 69% for Egypt and Ethiopia, 55% for Ghana, and 43% for Madagascar. As published by the United Nations [32], the predictions showed that 2023 might be the year for the tourism industry total recovery and return to normal operations as before the COVID-19 outbreak [33]. In terms of air travel, African airlines lost an estimated USD 10.21 billion in passenger revenue in 2020 and an additional USD 8.35 billion in 2021, according to the African Airlines Association [34].

4.1 Case Research on How COVID-19 Impacted the Tourism Industry in EAC

EAC is made up of six partner states that include Kenya, Rwanda, Burundi, Uganda, South Sudan, and Tanzania, with its headquarters in Arusha, Tanzania. Like the rest of the continent, EAC was immensely affected by the COVID-19 pandemic, e.g., Kenya's tourism receipts dropped by 80% in 2020 compared to 2019. According to the EAC secretariat, tourist arrivals in the region increased from 3.5 million people in 2006 to about seven million in 2019. Prior to the COVID-19 pandemic, the tourism sector contributed to GDP of EAC by an average of 9.5%. in 2019, it accounted for an average of 17.2% to EAC total export earnings and 7.1% to employment, according to official EAC data [35]. However, the upward trajectory in tourism was devastatingly affected by the onset of COVID-19 pandemic in March 2020. On October 9, 2021, EAC disclosed that the partner states lost 92% tourism revenue due to COVID-19. Hon. Dr. Peter Mathuki said that tourist arrivals to the region fell from 6.98 million before the pandemic to 2.25 million in 2020, adding that the tourism sector was the worst hit from the crisis. A report by the East African Business Council (EABC) [36], a bloc of private business and associations in the region, specified that 4.2 million foreign tourists were not able to travel to their preferred EAC destinations. As such, EABC commissioned a study that aimed at assessing the impact of COVID-19 on the tourism and hospitality industry, and generated policy options that the EAC partner states should adopt to protect sector players from COVID-19 disruptions and future shocks. An online survey was sent out to tourism businesses and business chambers across EAC (e.g., the East African Platform, Kenya Tourism Federation, Rwanda Chamber of Tourism, etc.); it disclosed that they lost between 25% and 100% of their projected revenue during the COVID-19 period. The respondents also indicated that their businesses undertook various operational changes including reducing staff by more than 50% and maintaining staff at partial pay. Others reduced staff by up to 50% and reduced working hours by 50%, while others closed down their business. According to key informants, businesses turned to borrowing to fund their running expenditures such as rent and utilities due to reduced operational capital during the pandemic. As a result, EAC's tourism sector lost millions of jobs in 2020 amid COVID-19 according to a number of articles written by Tasamba [37, 38] in 2021. EAC exemplifies the strain and suffering to the tourism sector during the first 2 years of the COVID-19 crisis.

5 Moving to a Post-COVID-19 Reality

Many African countries are set to boost tourist trust in the continent after the pandemic devastation. The tourism sector being a frontline sector was the worst affected by the onset of the COVID-19 pandemic. Since the pandemic hit Africa, many tourists chose to pause on travel due to various uncertainties that included the cancelations of flights and travel, closing of borders, imposed lockdowns, COVID-19 tests, quarantine, and fear of novel infections. The tourism sector relies on mobility and sociability, the two things that COVID-19 has undermined. As Butcher [39] observes "social distancing diminishes the pleasure of a holiday to the extent that many may choose to stay home." Consequently, the tourism sector, including commercial aviation, experienced amongst the worst socioeconomic complications of the pandemic [17, 39–43]. Assaf and Scuderi [44] observe that for tourism, COVID-19 "has been one of the most impactful and tragic pandemics of modern times." Within a period of only months "the framing of the global tourism system moved from over-tourism to non-tourism" [45].

As Africa moves to a post-COVID-19 reality, it is now generally accepted that the prerequisites for its tourism development will be attractions, accommodation, and accessibility. A combination of these elements often put destinations on the tourism map and, if not properly acknowledged, without them tourism cannot develop. As such, some African countries now entering the international markets are providing a wider range of destination options for tourists. In due course, standards of services and value for money will determine which countries and destinations will be most successful through the intense competition of the tourism market. There are many African countries which, for a number of reasons, have limited tourism development but have considerable potential. Some of the main tourism assets in Africa, are hard and expensive to access, poorly managed, and in poor condition, this led to low service standard levels, often resulting in tourism dissatisfaction. Even in well-known and successful destinations, public reinvestment in tourism attractions is often not enough to maintain and improve the quality of attractions. On the one hand, some tourism assets are underused due to insufficient funds, limited accessibility, operational and management expertise, marketing strategies, and tourism crowdedness. On the other hand, this can also lead to tourist attraction congestion, animal harm, and environmental degradation. As a result, local communities need to be featured through partnerships in community-based conservation and tourism projects, and government institutions need to reinvest tourism revenues effectively into conservation and local community-based development initiatives.

For tourism in Africa to be successful, it needs to engage as many stakeholders as possible in African countries. According to Christie and Cromption [20], airfares in Africa are among the highest in the world. The major obstacles to tourist arrivals in Africa in this regard are insufficient air transport, a shortage in facilities and accommodation, poor image and perceptions, poverty, disease, and conflict. Gauci et al. [46] include among the obstacles to tourism—sustainable development, undeveloped public health services, and fears of personal safety due to political instability. Eilat and Einav [47] found that political risk has a significant impact on tourism demand in both developed and developing countries. There are also "neighborhood effects" of instability, when the political instability in one country affects perceptions of the region as a whole, with "potential tourists often unable to distinguish between individual countries" [19]. In general, tourists will not travel to countries or areas within large countries where they feel threatened because of security matters. Over the long term, this explains why regions such as Africa, South Asia, and the Middle East have always received only a small share of international tourist arrivals. Socioeconomic and political stability is a key factor to sustainable tourism and economic growth in Africa. Insecurity, corruption, poor governance, poorly performing political institutions, and mismanagement of financial resources affect the political and investment image of a given country and the continent at large. Consequently, tourism requires much more investment to restore confidence in a destination, while a single event such as political and economic unrest, especially if continuous, will affect the industry heavily in which substantial efforts will be required to rebuild it. In a post-COVID-19 world, easing these problems in Africa will be challenging, and a much-needed effort in terms of the Africa Union's Agenda

2063 industry standards to prioritize "destination readiness" Africa-wide, and enhance the tourism industry so it can flourish in-line with individual policies from its member states. This chapter underscores these recommendations as requisites to sustainable tourism and economic development in Africa and considers them as essential in a tourism-led blueprint for future growth on the continent.

References

1. AUDA-NEPAD (2022) NEPAD home. In: African Union Development Agency. https://www.nepad.org/. Accessed 1 Aug 2022
2. UNCTAD (2017) Economic Development in Africa Report 2017: Tourism for Transformative and Inclusive Growth. United Nations Conference on Trade and Development, United Nations Publication, New York
3. Wikipedia (2007) Fichier: ECOWAS map. https://fr.wikipedia.org/wiki/Fichier:Ecowas_map.svg. Accessed 11 Aug 2022
4. Mason P (2003) Tourism impacts, planning and management. Butterworth Heinemann, Amsterdam
5. Poldrugovac K, Tekavcic M, Jankovic S (2016) Efficiency in the hotel industry: an empirical examination of the most influential factors. Econ Res Istraživanja 29:583–597. https://doi.org/10.1080/1331677X.2016.1177464
6. Park S, Woo M, Nicolau JL (2020) Determinant factors of tourist expenses. J Travel Res 59:267–280. https://doi.org/10.1177/0047287519829257
7. Dieke PUC (2020) Tourism in Africa: issues and prospects. Springer, Cham
8. UNWTO (2018) UNWTO Tourism highlights 2018 edition. United Nations World Tourism Organization, Madrid
9. WTTO (2019) You've reached your destination: best practices enabling the growth of travel and tourism. World Travel and Tourism Council, London
10. Durbarry R (2004) Tourism and economic growth: the case of mauritius. Tour Econ 10:389–401. https://doi.org/10.5367/0000000042430962
11. Ufomba HU (2020) The African Union development agenda 2063: can Africa get it right? Braz J Dev 6:62626–62648. https://doi.org/10.34117/bjdv6n8-627
12. Gowreesunkar V (2019) African Union (AU) Agenda 2063 and tourism development in Africa: contribution, contradiction and implications. Int J Tour Cities 5:288–300. https://doi.org/10.1108/IJTC-02-2019-0029/FULL/XML
13. Aniche ET (2020) African Continental Free Trade Area and African Union Agenda 2063: the roads to Addis Ababa and Kigali. J Contemp African Stud 1–16. https://doi.org/10.1080/02589001.2020.1775184
14. AfCFTA (2022) Home - AfCFTA. In: African Continental Free Trade Area. https://au-afcfta.org/. Accessed 2 Aug 2022
15. African Union (2022) Agenda 2063: The Africa we want. In: African Union. https://au.int/en/agenda2063/overview. Accessed 2 Aug 2022
16. UNCTAD (2017) Handbook on statisitics 2017. United Nations conference on trade and development. United Nations Publication, New York
17. UNCTAD (2020) World investment report 2020. United Nations, New York
18. Signé L (2018) African development, African transformation: How institutions shape development strategy. Cambridge University Press, Cambridge
19. Naudé WA, Saayman A (2005) Determinants of tourist arrivals in Africa: a panel data regression analysis. Tour Econ 11:365–391. https://doi.org/10.5367/000000005774352962
20. Christie I, Crompton DE (2001) Tourism in Africa. Africa Reg Find Good Pract Infobriefs, World Bank No. 187

21. UNWTO (2019) Global report on women in tourism, 2nd edn. United Nations World Tourism Organization, Madrid
22. UN Women (2022) UN Women. In: UN Women. https://www.unwomen.org/en. Accessed 3 Aug 2022
23. OECD (2022) Financing for sustainable development. In: Organization for economic co-operation and development. https://www.oecd.org/dac/financing-sustainable-development/. Accessed 3 Aug 2022
24. Signé L, Johnson C (2018) Africa's tourism potential trends, drivers, opportunities, and strategies. Brookings Institution, New York
25. World Bank (2005) World development indicators 2005. World Bank, New York
26. UNCTAD (2017) Economic development in Africa report 2017. United Nations conference on trade and development, New York
27. Jumia (2019) Jumia hospitality report Africa 2019, 3rd ed. Jumia, Lagos
28. World Economic Forum (2017) The Travel & Tourism Competitiveness Paving the way for a more sustainable and inclusive future. World Economic Forum, Geneva
29. UNWTO (2022) International tourism and covid-19: tourism dashboard. In: United Nations World Tourism Organization. https://www.unwto.org/tourism-data/international-tourism-and-covid-19. Accessed 8 Jul 2022
30. UNWTO (2022) Travel restrictions. In: World Tourism Organization. https://www.unwto.org/covid-19-travel-restrictions. Accessed 11 Feb 2022
31. UNWTO (2022) World Tourism Organization a UN Specialized Agency. In: United Nations World Tourism Organization. https://www.unwto.org/. Accessed 3 Aug 2022
32. UNWTO (2021) The Economic Contribution of Tourism and the Impact of COVID-19. In: Economic Contribution of Tourism and the Impact of COVID-19
33. Adepoju P (2022) Africa prepares for endemic COVID-19. Nat Med 28:876–878. https://doi.org/10.1038/D41591-022-00040-0
34. AFRAA (2022) African Airlines Associations. In: African Airlines Assoc. https://www.afraa.org/. Accessed 3 Aug 2022
35. EAC (2022) East African Community. In: East African Community. https://www.eac.int/. Accessed 3 Aug 2022
36. EABC (2022) East African Business Council. In: East African Bus. Counc. https://eabc-online.com/. Accessed 3 Aug 2022
37. Tasamba J (2021) African tourism ministers to work together to revitalize industry. In: Anadolu Agency. https://www.aa.com.tr/en/africa/african-tourism-ministers-to-work-together-to-revitalize-industry/2277927. Accessed 3 Aug 2022
38. Tasamba J (2021) East Africa pins hopes on intra-regional, domestic tourism. In: Anadolu Agency. https://www.aa.com.tr/en/africa/east-africa-pins-hopes-on-intra-regional-domestic-tourism/2375792. Accessed 3 Aug 2022
39. Butcher J (2020) Let the good times roll (as soon as possible): Why we need a post COVID convivial revolution. ATLAS Tour Leis Rev 2:26–29
40. Dube K (2020) Tourism and sustainable development goals in the African context. Int J Econ Financ Stud 12:88–102. https://doi.org/10.34109/IJEFS.202012106
41. Gursoy D, Chi CG (2020) Effects of COVID-19 pandemic on hospitality industry: review of the current situations and a research agenda. J Hosp Mark Manag 29:527–529. https://doi.org/10.1080/19368623.2020.1788231
42. ILO (2020) ILO: COVID-19 causes devastating losses in working hours and employment. In: Int Labour Organ. http://www.ilo.org/global/about-the-ilo/newsroom/news/WCMS_740893/lang%2D%2Den/index.htm. Accessed 11 Feb 2022
43. OECD (2022) International trade during the COVID-19 pandemic: big shifts and uncertainty. In: Organization for economic co-operation and development. https://www.oecd.org/coronavirus/policy-responses/international-trade-during-the-covid-19-pandemic-big-shifts-and-uncertainty-d1131663/. Accessed 24 Jul 2022

44. Assaf A, Scuderi R (2020) COVID-19 and the recovery of the tourism industry. Tour Econ 26: 731–733. https://doi.org/10.1177/1354816620933712
45. Corbisiero F, La Rocca RA (2020) Tourism on demand. New form of urban and social demand of use after the pandemic event. TeMA - J L Use, Mobil Environ:91–104. https://doi.org/10.6092/1970-9870/6916
46. Gauci A, Gerosa V, Mwalwanda C (2006) Tourism in Africa and the multilateral trading system: challenges and opportunities. Economic Commission for Africa, New York
47. Eilat Y, Einav L (2004) Determinants of international tourism: a three-dimensional panel data analysis. Appl Econ 36:1315–1327. https://doi.org/10.1080/0003684042000180897

Part II
Shocked Social Development: Mechanisms to Improve Community Robustness

Societal Shocks and Gender-Based Violence Among Vulnerable People in Kibra and Other Informal Settlements Around Nairobi, Kenya

Wyclife Ong'eta Mose and Giuseppe T. Cirella

1 Introduction

At present, one billion people live in urban informal settlements. These people are particularly vulnerable and susceptible to danger. They are, to varying degrees, deprived of adequate housing and access to basic services such as appropriate sanitation, fresh and potable water and storm drainage systems, reliable electricity supplies, and efficient affordable mobility [1]. According to the World Bank [2], these conditions have been aggravated by the COVID-19 pandemic. The pandemic has intensified existing drivers of fragility and conflict—worsening social tensions, widening inequalities, and heightening levels of gender-based violence (GBV) in many countries. The International Labor Organization (ILO) reports that for the first two quarters of 2021, the shortfall amounts to a reduction in global labor income of 5.3%, or USD 1.3 trillion [3]. Relative to 2019, an estimated additional 108 million workers are now extremely or moderately poor, meaning that they and their family members are having to live on less than USD 3.20 per day in purchasing power parity (PPP) terms. In 2021, the Institute for Economic and Peace [4] revealed that while some forms of violence declined in the short-term, growing unease with lockdowns and rising economic uncertainty, resulted in civil unrest and violence increasing in 2020. Over 5000 pandemic-related violent events were recorded between January 2020 and April 2021 [4]. They further indicated that the pandemic has had devastating impact in socioeconomic development in many developing countries, i.e., the economic impact of violence in 2020 in terms of the global

W. Ong'eta Mose (✉)
School of Security, Diplomacy and Peace Studies, Kenyatta University, Nairobi, Kenya

G. T. Cirella
Faculty of Economics, University of Gdansk, Sopot, Poland
e-mail: gt.cirella@ug.edu.pl

G. T. Cirella (ed.), *Uncertainty Shocks in Africa*, Advances in African Economic, Social and Political Development, https://doi.org/10.1007/978-3-031-21885-9_7

economy was USD 14.96 trillion in PPP. This figure is equivalent to 11.6% of the world's economic activity (i.e., the gross world product) or USD 1942 per person.

In Kenya, the National Crime Research Centre [5] revealed that due to socioeconomic shocks caused by COVID-19, there was increasing violence, especially GBV, among people living in Kibera, Nairobi's largest informal settlement, as well as other slums located in the city. The 71% of the 2416 cases of GBV reported between January and June of 2020 were female victims. The main perpetrators of GBV are youthful males aged 18–33 years who are in a family or intimate partner relationship context. ILO [3] attributes GBV to disproportionate job losses and the disruption of labor markets in which women's employment declined by 5% in 2020 compared with 3.9% for men. However, in Kenya's case, this figure does not fully integrate the social structures that increasing effect the most vulnerable—such as people living in Kibra compared to the other parts of the country. This chapter applies Galtung's [6] classification of direct, structural, and cultural violence framework by analyzing the constructs to reduce the resilience of people in such areas in the context of COVID-19. It will then suggest policy directions in hope of creating and sustaining a peaceful society. When considering the United Nations Human Settlements Program's (UN-Habitat) [7] projection for 2050, 68% of the world's population or 6.7 billion people will live in cities, with most of this growth being in poorly serviced and underdeveloped urban slums. This projection amplifies the importance and urgency of building stronger communities that are safe, economically prosperous, and environmentally sound. A breakdown of this chapter will first look at Galtung's framework by integrating it with COVID-19, socioeconomic shocks, and violence, before piecing together how such shock events effect Nairobi's informal settlements in terms of their GBV levels. To end, recommendations are presented to reduce GBV with a far-sighted vision on how to better handle future shocks from an international and national perspective.

2 Galtung's Classification of Direct, Structural, and Cultural Violence Framework

According to Galtung [6, 8], direct violence is a kind of violence with a clear subject-object relation that manifests because it is visible as action. It corresponds to an idea of what drama is, i.e., it is personal, because there are persons committing the violence. For example, Galtung [6] notes when a husband beats his wife, there is a clear case of personal violence, but when one million husbands keep one million wives in ignorance, there is structural violence. Galtung also points out that violence in the structure is calm and still. This violence, most of the time, is present but it is seen as normal, e.g., where a mother dies while doing home delivery because the hospital is several kilometers away, or where a child dies because of malnutrition even though people nearby have too much food that they can afford to throw it out. These types of violence are emblematic among the vulnerable members of society.

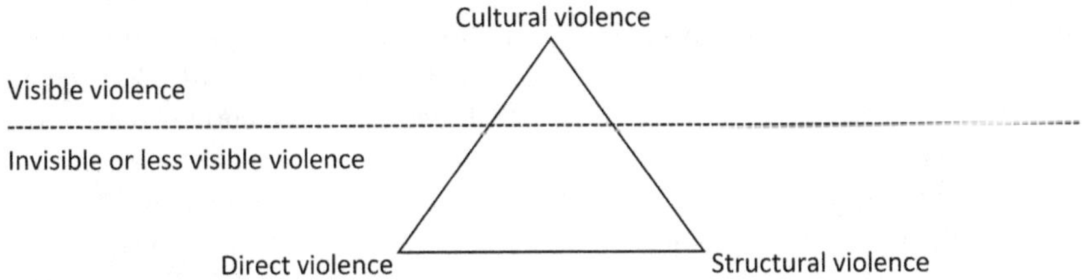

Fig. 1 Galtung's triangle—classification of direct, structural, and cultural violence framework. Source: adapted from Galtung [6, 8]

For direct violence, it is always visible, i.e., people can easily call it harmful and wrong as they strive to stop it. Sometimes even people do not realize direct violence is a manifestation of structural violence in their society [6].

To expand on his early work, Galtung came up with another kind of violence called cultural violence. This violence is defined as any facet of traditions that can be used to regularize violence in its direct or structural shape. Symbolic violence assembled into a culture does not kill akin to direct violence or the violence built into the structure [8]. Cultural violence works in a way that could right a wrong. For instance, if there are two warring communities and warriors from one community kill members from the other, this is seen as right by the community where the warriors come from but wrong from the affected one. Hence, the perpetrators do not see the violent act or harm they have caused the opposing community—instead they are celebrated as heroes [8]. The three types of violence are connected in a triangular manner called the classification of direct, structural, and cultural violence framework (Fig. 1).

3 COVID-19, Socioeconomic Shocks, and Violence

The measures to tackle the COVID-19 pandemic have had a devastating impact to lives of millions worldwide [9–12]. The pandemic has also revealed, and sometimes aggravated, existing patterns of abuses and inequalities. Some had roots in discrimination based on gender, race, and other grounds, which often intersected and rendered certain populations uniquely vulnerable [13]. For example, lockdowns and curfews led to particularly high numbers of workers in the informal economy losing their incomes without recourse to adequate social protection. Since they dominated the sector, women and girls were disproportionately affected [13]. ILO underlines that informal employees were three times more likely than their formal counterparts, and 1.6 times more likely than the self-employed, to lose their jobs as a result of the crisis, thereby contributing to the observed shift towards self-employment [3]. Moreover, because of their informal status, they were less likely to benefit from any form of social welfare. This is what we call structural violence as discussed earlier. Similarly, the United Nations Development Program (UNDP) reiterates that for informal workers, a feeling of insecurity can arise from worries about daily life versus the dread of a cataclysmic world event [14]. Job security, income security, health security, environmental security, and security from crime are the emerging concerns.

According to UN-Habitat [7], inequality remains a persistent trend in urban areas. For more than two-thirds of the world's urban population, income inequality has increased since 1980. This widening gap means that about 2.9 billion people are living in cities where income inequalities are currently more pronounced than they were a generation ago. The situation is dire for women living in urban areas—more specifically in slums. OXFAM [15] and the Mo Ibrahim Foundation [16] report that women are overrepresented in low-paid, precarious sectors such as retail, tourism, and food services, that have been hardest hit by the pandemic. Across South Asia, sub-Saharan Africa, and Latin America, the majority of women work in informal employment. Women also make up roughly 70% of the world's health and social care workforce—i.e., essential but often poorly paid jobs—that put them at greater risk from COVID-19. In other words, ILO estimates that 327 million wage earners are paid at or below the applicable hourly minimum wage [17]. This figure represents 19% of all wage earners and includes 152 million women. Although, in absolute terms, more men than women earn the minimum wage or less, women are overrepresented among this category of workers—i.e., while women make up 39% of the world's employees paid above the minimum wage, they represent 47% of the world's sub-minimum and minimum wage earners. This is in-line with the 2021 World Economic Forum [18] report that shows, globally, the average distance completed to parity is at 68%, a step back compared to 2020 (i.e., −0.6 percentage points). The slow progress seen in closing the economic participation and opportunity gap is the result of two opposing trends. On the one hand, the proportion of women among skilled professionals continues to increase, as does progress towards wage equality, albeit at a slower pace. On the other hand, overall income disparities are still only part way towards being bridged and there is a persistent lack of women in leadership positions, with women representing just 27% of all managerial positions [18]. This concurs with the Lloyd's Register Foundation [19] report contending that 27% of women across the globe felt less safe than they did 5 years ago. As such, significant numbers of working women around the world fear violence and harassment in the workplace and at home.

In the face of these global challenges, countries already threatened by conflict and crisis are among the most vulnerable. In 2020, many lacked the tools needed to respond to the pandemic's far-reaching impact because of pre-existing vulnerabilities and gaps in social safety nets, health systems, deep regional disparities, and low levels of public trust. In several countries, the crisis has therefore exacerbated risks and grievances, leading to greater deprivation and social unrest [2]. For example, the global political conflict panorama in 2020 was marked by a rise in the number of wars and violent crises. The overall number of wars increased significantly from 15 to 21 [20]. In Europe, two conflicts escalated to full scale wars, while in sub-Saharan Africa six ongoing wars continued and another five violent conflicts escalated to the level of war, making it the region with the highest number of conflicts on war level in 2020. However, it is difficult to tell whether the rise of violent conflict was caused by the COVID-19 pandemic. Perhaps, the pandemic aggravated already existing structural violence that then transformed to direct violence. However, in various conflicts, the number and extent of demonstrations, at least temporarily, decreased compared to the previous year, possibly in connection with COVID-19 or restrictive government policies, e.g., Algeria (i.e., the opposition party), Brazil (i.e., the Landless Workers Movement), China (i.e., Hong Kong), Chile (i.e., several social movements); India (i.e., Nagalim), Indonesia (i.e., the Free Papua Movement), Iraq (i.e., the opposition party), Kenya (i.e., the opposition party), and Lebanon (i.e., inner-Palestinian tensions) [20]. The International Monetary Fund (IMF) contends that while the pandemic continues, governments should formulate policies focusing on escaping the crisis, prioritizing healthcare spending, providing well-targeted fiscal support, and maintaining accommodative monetary policy while monitoring financial stability risks [21]. Then, as the recovery progresses, policymakers will need to limit long-term economic scarring with an eye towards boosting productive capacity (e.g., public investment) and increasing incentives for an efficient allocation of productive resources. IMF further notes that the international community needs to work together to ensure that financially constrained economies have adequate access to international liquidity so that they can continue needed healthcare as well as other social and infrastructure spending required for development and convergence to higher levels of income per capita. To achieve this goal, the assertion from UNDP [14] that economic partnership should be based on mutual interests, not charity; cooperation, not confrontation; equitable sharing of market opportunities, not protectionism; and far-sighted internationalism, not stubborn nationalism—is central to developing, transforming, and putting behind us the COVID-19 era difficulties.

4 Economic Shocks in Nairobi's Informal Settlements and GBV: Analysis Using Galtung's Framework

To understand how COVID-19 triggered weak social and physical structures in informal settlements, i.e., often propped with backward cultural elements that transform into direct violence and the manifestation of GBV, Galtung's [6, 8] framework is applied. Guided by the framework, i.e., addressing what the concept of peace means, the larger picture of peace is equivalent to the absence of structural violence, the absence of cultural violence, and the absence of direct violence. This implies the absence of direct violence does not necessarily equate to peacefulness in a society. If there is the presence of structural and cultural violence, then this can be equated to an inactive volcano which could erupt if triggered. Hence, to speak of peace, structural and cultural violence must be abolished even though these kinds of violence, most often than not, appear as part and parcel of life. When we speak of

Fig. 2 Kibra, informal settlement located in Nairobi, Kenya. Source: Google Maps [22]

Fig. 3 Poor housing, poor water and sanitation, and poor drainage in the informal settlement of Kibra, Nairobi. Source: Photographs by Wyclife Ong'eta Mose, July 16, 2022

urban slums, the question of what is structural violence needs to be carefully considered and, contemporarily, in terms of COVID-19, how this kind of violence has been aggravated by the pandemic?

To elucidate on the shock of COVID-19, case research on the informal settlement of Kibra as well as other slums located in Nairobi are looked at through the lens of Galtung's framework (Fig. 2). At present, 14 out of 25 of Nairobi's residents live in slums [23, 24]. These crowded informal settlements are characterized by poor housing, poor water and sanitation, poor drainage, poor street lighting, insecurity, poor recreational facilities, inadequate education and health services, and a large majority of people doing low-cadre jobs for survival [25] (Fig. 3). To make matters worse, education which is believed to have the potential to lift people out of poverty, appears to be a luxury to a fairly large portion of the population, i.e., one of five men have attained tertiary education while for women it is three of twenty. Sadly, two out of five people have not gone past primary education [26]. This implies that

Fig. 4 Poor facilities and standard of living in the informal settlements of Nairobi: (*top*) inadequate and poor schooling facility in the informal settlement of Juja, on the outskirts of Nairobi and (bottom) insufficient housing and infrastructure in the informal settlement of Kibra, Nairobi. Source: (top) Photograph by Wyclife Ong'eta Mose, 17 July 2022; (bottom) photograph by klndonnelly on Flickr, Creative Commons Public Domain, 21 May 2007

transforming these people's lives will need to be premeditated, i.e., a deliberate effort, from the outside-in. It is well documented that if the majority of individuals from informal settlements are able to attain at least secondary education, more opportunities become available [27–32]. In this instance, the picture being depicted is what Galtung referred to as structural violence, i.e., where the informal settlement residents are taxpayers like normal residents, yet they are missing essential services from their government. In this case, a lack of educational services compounded by a lack of social and physical infrastructure to advance well-being (Fig. 4).

In terms of structural and cultural violence, this further manifests itself between the male-to-female ratio of Kenya's total population which currently stands at 98.76 males per 100 females [33]. Moreover, this is perpetuated by the culture of patriarchy, i.e., families are more prone to giving opportunities to the boy child rather than the girl child. This is demonstrated by the Trends and Insights for Africa (TIFA) report that elucidates women and girls as heavily disadvantaged—especially in terms of education—for Nairobi's slum-dwelling residents [26]. TIFA states that girls take more of the homely and nurturing roles than boys, who are believed to be tasked with important duties to prepare them as leaders and breadwinners who are expected to utilize the available education and trade training each family can afford. At the end of the day, boys end up getting better job opportunities compared to girls when they

Fig. 5 Limited health services in the informal settlement of Kibra, Nairobi: (*left*) chemist and (*right*) medical clinic. Source: Photographs by Antonella Sinopoli on Flickr, Creative Commons Public Domain, May 21, 2008

become adults. OXFAM suggests that the current economic system exacerbates the patriarchy—transforming society via a narrow extreme level of inequality, injustice, and poverty which renders humans more vulnerable when a crisis occurs [34]. As a result, it is evident that structural and cultural violence is emblematic and part of the lives of people living in Kibra and other slums in Nairobi. When the COVID-19 pandemic entered the borders of Kenya, the government put in place a set of measures to cope with the shock. These included lockdowns, curfews, handwashing, social distancing, closures of learning institutions, working from home, and so forth. The containment measures caused three critical outcomes, according to the Kenya Institute for Public Policy Research and Analysis [35]. First, 6.2 million people in Kenya were consigned into poverty. This was attributed to loss of income and job opportunities. Second, revenue collection diminished from 17.8% in 2020 to 16.3% in 2021 which led to increasing public debt. Third, it worsened the existing gender inequality as many women lost jobs compared to men. This especially was dominated by the lower echelons of society and lower paying job goers [16, 34, 36]. For example, across the slums one out of five men lost a job, while for women it was one out of four. In full-time employment, only 12% of men retained work, while for women, it was a marginal 3% [26]. The economic shock caused by COVID-19 had limited government support. This lack of social safety generated into violence and manifested in the form of GBV. From the beginning of 2020 to the end of 2021, i.e., the first 2 years of COVID-19, a reported increase in cases of sexual and physical violence against women and girls was reported [37]. The forms of violence included rape, physical assault, psychological abuse, murder, and child marriage. The perpetrators were close members of the family, particularly young men [5]. This kind of violence is attributed to pressure via the family breadwinner, who was subjected to the containment measures from COVID-19. As such, families were compelled to stay at home at all times, despite the very overcrowded home environment in slums. This measure alone could be regarded as a form of psychological torture due to the often small and unlivable circumstances of not being able to leave a slum area.

Often, relief from health services are minimal and too expensive or nonexistent in informal settlements (Fig. 5).

As previously mentioned, the aspect of the patriarchy where a man is looked at as a sole breadwinner resulted in a problematic circumstance. It can be inferred that this could help explain why most young men were the perpetrators of violence during this period. Again, the aspect of structural violence is clear in this situation. Despite the fact that most people in varying slums of Nairobi face economic hardships, the government is not able to reach them in times of crisis with social safety support. Hence, structural and cultural violence, as seen in this context, legitimize direct violence in the form of GBV—without consequence. However, according to Galtung's framework, the aspect of gender is increasingly absent. That is why Standish [38] is of the view that neglecting the aspect of GBV in the theory collapses the experience of violence. Galtung, nonetheless, identifies ideological facets in which he refers to male supremacy which can result in sexism. Standish is of the opinion that male's use violence as a tool to control women [38].

5 Conclusion and Recommendations

Following this analysis, to address the issue of violence across informal settlements, a multi-prong approach is needed. First, the government needs to confront the issue of social inequality through continuous taxation on income from capital. Education, touted as an equalizer, should be made free from primary to the end of secondary school. This could also be extended to higher institutions under certain conditions for exceptionally favorable students. This will aid in guaranteeing that all vulnerable people are reached with social protection to boost their resilience in times crisis such as the COVID-19 pandemic [39]. Second, the issue of gender inequality should be given maximum attention. At present, there are very influential instruments that are seeking to abolish gender inequality, including internationally (i.e., the 1979 UN convention on the elimination of all forms of discrimination against women; the United Nations Beijing Declaration and Platform for Action, 1995; the United Nations Resolution 1325 on Women, Peace, and Security; the United Nations Sustainable Development Goals; the Maputo Protocol; and the Generation Equality Forum) and nationally (i.e., the 2010 Constitution of Kenya that speaks of the two-thirds gender rule; the Sexual Offences Act of 2006; the Protection against Domestic Violence Act, 2015; and the Matrimonial Property Act). These instruments are dedicated to abolishing violence against women on the one hand, while advancing the goals of equality, development, and peace for all women and men on the other. The question of how and why GBV continues to happen—i.e., with these powerful instruments—is in part an ongoing struggle. There is a need to regularly monitor and evaluate all government institutions, frameworks, and structures advancing equality to establish gaps and take action. Success stories need to be amplified and best practices replicated. It should be noted that the issue of social inequality and patriarchy partly sustain social violence and they are as old as man himself. To aid in abolishing these problems, it should be a gradual and sustained process.

In conclusion, it is becoming increasingly clear that structural and cultural violence stands in the way of the people living across informal settlements, such as in Kibra, from achieving a dignified life worth living. It has weakened their resilience against hardships and crises, e.g., the COVID-19 pandemic. To address this, the government should make deliberate policy initiatives to narrow the gap of social and gender inequality especially for vulnerable people living in slums as a way to address violence, including GBV. As such, the following recommendations are pertinent for the Government of Kenya: (1) make education free for vulnerable groups including those living in informal settlements as a way to lessen structural violence and boost social and gender equality; (2) in cooperation with development partners, ensure that all vulnerable people are qualified for social protection schemes in order to boost their resilience in time of uncertainties; (3) make deliberate efforts to enhance social and physical infrastructure across informal settlements including adequate water and sewerage systems, good road networks, street lights connections, establish more schools to accommodate all children in crowded settlements, more health facilities, and develop recreation facilities to nurture talents; and (4) in cooperation with development partners, ensure women are provided meaningful opportunities to participate in leadership and development initiatives to promote the well-being of people by adopting and implementing the international legal frameworks advancing gender equality.

References

1. UN-Habitat (2021) Adapting cities for climate resilience. United Nations Human Settlements Programme, Nairobi
2. World Bank (2020) Partnership in crisis-affected situations. World Bank: UN-WB Partnership Monitoring Report, Washington, DC
3. ILO (2021) World employment and social outlook: trends 2021. International Labour Organization, Geneva
4. Institute for Economic and Peace (2021) Global peace index 2021: measuring peace in complex world. Institute for Economic and Peace, Sydney
5. National Crime Research Centre (2020) Protecting the family in the time of COVID-19 pandemic: addressing the escalating cases of gender-based violence, girl child disempowerment and violations of children's rights in Kenya. Government Press, Nairobi
6. Galtung J (1969) Violence, peace, and peace research. J Peace Res 6:167–191. https://doi.org/10.1177/002234336900600301
7. UN-Habitat (2020) World cities report 2020: the value of sustainable urbanization. United Nations Human Settlements Programme, Nairobi
8. Galtung J (1990) Cultural violence. J Peace Res 27:291–305. https://doi.org/10.1177/0022343390027003005
9. Simon J, Helter TM, White RG et al (2021) Impacts of the Covid-19 lockdown and relevant vulnerabilities on capability well-being, mental health and social support: an Austrian survey study. BMC Public Health 21:1–12. https://doi.org/10.1186/S12889-021-10351-5/TABLES/4
10. Zhou M, Kan MY (2021) The varying impacts of COVID-19 and its related measures in the UK: a year in review. PLoS One 16:e0257286. https://doi.org/10.1371/JOURNAL.PONE.0257286

11. Poudel AN, Zhu S, Cooper N et al (2021) Impact of Covid-19 on health-related quality of life of patients: A structured review. PLoS One 16:e0259164. https://doi.org/10.1371/JOURNAL.PONE.0259164
12. Shukla M, Pandey R, Singh T et al (2021) The effect of COVID-19 and related lockdown phases on young peoples' worries and emotions: novel data from India. Front Public Heal 9: 594. https://doi.org/10.3389/FPUBH.2021.645183/BIBTEX
13. Amnesty International (2021) The state of the world's human rights. Amnesty International Report, London
14. UNDP (1994) Human development report. Oxford University Press, New York
15. OXFAM (2021) COVID-19 cost women globally over $800 billion in lost income in one year. Oxfam International, London
16. Mo Ibrahim Foundation (2021) COVID-19 in Africa one year on: impact and prospects. Mo Ibrahim Foundation, London
17. ILO (2020) Global wage report 2020–21: wages and minimum wages in the time of COVID-19. International Labour Organization, Geneva
18. World Economic Forum (2021) Global gender gap report. World Economic Forum, Geneva
19. Lloyd's Register Foundation (2019) World risk poll. Lloyd's Register Foundation, London
20. Heidelberg Institute for International Conflict Research (2021) Conflict barometer 2020. Heidelberg Institute for International Conflict Research, Heidelberg
21. IMF (2021) World economic outlook: managing divergent recoveries. International Monetary Fund, Washington, DC
22. Google Maps (2022) Google maps. https://www.google.com/maps/. Accessed 4 Mar 2022
23. Desgroppes A, Taupin S (2011) Kibera: the biggest slum in Africa? Les Cah d'Afrique l'Est/ East African Rev 23–33. https://doi.org/10.4000/EASTAFRICA.521
24. APHRC (2014) Population and health dynamics in Nairobi's informal settlements: report of the nairobi cross-sectional slums survey. African Population and Health Research Center, Nairobi
25. UNICEF (2021) Sub-Saharan Africa: growing up in crisis in a world of opportunities. United Nations International Children's Emergency Fund, Paris
26. TIFA (2020) COVID-19 global pandemic in Nairobi's low-income areas: effectiveness of preventive measures, curfew and mask-wearing compliance and enforcement. Trends and Insights for Africa, Nairobi
27. Zhang AT, Patnaik S, Jha S et al (2022) Evidence of multidimensional gender inequality in energy services from a large-scale household survey in India. Nat Energy 1–10. https://doi.org/10.1038/s41560-022-01044-3
28. Maemeko E, Mukwambo M, Nkengbeza D (2021) Social challenges learners residing in informal settlements in Katima Mulilo Town face in learning. J Curric Teach 10:36–46. https://doi.org/10.5430/jct.v10n3p36
29. de Jager T, Maserumule MH (2021) Innovative community projects to educate informal settlement inhabitants in the sustainment of the natural environment. Sustainability 13:6238. https://doi.org/10.3390/SU13116238
30. Cervantes NG, Hinojosa KH (2022) Opportunities and challenges for service-learning experiences in informal urban settlements. J Archit Res e0348. https://doi.org/10.1108/ARCH-12-2021-0348
31. Tikly L, Barrett AM (2011) Social justice, capabilities and the quality of education in low income countries. Int J Educ Dev 31:3–14. https://doi.org/10.1016/J.IJEDUDEV.2010.06.001
32. Mitchell A, Del Monte P, Deneulin S (2018) School completion in urban Latin America: the voices of young people from an informal settlement. Oxford Dev Stud 46:45–56. https://doi.org/10.1080/13600818.2017.1387242
33. Statista (2022) Kenya: population's gender ratio 2000–2020. In: Statistica. https://www.statista.com/statistics/1226942/male-to-female-ratio-of-the-total-population-in-kenya/. Accessed 13 Jul 2022
34. OXFAM (2020) COVID-19 and vulnerable, hardworking Kenyans: why it's time for a strong social protection plan. Oxfam International, Nairobi

35. KIPPRA (2021) Kenya in COVID-19 era: fast-tracking recovery and delivery of the "big four" agenda. Kenya Institute for Public Policy Research and Analysis, Nairobi
36. Government of Kenya, United Nations (2020) COVID-19 gender assessment. United Nations, Nairobi
37. Human Right Watch (2021) "I had nowhere to go" violence against women and girls during the COVID-19 pandemic in Kenya. Human Right Watch, Nairobi
38. Standish K (2021) Suicide, femicide, and COVID-19. Peace Rev 33:71–79. https://doi.org/10.1080/10402659.2021.1956132
39. United Nations Conference on Trade and Development (2021) Technology and innovation: catching technological waves innovation with equity. In: United Nations Conference on Trade and Development, Geneva

Contraceptive Utilization Among Married Couples in Nigeria: Socio-cultural Factors

Dominic E. Azuh, Paul O. Adekola, Adebanke Olawole-Isaac, Gideon A. Adeyemi, Giuseppe T. Cirella, and Chelsea R. Spring

1 Introduction

Given the slow progress made in reducing the high fertility rate, there is an urgent need to increase contraception use among couples in Nigeria, particularly in rural areas. Understanding the influence of socio-cultural factors on contraceptive use is

D. E. Azuh (✉) · A. Olawole-Isaac
Demography and Social Statistics Programme, Department of Economics and Development Studies, Covenant University, Ota, Ogun State, Nigeria

Centre for Economic Policy and Development Research, Covenant University, Ota, Ogun State, Nigeria
e-mail: dominic.azuh@covenantuniversity.edu.ng; adebanke.olawole-isaac@covenantuniversity.edu.ng

P. O. Adekola
Demography and Social Statistics Programme, Department of Economics and Development Studies, Covenant University, Ota, Ogun State, Nigeria

Centre for Economic Policy and Development Research, Covenant University, Ota, Ogun State, Nigeria

Research Centre for Anthropology and Health, Department of Life Sciences, University of Coimbra, Coimbra, Portugal
e-mail: paul.adekola@covenantuniversity.edu.ng

G. A. Adeyemi
Centre for Economic Policy and Development Research, Covenant University, Ota, Ogun State, Nigeria

Department of Civil Engineering, Covenant University, Ota, Ogun State, Nigeria
e-mail: gideon.adewale@cu.edu.ng

G. T. Cirella · C. R. Spring
Faculty of Economics, University of Gdansk, Sopot, Poland
e-mail: gt.cirella@ug.edu.pl

G. T. Cirella (ed.), *Uncertainty Shocks in Africa*, Advances in African Economic, Social and Political Development, https://doi.org/10.1007/978-3-031-21885-9_8

crucial to embracing the use of contraceptive practices [1–4]. The application of birth control methods will beneficially reduce the unmet need for services by preventing unplanned pregnancies and saving women's lives from premature death resulting from abortion or multiple births [5–8]. Contraception is merely a procreation-regulating practice, which negates most people's opinion, especially those in rural areas. Reproductive health beliefs and attitudes are vital for the acceptance of contraception. Besides religious misconceptions, taboos are strong influencing forces that sustain high rates of childbearing [9–11]. The large family size in Africa is probably the highest in the world, e.g., Djibouti—9.33 per household, Senegal—7.7, and Nigeria—4.63 [12]. Traditional Nigerian socio-cultural norms view marriage as a sacred bond for the purpose of procreation, lineage, and polygyny—a belief which is still widespread. Nigeria's current contraceptive prevalence rate among married couples is low (i.e., 12%), according to the 2018 Nigerian Demographic and Health Survey (NDHS) [13]. This is far from the goal of the Federal Government of Nigeria, even though the Federal Ministry of Health has set a prevalence rate target of 27% by the end of 2022. In 2020, 1.9 billion women of reproductive age (i.e., 15–49 years) were living in the world, with 1.1 billion of them in need of contraception [14]. In Nigeria, 36% of married women demand family planning in the form of limiting the number of children they bear (i.e., 14%) and for spacing the length of time between pregnancies (i.e., 22%) [13]. Traditionally, men in most developing countries are the head of the household, sole providers, and control their family's economic resources. This control makes the patrilineal system significant and plays an essential role in reproductive health and household decision-making [15–18]. Rapid scale-up of contraceptive programs and medical facilities will be essential to reducing the unmet need for information and services, which requires a thorough understanding of the factors influencing contraception use [19–21], particularly socio-cultural factors (Fig. 1).

Several social and cultural factors mitigate the practice of contraception in developing countries. However, not much has been written about this, specifically, why cultural norms disapprove of contraceptive implementation. Informed intervention aimed at contraceptive acceptance and practice revolves around a complete understanding of the societal and contextual factors against fertility regulation, especially among low social strata in semi-urban and rural communities where over 65% of the population of Nigeria resides. In 2013, Viswan et al. [22] observed that the prevalence rate for the use of modern contraception was 2.6 times higher among women who had high sexual autonomy and 11.8 times higher for women with secondary or higher education compared with women who had no formal education. Education seems to break the veil of ignorance, superstition, and conservatism on contraceptive acceptance in developing countries. Current misconceptions about birth control in Nigeria are contraceptives can cause cancer and lead to physical and mental deformities. Conversely, education effectively lowers the level of adverse myths and rumors about family planning. Furthermore, it facilitates effective husband–wife communication and the reduction of misconceptions arising from social norms. Additionally, it enhances perceived self-efficacy to use contraception and starts a conversation with a partner about family planning benefits [23].

Fig. 1 Medical facilities throughout Nigeria: (*top left*) entrance to Reference Hospital, Okene, during its construction, (*top right*) ECWA Hospital Egbe, a Christian hospital located in Egbe, Kogi, (*bottom left*) medical supply vendor supported by the World Health Organization (WHO) and the World Bank, and (*bottom right*) Dr. Dan C. Nwankwo Memorial Infant Welfare Clinic, partner in the Stand to End Rape Initiative. Source: (*top left*) Photograph by Francis Tokede on Upsplash, Creative Commons Public Domain, 9 June 2022; (*top right*) photograph by SIM USA on Flickr, Creative Commons Public Domain, 21 August 2015; (*bottom left*) photograph by Arne Hoel on Flickr, Creative Commons Public Domain, 23 May 2008; (*bottom right*) photograph by Matthew Greer on Flickr, Creative Commons Public Domain, 30 August 2007

In a Nigerian study to determine factors influencing urban men and their readiness to adopt contraceptive methods, Babalola et al. [23] found key correlations between its use and exposure to family planning, promotional campaigns, education, age, religion, marital status, and community norms. Adanikin et al. [24], correspondingly, reported that the slow progress in family planning uptake, despite programmatic interventions, was due to the fear that women who use family planning may become promiscuous. As such, the use of contraceptives is relatively low and varies across 17 of the sub-Saharan African countries [25]. In a recent study, Owoyemi et al. [26] revealed that despite family planning benefits, perceived side effects, disapproval from friends, age, culture, and poor level of education were key factors that cause low utilization of family planning in the state of Kogi. Similarly, Alabi et al. [27] found that female autonomy, education, wealth status, and desire for no more children were associated with higher contraceptive use. Exposure to family planning messages from religious leaders and engaging spiritual leader support was significantly associated with higher implementation of modern contraceptive use, regardless of myths and misconceptions [28]. Contrary to the widely circulated negative fallacies that surround Islamic beliefs of contraception emerging knowledge proves it is acceptable as long as the type follows Islamic ethics [29–31]. In similar studies, low utilization of contraception in core Islamic nations, especially in rural areas, correlated to poverty, illiteracy, and religious misconceptions [30, 31]. Interestingly, numerous studies show that in Nigeria, Christians are more likely to use contraception than their Muslim counterparts [32–34].

According to WHO [35], reducing the vast unmet need for family planning remains a massive challenge to countries and the global health community as services are still of poor quality or unavailable in many settings, while service delivery and social constraints persist. Lasong et al. [36] revealed that modern contraceptive use in rural Zambia among married women of reproductive age is relatively low, with education, wealth index, and high parity as factors positively associated with contraceptive use. The odds that women used a contraceptive method increased significantly by level of education, wealth status, and having several living children [37]. This chapter uniquely ties socio-cultural factors—such as child preference, household decision autonomy, and healthcare decision-making in the family—with Nigeria's geopolitical zones. Most of the variables, not used in the previous NDHS, were introduced in the 2018 data. The updated data allowed for an inter-geopolitical assessment of the socio-cultural factors obstructing contraceptive deployment in the country and sheds light on the different intervention measures noted in the United Nations Sustainable Development Goals (SDGs) 3, 5, and 10 [38].

2 Methodological Background

2.1 Data

This chapter utilized representative cross-sectional secondary data from the 2018 NDHS, i.e., the sixth cohort in a series of population and health surveys conducted in Nigeria as part of the global Demographic and Health Surveys (DHS) project. NDHS used a multi-stage sampling technique that had broken down the country by way of state and local government areas (LGAs). Each LGA was further divided into different census enumeration areas which were classified between rural and urban. The sample for this chapter was selected using a stratified three-stage cluster design consisting of 904 clusters—i.e., 372 in urban areas and 532 in rural areas. Three sets of questionnaires were used in the 2018 NDHS, i.e., a household questionnaire, a women's questionnaire, and a men's questionnaire. These questionnaires were modeled by the Monitoring and Evaluation to Assess and Use Results of Demographic and Health Surveys project in which the target groups were married women aged 15–49 and married men aged 15–59 in randomly selected households across Nigeria. A representative sample of approximately 42,000 households was selected from NDHS [13] in which 8061 married couples were used for this chapter's study. All the data used was fully anonymized since NDHS does not contain any name or address of the survey's respondents.

2.2 Study Variables and Measures

The outcome variable was derived based on women and men (i.e., matched couples) currently using contraceptives. All the categories and responses from women and men were used and classified based on the 2018 NDHS, i.e., 0 = no (i.e., not using) and 1 = yes (i.e., using). The predictor variables comprised of household wealth and status, as reported by DHS, and were classified into five categories; however, for simplicity and ease this chapter reduced them to three. The first and second groups (i.e., poorest, and poorer) were classified as poor, the third (i.e., middle) and fourth group were classified as intermediate, and the fifth group (i.e., richest) were classified as rich. Moreover, other socio-demographic variables included: educational attainment (i.e., no education, primary, secondary, and higher), work status (i.e., working and not working), number of children born (i.e., 0, 1–2, 3–4, and 5+), religion (i.e., Christian and Muslim), and place of residence (i.e., urban and rural). These were all categorized as control variables. Furthermore, at the aggregate level, additional contextual factors that could affect modern contraceptive use were integrated in the analysis. They included: child preference, wife's rank, household decision autonomy, and opinion on whether contraceptive use leads to promiscuity. Additional opinion on whether contraceptive use is a woman's business, has regional differences, effects healthcare decision-making autonomy, and is generally understood was considered. These explanatory variables were selected based on the extant empirical literature on the subject. The data was weighted to adjust for sampling selection biases.

2.3 Analytic Procedure

Descriptive statistics were applied to assess the full range of the socio-demographic and exploratory variables from NDHS. The chi-square test was adopted to associate the prevalence of contraceptive use to each of the socio-cultural characteristics. To understand variability, binary logistic regression was used to identify the socio-cultural factors that accurately influence contraceptive use. All the analyses were done using the software program STATA Version 15 in which a 5% sample error was adopted. Each of the variables was assessed with the outcome variable by way of logistic regression modeling using Eq. 1.

$$\log\left(\frac{p}{1-p}\right) = \alpha + \beta_1 X_1 + \beta_2 X_2 + \ldots + \beta_n X_n + e \tag{1}$$

where: p = probability that a woman (or man or couple) uses contraceptives given the covariate $\beta_n X_n$, $1 - p$ = probability of non-use, and e = error term.

The model was used to control demographic and socio-cultural factors that could potentially influence individual-level contraceptive use. Odds ratio (OR) and confidence interval (CI) were then calculated for estimation.

3 Results

3.1 Socio-demographic Characteristics

The distribution of married couples, shown in Table 1, indicates that a large proportion of the population surveyed was between 25 and 34 years while about two out of every ten couples were between 15 and 24 years. The distribution by region shows that six out of every ten respondents interviewed were from the northern part of Nigeria, while less than 40% were from the southern part. Results further indicate that 62.7% of the respondents resided in rural areas at the time of the survey. Approximately 56% of the couples were Muslim, while the others were Christian. Seven out of every ten were in a monogamous marriage (i.e., 72.8%), while the rest were in a polygamous marriage. Furthermore, the result shows that over 40% of the respondents had no formal education, 16.5%—primary education, 32.4% a—secondary education, and less than 10%—higher education. The distribution of the number of children born shows that a little over one-quarter of the respondents had 3–4 children, while another quarter had six or more children, and 45% had 1–3 children. Also, seven out of every ten respondents desire an additional child. Moreover, 59.6% of respondents indicated that the ideal number of children a couple should have is six or more, while only 6.2% believe that a couple should not have more than three children. To further establish the level of closeness among couples, questions were asked about household decision-making status. The result shows that 58.7% of men are the sole decision-makers in the household, while 36.8% take joint decisions, and less than 5% of women make decisions by themselves. Also, questions on health issues were asked in which 56% of the couples take joint health decisions while 36% of the men take sole decisions on health matters. In terms of contraception knowledge, the result shows that 94.4% of the studied population knew about contraceptives. However, despite the high understanding of contraceptives among the respondents, the usage level is very low, as only 18.6% of married couples are using them. At length, the result shows that 37.7% of the respondents believe that women who use contraceptives are promiscuous, while 34.8% believe that contraceptive use is solely women's business.

3.2 Contraceptive Use among Married Couples

Contraceptive use varies considerably by age amongst married couples in Nigeria. The prevalence of contraceptive use was highest for women aged 35–44 (i.e.,

Table 1 Percentage distribution of respondents by socio-demographic and cultural variables

Variable	Frequency	Percentage	Variable	Frequency	Percentage
Age			*Age at first birth*		
15–24	1745	21.6	12–18	3585	56.2
25–34	3554	44.1	19–25	3130	41.2
35–44	2223	27.6	26–32	784	10.3
45+	539	6.7	33+	89	1.2
Religion			*Number of wives*		
Christian	3528	44.1	One wife	5846	72.8
Muslim	4474	55.9	More than one	2188	27.2
Region			*Wealth index*		
North-central	1451	18.0	Poor	3346	41.5
North-east	1574	19.5	Middle	1682	20.9
North-west	2101	26.1	Rich	3033	37.6
South-east	943	11.7	*Fertility preference*		
South-south	793	9.8	Want another child	5602	69.5
South-west	1199	14.9	Undecided	510	6.3
Residence			Sterile or other	1949	24.2
Urban	3009	37.3	*Ideal number of children*		
Rural	5052	62.7	1–3 children	483	6.2
Education			4–5 children	2687	34.3
No formal education	3371	41.8	6+	4671	59.6
Primary	1329	16.5	Rank among wives		
Secondary	2615	32.4	First rank	993	44.8
Higher	746	9.3	Second or other	1222	55.2
Number of children born			*Contraceptive use is a woman's business*		
1–3 children	3630	45.0	Disagree	5257	65.2
4–5 children	2297	28.5	Agree	2804	34.8
6+	2134	26.5	*Contraceptive use leads to promiscuity*		
			Disagree	5020	62.3
Household decision			Agree	3041	37.7
Wife alone	361	4.5	*Use of contraceptive*		
Husband alone	4716	58.7	Not using	6560	81.4
Joint decision	2953	36.8	Using	1501	18.6
			Decision on health		
Knowledge of contraceptive			Wife alone	643	8.0
No knowledge	450	5.6	Husband alone	2893	36.0
Yes knowledge	7611	94.4	Joint decision	4509	56.0

Source: Authors' own computation from 2018 NDHS

23.9%), followed by those aged 25–34 (i.e., 19.9%). Women aged 15–24 years had the lowest contraceptive use. Furthermore, the prevalence of contraception varies by women's education level. This is, probably, because 36.8% with higher education had the highest usage of contraceptive, followed by secondary (i.e., 29.4%), then primary (i.e., 20.6%), and lastly, by women who had no formal education (i.e.,

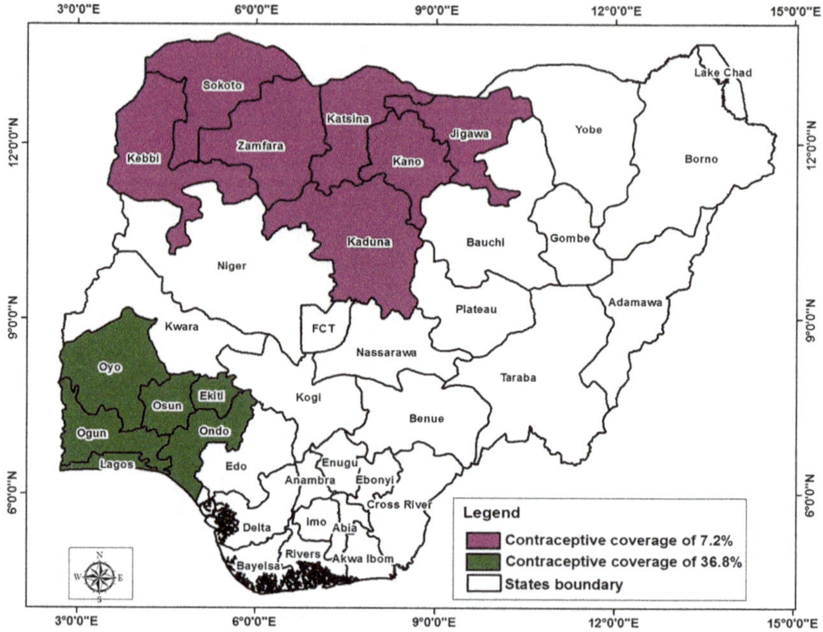

Fig. 2 Map of Nigeria showing disparity in contraceptive use between North-West and South-West

5.8%). It was found that married couples from North-Central had the highest prevalence of contraceptive use (i.e., 19%) in the northern part of the country. In comparison, those from South-South recorded the least utilization of contraceptive use (i.e., 22.2%) in the southern part of the country. Moreover, the region with the lowest prevalence in the southern part was 3.2% higher than the area with the highest in the northern part. This implies that there is a stack of geopolitical variation in contraceptive use in Nigeria. For example, while 92.8% of married couples in North-West do not use contraceptives, 36.8% of married couples in the South-West do (Fig. 2).

Whether contraceptive usage promoted promiscuity was another socio-cultural factor of importance among married couples in Nigeria. As captured by the chi-square analysis, results showed that 83.1% of those who agreed that contraceptive use promoted promiscuity among married couples did not use it versus 16.9% that did. Nonetheless, 80.4% still disagreed that contraceptive use is linked with promiscuity. However, despite their disagreement, only 19.6% of them used it. Also, couples who believed that 1–3 children are the ideal number to have, had the highest prevalence of using contraceptives, while those with 4–5 children had a 71.3% prevalence of not using them. The majority of contraceptive use was highest among couples who took joint household decisions (i.e., 27.4%), while teams whose husband is the sole decision maker recorded the lowest contraceptives prevalence (i.e., 12.7%). A similar trend was observed among the couple's decisions on health. Husbands with only one wife had a 21.9% prevalence of contraceptive use, while those with more than one had a 90.2% prevalence of not using a contraceptive. Moreover, couples who fell into the most affluent wealth index had the highest prevalence of using contraceptives (i.e., 31.1%). As such, those categorized as inferior based on the index recorded the highest majority of not using contraceptives (i.e., 92.1%). Also, couples who are Christians recorded a 30% prevalence rate of using a contraceptive, while Muslims recorded a 9.7% prevalence rate of using a contraceptive. Hence, there is a significant relationship between the use of contraceptives and socio-cultural variables (i.e., $p < 0.05$) (Table 2).

3.3 Socio-cultural Factors Associated with Contraceptive Use

An individual assessment of each of the covariates concerning the use of contraception is presented in Table 3. Significant variation was observed in age at first birth and education. Also, religion, region, household wealth quintile, total number of children born, ideal number of children, fertility preference, residence, and health decisions showed moderate to significantly high association with current contraception use among married couples in Nigeria. On the other hand, the ideology that the number of wives a man had, household decisions, and contraceptive use is a "woman's business" as well as contraceptive use leads to promiscuity showed no significant association. In detail, the adjusted effects of the socio-cultural factors associated with contraceptive use indicated variation in terms of geopolitical zone. A couple from South-West had approximately a two times higher chance of using contraception than couples from the northern part of Nigeria (i.e., OR: 2.47, 95% CI: 1.37–4.60). On the other hand, a couple from North-East had 12% less chance of using contraception than a couple from North-Central (i.e., OR: 0.88, 95% CI: 0.71–1.07). An educated woman with higher education had an 81% higher chance of using contraception than an uneducated woman (i.e., OR: 1.81, 95% CI: 1.66–2.15). Moreover, a woman who completed her primary education had a 68% higher chance of not using contraceptives than a woman who had no formal education (i.e., OR: 0.32 and 1.12, 95% CI: 0.24–0.43). A married couple from an urban setting had a 32% higher chance of contraception of using practices versus a woman from a rural setting (i.e., OR: 1.32, 95% CI: 1.13–1.53). It was also found that Muslim women had a 10% lesser chance of using contraception than Christian women (i.e., OR: 0.90, 95% CI: 1.65–2.37). Age, as expected, played a vital role in contraception use. Women aged 25–34 years had a 106% higher chance of using contraception than a group aged 15–24 year (i.e., OR: 2.06, 95% CI: 1.73–2.45), whereas, this difference was close to twice as high for women ages 35–44 years (i.e., OR: 2.60, 95% CI: 2.17–3.12). To conclude, after the age of 45, contraceptive use decreased and was just 29%. Lastly, a couple who took joint decisions on health matters had a 48% higher chance of using contraception than women who took the sole judgment, while the probability was 19% more for a family whose husband is the only decision maker (i.e., OR: 1.48 and 1.19, 95% CI: 1.17–1.88 and 0.96–1.45,

Table 2 Married couple contraceptive use and socio-cultural characteristics

Variable	Category	Contraceptive use		Chi-square	*p*-value
		Not using (%)	Using (%)		
Age	15–24	1557 (89.2)	188 (10.8)	125.423	0.000
	25–34	2846 (80.1)	708 (19.9)		
	35–44	1691 (76.1)	532 (23.9)		
	45+	466 (86.5)	73 (13.5)		
Religion	Christian	2469 (70.0)	1059 (30.0)	535.017	0.000
	Muslim	4039 (90.3)	435 (9.7)		
Region	North-Central	1175 (81.0)	276 (19.0)	591.738	0.000
	North-East	1401 (89.4)	173 (11.0)		
	North-West	1950 (92.8)	151 (7.2)		
	South-East	659 (69.9)	284 (30.1)		
	South-South	617 (77.8)	176 (22.2)		
	South-West	758 (63.2)	441 (36.8)		
Residence	Urban	2142 (71.2)	867 (28.8)	329.191	0.000
	Rural	4418 (87.5)	634 (12.5)		
Education	No formal education	3177 (94.2)	194 (5.8)	710.153	0.000
	Primary	1055 (79.4)	274 (20.6)		
	Secondary	1845 (70.6)	770 (29.4)		
	Higher	483 (64.7)	263 (35.3)		
Number of children born	0	469 (99.2)	4 (0.8)	164.650	0.000
	1–3	2779 (81.0)	651 (19.0)		
	4–5	1517 (75.0)	507 (25.0)		
	6+	1795 (84.1)	339 (15.9)		
Household decision	Wife alone	272 (75.3)	89 (24.7)	265.595	<0.001
	Husband alone	4116 (87.3)	600 (12.7)		
	Joint decision	2145 (72.6)	808 (27.4)		
Number of wives	One wife	4568 (78.1)	1278 (21.9)	153.648	0.000
	More than one	1974 (90.2)	214 (9.8)		
Fertility preference	Have another	4818 (86.0)	784 (14.0)	293.397	0.000
	Undecided	407 (79.8)	103 (20.2)		
	Sterile and other	1335 (68.5)	614 (31.5)		
Wealth index	Poor	3080 (92.1)	266 (7.9)	566.288	0.000
	Middle	1391 (82.7)	291 (17.3)		
	Rich	2089 (68.9)	944 (31.1)		
Ideal number of children	1–3	307 (63.6)	176 (36.4)	429.271	0.001
	4–5	1916 (71.3)	771 (28.7)		
	6+	4132 (88.5)	539 (11.5)		
Contraceptive use is woman's business	Disagree	4220 (80.3)	1037 (19.7)	12.190	<0.001
	Agree	2340 (83.5)	464 (16.5)		

(continued)

Table 2 (continued)

Variable	Category	Contraceptive use		Chi-square	*p*-value
		Not using (%)	Using (%)		
Contraceptive use leads to promiscuity	Disagree	4034 (80.4)	986 (19.6)	9.153	0.002
	Agree	2526 (83.1)	515 (16.9)		
Decision on health	Wife alone	455 (70.8)	188 (29.2)	359.293	<0.001
	Husband alone	2094 (72.4)	799 (27.6)		
	Joint decision	3997 (88.6)	512 (11.4)		

Source: Authors' own computation from 2018 NDHS

respectively). Couples who agreed that contraceptive use is a "woman's business" had a 7% lesser chance of using contraception (i.e., OR: 0.93, 95% CI: 0.80–1.08). It was also deduced that since no significant association was found regarding contraceptive use leading to promiscuity, it was surprising to see that married couples who agreed that contraception made women more promiscuous had a 4% higher chance of using them (i.e., OR: 1.04, 95% CI: 0.90–1.20).

4 Discussion

This chapter has looked at practical information on the socio-cultural factors affecting contraceptive use among married couples in Nigeria. The research, in general, showed considerably low levels of contraceptive use among married couples with a clear geopolitical (i.e., regional) difference. One of the regression model results showed that married couples from South-West are twice as likely to use contraceptives than married couples from the northern regions of Nigeria. The socio-cultural reasons for this north-south divide may be connected to the disparity level in literacy between the two geopolitical zones. As such, southern Nigeria has a higher percentage of educated women than the north. This can be further elevated with the religious misconceptions against contraceptive use among rural women in the north. This study and many other previous studies [39–42] have shown positive relationships between education level and contraception. On religious grounds, a higher percentage of married couples in northern Nigeria practice Islam. As earlier stated, previous studies have clearly shown that Islam is not opposed to contraceptive adoption as long as it is done within the ambience of proper Islamic ethics, especially among married couples [29, 30, 43]. However, this study showed that Muslim women are 10% less likely to use contraceptives than their Christian counterparts. On the other hand, in southern Nigeria, Christianity is widely practiced, and contraceptive use is not religiously condoned except for some of the Catholic faith, which are few in numbers. This is corroborated by a study in Tanzania that showed that religion influences family planning decisions. Respondents who found family planning

Table 3 Estimated effects and corresponding 95% CI from the logistic regression model for contraceptive use

Variable	Category	OR	*p*-value	CI
Age	15–24	1.00		
	25–34	2.06*	0.000	1.73–2.45
	35–44	2.60*	0.000	2.17–3.12
	45+	1.29	0.078	0.97–1.73
Religion	Christian	1.00		
	Muslim	0.90*	0.000	1.65–2.37
Region	North-Central	1.00		
	North-East	0.88	0.207	0.71–1.07
	North-West	1.09	0.513	0.84–1.41
	South-East	1.81	0.111	1.62–2.05
	South-South	1.66*	0.000	1.53–1.81
	South-West	2.47*	0.000	1.37–4.60
Residence	Rural	1.00		
	Urban	1.32*	0.000	1.13–1.53
Education	No formal education	1.00		
	Primary	0.32*	0.000	0.24–0.43
	Secondary	1.64*	0.001	1.50–1.93
	Higher	1.81*	0.048	1.66–2.15
Number of children born	1–3	1.00		
	4–5	0.58*	0.000	0.46–0.74
	6+	1.01	0.931	0.83–1.23
Household decision	Wife alone	1.00		
	Husband alone	1.11	0.275	0.92–1.35
	Joint decision	0.83	0.216	0.61–1.11
Number of wives	One wife	1.00		
	More than one	1.16	0.119	0.96–1.40
Wealth index	Poor	1.00		
	Middle	1.55*	0.000	1.45–1.68
	Rich	1.75*	0.001	1.63–1.90
Fertility preference	Have another	1.00		
	Undecided	0.50*	0.000	0.42–0.60
	Sterile and other	0.70*	0.011	0.53–0.92
Ideal number of children	1–3	1.00		
	4–5	1.87*	0.000	1.44–2.43
	6+	1.47*	0.000	1.25–1.73
Contraceptive use is woman's business	Disagree	1.00		
	Agree	0.93	0.336	0.80–1.08
Contraceptive use leads to promiscuity	Disagree	1.00		
	Agree	1.04	0.604	0.90–1.20
Decision on health	Wife alone	1.00		
	Husband alone	1.19	0.098	0.96–1.45
	Joint decision	1.48*	0.001	1.17–1.88

* Significant variables (i.e., $p < 0.05$); Source: Authors' own computation from 2018 NDHS

incompatible with their faith consented to giving birth to as many children as they wanted [42] perhaps because of illiteracy and religious misconception as earlier stated. This spatial (i.e., north-south) variation revealed that contraceptive utilization in Nigeria corroborates with the study by Nyako [44] in Ghana. That study showed that notable regional disparities in modern contraceptive use were due to varying socioeconomic status among Ghana's population.

The age of married couples was one of the factors which significantly affected contraceptive usage in this study. In the descriptive analysis, the result showed that not using contraception is almost 44%, i.e., peaking, in the reproductive years before (i.e., 25–34 years old) dropping as married couples get older. The regression model also illustrated a significant relationship between the age of couples and contraception, especially the age of the woman when she birthed her first child. As such, age is crucial to childbirth and the nurturing time for any mother, so it is an important issue whenever contraceptive usage is considered. In Bangladesh, for example, the desire to have another child 2 years after the last birth and no more children were the most significant factors affecting contraceptive use among young women from several identical factors examined in this study [45]—i.e., it was noted that a woman who still desired to have another child and had not given birth in the last 1 or 2 years may not use (or want to use) contraceptives. Studies in Ethiopia on factors associated with modern contraceptives among reproductive women also found age, the husband's view about contraceptives, and the husband's level of education are strongly associated with current contraceptive adoption in rural communities [13, 37]. In another study in South Sudan, it showed that modern contraceptive use was significantly associated with socioeconomic variables like age, educational attainment, work status, religious affiliation, and social status [46]. As stated, the issue of age and modern contraceptive use can closely be interlinked with the need to have an additional child or children. For example, a couple of advanced age who desire to have another child may not use contraceptives since their childbearing biological clock is ending. As a result, age, and the desire to have additional children work intricately together to affect couples' contraception decisions in Africa.

The bivariate result showed a higher prevalence (i.e., 27.4%) of contraceptive use among married couples who take joint decisions on contraceptive use than families where the husband is the imperial decision maker (i.e., 12.7%). The regression model showed that households, where decisions on contraception are jointly taken among couples have a 48% higher prevalence of contraception use than those where the wife or husband alone makes such decisions. In a similar study in Nigeria, married couples' communication and inter-spousal decision-making were positively associated with improved contraceptive acceptance [47]. Studies from Bangladesh and Tanzania also found that couples' joint decision-making was a very influential determinant of modern contraception and family planning [39, 41]. Studies recently carried out in Ethiopia found that the husband's approval, among other factors, especially postpartum amenorrhea, was a significant determinant of modern contraceptive use. This was especially validated if the postpartum period among women who had given birth in the last 12 months [48–51]. Still, in Ethiopia, a study found that intra-uterine contraceptive device (IUCD) usage, among the few reproductive women using it, was strongly associated with a supportive spouse, literacy level, access to IUCD, and assurance of no side effects [47]. In this case, husband approval was crucial for the couple's usage of such contraception. This is very important because partner refusal, for example, has been one of the critical factors affecting condom use in a study in Botswana [48]. Conversely, a study in South Sudan showed that although there are social norms, which give a woman room to birth as many children as she wants, an increase in the desire to have a modernized lifestyle as well as pressure from social norms via education, household spacing, and family planning have aided in expanding women's options and contraceptive usage [49]. Hence, modern contraceptive use can be significantly associated with socio-economic variables. In Nepal, the utilization of family planning methods among postpartum mothers showed that the husband's education, occupation, and previous utilization of contraceptives were the most significant variables [50]. It is therefore partly implicit in Africa, and beyond, that educational level significantly affects contraceptive utilization.

5 Conclusion

Other unconfirmed myths surrounding contraceptive usage among reproductive women in some regions of the world is still prevalent. In this chapter, 83.1% of the sampled married couples who agree that contraceptive use promoted promiscuity do not use it. Similarly, research in Ethiopia on contraceptive usage among married women showed that the fear of side effects is an unconfirmed myth preventing women from using IUCD in that county [51]. In Africa as a whole, fear of unconfirmed side effects must be doused if modern contraception is to have any chance of optimum utilization on the continent. This chapter unearthed socio-cultural factors affecting contraceptive usage among married couples in Nigeria with a clear north-south divide. Contraceptive adoption in Nigeria differed greatly due to the level of education among the differing geopolitical zones in the country. Age, religious misconceptions, and inter-spousal communication are other socio-cultural factors that significantly influenced contraceptive approval among married couples. This research, in conjunction with other cited literature, has shown almost no socio-cultural factor can match a woman's education level which culminates into gender equality and empowerment for women. In Nigeria, the unmet need for contraceptive utilization, especially among married couples in rural areas, is glaring. Conclusive findings emphasize that there is still a lot of room for improvement in contraceptive implementation in rural Nigeria. The research is aimed at bettering women's health and well-being as noted in SDGs 3, 5, and 10. As the world gradually approaches 2030, the ending period for SGDs, the above narratives on contraceptive usage in Nigeria hint at some important recommendations for the immediate future. First, access to higher education for women in the north of the country is vital because it has the most negligible percentage of illiteracy and contraceptive use among women. Second, in northern Nigeria, the patriarchal system, which makes men the imperial decision maker even on contraceptive issues is concerning and needs to be revisited. Third, public awareness on the subject matter should be tailored toward enhancing husbands' and partners' involvement in their spouses' usage of contraceptives. Finally, proper orientation carried out in local languages (and dialects) that can speak better to the inner consciousness of reproductive mothers, especially the illiterate, needs to be developed to tackle the myths surrounding contraceptive use to reassure them of its importance for their health and that of their children.

References

1. Sinai I, Omoluabi E, Jimoh A, Jurczynska K (2019) Unmet need for family planning and barriers to contraceptive use in Kaduna, Nigeria: culture, myths and perceptions. Cult Health Sex 22:1253–1268. https://doi.org/10.1080/13691058.2019.1672894
2. Eborka K, Akarawak EE, Owolabi TJ et al (2021) Chawhanda et al. examining males' perceptions and concerns about adopting modern family planning methods in Delta state, Nigeria. Afr J Reprod Health 25:75. https://doi.org/10.29063/ajrh2021/v25i6.8
3. Ajayi AI, Adeniyi OV, Akpan W (2018) Use of traditional and modern contraceptives among childbearing women: findings from a mixed methods study in two southwestern Nigerian states. BMC Public Health 18:1–9. https://doi.org/10.1186/S12889-018-5522-6/TABLES/3
4. Sanchez EK, Speizer IS, Tolley E et al (2020) Influences on seeking a contraceptive method among adolescent women in three cities in Nigeria. Reprod Health 17:1–11. https://doi.org/10.1186/S12978-020-01019-1/FIGURES/2
5. Atuhairwe S, Gemzell-Danielsson K, Byamugisha J et al (2021) Abortion-related near-miss morbidity and mortality in 43 health facilities with differences in readiness to provide abortion care in Uganda. BMJ Glob Heal 6:e003274. https://doi.org/10.1136/BMJGH-2020-003274
6. Qureshi Z, Mehrtash H, Kouanda S et al (2021) Understanding abortion-related complications in health facilities: results from WHO multicountry survey on abortion (MCS-A) across 11 sub-Saharan African countries. BMJ Glob Heal 6:e003702. https://doi.org/10.1136/BMJGH-2020-003702
7. Benson J, Andersen K, Samandari G (2011) Reductions in abortion-related mortality following policy reform: evidence from Romania, South Africa and Bangladesh. Reprod Health 8:1–12. https://doi.org/10.1186/1742-4755-8-39/FIGURES/4
8. Hord C, Wolf M (2004) Breaking the cycle of unsafe abortion in Africa. Afr J Reprod Health 8:29–36. https://doi.org/10.2307/3583302
9. Turner N (2021) Influence of religion and religiosity on fertility and contraceptive use in continental sub-Saharan Africa: a comprehensive review. University of Gothenburg
10. Gueye S, Corroon O (2015) Belief in family planning myths at the individual and community levels and modern contraceptive use in urban Africa. Int Perspect Sex Reprod Health 41:199. https://doi.org/10.1363/INTSEXREPHEA.41.4.0191
11. Obasohan PE (2015) Religion, ethnicity and contraceptive use among reproductive age women in Nigeria. Int J MCH AIDS 3:63. https://doi.org/10.21106/ijma.39
12. Statista (2022) Africa: average household size by country 2021. Statista. https://www.statista.com/statistics/1228286/average-household-size-in-africa-by-country/. Accessed 25 Jul 2022
13. NPC, ICF International (2019) Nigeria demographic and health survey 2018. National Population Commission and ICF International, Rockville, MD
14. UN (2019) Family Planning and the 2030 Agenda for Sustainable Development: Data Booklet ST/ESA/SER.A/429. United Nations Department of Economic and Social Affairs, Population Division, New York

15. Azuh D, Fayomi O, Ajayi L (2015) Socio-cultural factors of gender roles in Women's healthcare utilization in Southwest Nigeria. Open J Soc Sci 3:105–117. https://doi.org/10.4236/JSS.2015.34013
16. Azuh D, Amodu L, Azuh AE et al (2017) Factors of gender inequality and development among selected low human development countries in sub-Saharan Africa. IOSR J Humanit Soc Sci 22: 01–07. https://doi.org/10.9790/0837-2202040107
17. Duze MC, Mohammed IZ (2007) Male knowledge, attitude, and family planning practices in northern Nigeria. Afr J Reprod Health 10:53–65. https://doi.org/10.4314/ajrh.v10i3.7899
18. Dudgeon MR, Inhorn MC (2004) Men's influences on women's reproductive health: medical anthropological perspectives. Soc Sci Med 59:1379–1395. https://doi.org/10.1016/J.SOCSCIMED.2003.11.035
19. Hlongwa M, Mashamba-Thompson T, Makhunga S et al (2020) Evidence on factors influencing contraceptive use and sexual behavior among women in South Africa: a scoping review. Medicine (Baltimore) 99. https://doi.org/10.1097/MD.0000000000019490
20. Alo OD, Daini BO, Omisile OK et al (2020) Factors influencing the use of modern contraceptive in Nigeria: a multilevel logistic analysis using linked data from performance monitoring and accountability 2020. BMC Womens Health 20:1–9. https://doi.org/10.1186/S12905-020-01059-6/TABLES/3
21. Afriyie P, Tarkang EE (2019) Factors influencing use of modern contraception among married women in Ho west district, Ghana: descriptive cross-sectional study. PAMJ 33. https://doi.org/10.11604/PAMJ.2019.33.15.17500
22. Viswan SP, Ravindran TKS, Kandala NB et al (2017) Sexual autonomy and contraceptive use among women in Nigeria: findings from the demographic and health survey data. Int J Women's Health 9:581–590. https://doi.org/10.2147/IJWH.S133760
23. Babalola S, Kusemiju B, Calhoun L et al (2015) Factors associated with contraceptive ideation among urban men in Nigeria. Int J Gynaecol Obstet 130(Suppl 3):E42–E46. https://doi.org/10.1016/J.IJGO.2015.05.006
24. Adanikin AI, McGrath N, Padmadas SS (2017) Impact of men's perception on family planning demand and uptake in Nigeria. Sex Reprod Healthc Off J Swedish Assoc Midwives 14:55–63. https://doi.org/10.1016/J.SRHC.2017.10.002
25. Ba DM, Ssentongo P, Agbese E, Kjerulff KH (2019) Prevalence and predictors of contraceptive use among women of reproductive age in 17 sub-Saharan African countries: a large population-based study. Sex Reprod Healthc Off J Swedish Assoc Midwives 21:26–32. https://doi.org/10.1016/J.SRHC.2019.06.002
26. Owoyemi JO, Ifatimehin OI, Egwuaba E, Obaka PI (2020) Accessibility and utilization of family planning services among married couples in Kogi state, north Central Nigeria. Cent African J Public Heal 6:121. https://doi.org/10.11648/J.CAJPH.20200603.12
27. Alabi O, Odimegwu CO, De-Wet N, Akinyemi JO (2019) Does female autonomy affect contraceptive use among women in northern Nigeria? Afr J Reprod Health 23:92–100
28. Adedini SA, Babalola S, Ibeawuchi C et al (2018) Role of religious leaders in promoting contraceptive use in Nigeria: evidence from the Nigerian urban reproductive health initiative. Glob Heal Sci Pract 6:514. https://doi.org/10.9745/GHSP-D-18-00135
29. Serour G (2008) Islamic perspectives in human reproduction. Reprod Biomed Online 17(Suppl 3):34–38. https://doi.org/10.1016/S1472-6483(10)60328-8
30. Shaik B, Azmat S, Mazhar A (2013) Family planning and contraception in Islamic countries: a critical review of the literature. J Pakistan Med Assoc 63:67–72
31. Mallick J (2017) Structural change and productivity growth in India and the People's republic of China. Asian Development Bank Institute, Tokyo
32. Oye-Adeniran BA, Adewole IF, Umoh AV et al (2006) Community-based study of contraceptive behaviour in Nigeria. Afr J Reprod Health 10:90–104. https://doi.org/10.2307/30032462
33. Sanchez EK, McGuire C, Calhoun LM et al (2021) Influences on contraceptive method choice among adolescent women across urban centers in Nigeria: a qualitative study. Contracept Reprod Med 6:1–10. https://doi.org/10.1186/S40834-020-00146-1

34. Osuafor G, Mturi A (2013) Do religious beliefs influence use of contraception among currently married women in Nigeria? J Soc Dev Afr 28:187–212. https://doi.org/10.4314/jsda.v28i1
35. WHO (2018) Family planning: a global handbook for providers—evidence-based guidance developed through worldwide collaboration, 3rd edn. World Health Organization Department of Reproductive Health and Research, Baltimore, MD
36. Lasong J, Zhang Y, Gebremedhin SA et al (2020) Determinants of modern contraceptive use among married women of reproductive age: a cross-sectional study in rural Zambia. BMJ Open 10:e030980. https://doi.org/10.1136/BMJOPEN-2019-030980
37. Salami IC, Oladosu M (2016) Socio-demographic factors, contraceptive use and fertility preference among married women in South-South Region of Nigeria. 3rd International Conference on African Development Issues. CU-ICADI 2016, Ota, Ogun State, Nigeria, pp 504–510
38. UN (2015) United Nations Sustainable Development Goals. In: United Nations Resolution. A/RES/70/1 25 Sept 2015. http://www.un.org/ga/search/view_doc.asp?symbol=A/RES/70/1&Lang=E. Accessed 3 May 2019
39. Pokharel R, Bhattarai G, Shrestha N, Onta S (2018) Knowledge and utilization of family planning methods among people living with HIV in Kathmandu. Nepal BMC Health Serv Res 18:1–12. https://doi.org/10.1186/S12913-018-3643-3/TABLES/6
40. Debebe S, Limenih MA, Biadgo B (2017) Modern contraceptive methods utilization and associated factors among reproductive aged women in rural Dembia District, Northwest Ethiopia: community based cross-sectional study. Int J Reprod Biomed 15:374. https://doi.org/10.29252/ijrm.15.6.367
41. Tukue D, Gebremeskel TG, Gebremariam L et al (2020) Prevalence and determinants of modern contraceptive utilization among women in the reproductive age group in Edaga-hamus town, eastern zone, Tigray region, Ethiopia, June 2017. PLoS One 15:e0227795. https://doi.org/10.1371/JOURNAL.PONE.0227795
42. Sundararajan R, Yoder LM, Kihunrwa A et al (2019) How gender and religion impact uptake of family planning: results from a qualitative study in Northwestern Tanzania. BMC Womens Health 19:1–10. https://doi.org/10.1186/S12905-019-0802-6/FIGURES/1
43. Abdi B, Okal J, Serour G, Temmerman M (2020) "Children are a blessing from god"- a qualitative study exploring the socio-cultural factors influencing contraceptive use in two Muslim communities in Kenya. Reprod Health 17:1–11. https://doi.org/10.1186/S12978-020-0898-Z/TABLES/1
44. Nyako AM (2015) Concept note on north-east development commission: an institutional framework for a sustainable solution to the north-east National Security Challenge. Statehouse Government of Nigeria, Abuja
45. Islam AZ (2018) Factors affecting modern contraceptive use among fecund young women in Bangladesh: does couples' joint participation in household decision making matter? Reprod Health 15:1–9. https://doi.org/10.1186/S12978-018-0558-8/TABLES/2
46. Kane S, Kok M, Rial M et al (2016) Social norms and family planning decisions in South Sudan. BMC Public Health 16:1–12. https://doi.org/10.1186/S12889-016-3839-6/TABLES/1
47. Olawole-Isaac A, Oni Gbolahan A, Oladosu M et al (2017) Inter-spousal communication as a determinant of contraceptive use in Nigeria: a mixed-method. IJASOS- Int E-journal Adv Soc Sci 3:645–654. https://doi.org/10.18769/IJASOS.337324

48. Berta M, Feleke A, Abate T et al (2018) Utilization and associated factors of modern contraceptives during extended postpartum period among women who gave birth in the last 12 months in Gondar town, Northwest Ethiopia. Ethiop J Health Sci 28:207–216. https://doi.org/10.4314/ejhs.v28i2.12
49. Ahmed M, Seid A (2020) Survival time to modern contraceptive uses from the resumption of sexual intercourse among postpartum women in Ethiopia. Int J Women's Health 12:641–647. https://doi.org/10.2147/IJWH.S266748
50. Dereje N, Engida B, Holland RP (2020) Factors associated with intrauterine contraceptive device use among women of reproductive age group in Addis Ababa, Ethiopia: a case control study. PLoS One 15:e0229071. https://doi.org/10.1371/JOURNAL.PONE.0229071
51. Joshi AK, Tiwari DP, Poudyal A et al (2020) Utilization of family planning methods among postpartum mothers in Kailali District. Nepal Int J Womens Health 12:487. https://doi.org/10.2147/IJWH.S249044

COVID-19 and the Built Environment: Informal Sector, Housing, and Shock Challenges in Nigeria

Adewale O. Yoade, Solomon A. Olatunji, and Giuseppe T. Cirella

1 Introduction

Africa is the continent where the greatest proportion of the population does not have access to social protection and adequate healthcare [1]. It also has the largest share of poverty [2] and regularly deals with the heavy burden of diseases that are exacerbated by recurring natural disasters, poor economic performance, and military conflicts [3]. In COVID-19 terms, the impact on the continent, especially for marginalized groups, has been damaging. COVID-19 has taken more lives among the older population even though, i.e., comparatively, Africa has a younger population than other continents. Sadly, higher levels of malnutrition and disease mean COVID-19 could turn out to be deadlier for the African population. Since Africa is en route as the most rapidly urbanizing region in the world, i.e., with 60% of urban settlements being informal, the population of these informal settlements often live in precarious housing conditions. For example, such residents in African countries often share rooms and houses with multiple families that are accustomed to overcrowded public spaces (e.g., buses and markets) which may also affect the pandemic in unpredictable ways. The lack of access to land, shelter, basic services, and transport drives higher risk and makes the countries less resilient to shock events. The real estate industry, as a result, is facing great uncertainty due to the COVID-19 pandemic.

A. O. Yoade (✉)
Department of Urban and Regional Planning, Wesley University Ondo, Ondo, Nigeria

S. A. Olatunji
Department of Urban and Regional Planning, Federal University Oye-Ekiti, Oye-Ekiti, Nigeria
e-mail: solomon.olatunji@fuoye.edu.ng

G. T. Cirella
Faculty of Economics, University of Gdansk, Sopot, Poland
e-mail: gt.cirella@ug.edu.pl

G. T. Cirella (ed.), *Uncertainty Shocks in Africa*, Advances in African Economic, Social and Political Development, https://doi.org/10.1007/978-3-031-21885-9_9

At the individual level, social distancing precautions have reduced property views, a key part of the selling process, where both buyers and sellers are reconsidering market price fluctuation and instability due to the pandemic. Moreover, sellers are looking for reassurance regarding the health of potential buyers coming to view properties [4]. As a result, thousands of workers from around the world have been made redundant or have been placed on temporary, unpaid leave of absence. Correspondingly, this has had a sizable impact on individuals' ability to pay rent, make mortgage repayments, and keep up with ongoing household expenses. To tackle this, in the United Kingdom (UK) the government released a GBP 350 billion (i.e., USD 415 billion) lifeline to allow mortgage lenders the option of a 3-month mortgage delay to those in financial difficulty [5]. The UK Government also recommended that buyers and lenders delay negotiations during the lockdown, bringing transactions to a halt [6]. During the initial stages of the pandemic, many worried that another financial crisis, similar to that of 2008, would impact confidence in the property market. Banks within the UK, for instance, began to take precautions, i.e., high street lenders required up to 40% deposits for a new mortgage to be approved [7]. Housing conditions in Nigeria, on the other hand, regularly need to deal with overcrowding and are at risk, i.e., the perception of quality housing, of decline. The congestion and low quantity of comfortable housing in Nigeria has led several people, especially in informal settlements, to sleep outside amid dangers. The architectural quality of houses in Nigeria is also often alienating and bleak in which local bylaws are often negated or violated by building authorities. This is frequently worsened by low-quality rental properties in which landlords do not consider the negative effects to end-users and the environment. Outdated housing laws vis-à-vis noncompliance to housing guidelines has created a need to rethink, reconsider, and properly promote higher quality standards and awareness for improved housing environments. A novel sustainability-friendly perspective is proposed to curb the spread of disease outbreaks and help develop a best practice way forward. When people are made to stay at home, the definition of adequate and standard housing should be properly explored. This chapter investigates the existing situation of housing with a detailed look at informal settlements, housing environments, and the definition of a safe house in terms of planning and design in the context of the COVID-19 pandemic in Nigeria.

2 Population Density and Informal Settlements

Half of Nigeria's total urban population (i.e., approximately 42 million people) live in informal settlements [8]. Informal settlements, i.e., "areas where groups of housing units have been constructed on land that the occupants have no legal claim to and unplanned settlements, [as well as] areas where housing is not in compliance with current planning and building regulations" [9], by definition are usually overcrowded and cut off from the services associated with big cities. People living in these settlements are more likely to be affected by untreated health issues,

Fig. 1 Informal settlements in Nigeria: (*top left*) slum area in Lagos—26 March 2020, (*top middle*) poor people scavenging Igando Landfill in Lagos—17 May 2020, (*top right*) open drainage and waste dump in Apete area in Ibadan—14 April 2020, and (*bottom*) open channelization in Osogbo—21 May 2020. Source: Photographs by Adewale O. Yoade

including malnutrition, with limited means to access health services and food [10–12]. In Nigeria, large cities like Lagos and Ibadan have several populated slums. In Lagos, an estimated 60% of the population live in informal settlements, including floating slums such as Makoko. These settlements are characterized by a lack of proper water, sanitation, and hygiene (WASH) facilities, electricity, and other support services [13–16] (Fig. 1). Overcrowding and poor WASH conditions are also common in internally displaced person (IDP) camps across the country as well as garrison towns in North-East, Nigeria, where people fleeing conflict and insecurity have found refuge. In 2018, over 600,000 IDPs (i.e., one-third of the total IDP population in North-East) were living in congested informal IDP settlements—at a total of 5 m^2 per person. Note, sphere standards indicate a roofed shelter should have at least 3.5 m^2 per person, excluding cooking space, bathing area, and sanitation facility [16]. Medical research and recent studies on the pandemic in the congested Rohingya refugee camps have shown strong links between overcrowded spaces and

Fig. 2 European Union humanitarian aid camp in North-East: (*top left*) field mission providing nutrition support and healthcare to mothers and their children, (*top right*) living conditions are poor at overcrowded camps and settlements hosting displaced people, (*bottom left*) adult education classes for women, and (*bottom right*) aerial view of a camp hosting displaced people. Source: Photographs by Samuel Ochai on Flickr, Creative Commons Public Domain, 14 August 2018

the risk of spread of various diseases [17–22]. As such, co-morbidities in highly congested IDP camps are common, including high incidence of endemic and waterborne diseases and malnutrition [20, 22–24]. Moreover, people living in congested and unsanitary camps, slums, and garrison towns are more vulnerable to the spread of infectious outbreaks [18]. Making things more complicated, many IDP camps and garrison towns, e.g., in North-East, are not easily accessible by humanitarian organizations (Fig. 2). In the states of Borno, Adamawa, and Yobe (BAY), vaccination campaigns and health services are often disrupted because of conflict and insecurity. In densely populated areas and overcrowded spaces it is extremely challenging to respect physical distancing, or strictly follow hygiene practices due to limited access to clean water. Consequently, people are more likely to be exposed to disease outbreaks and may have limited access to healthcare and medicine if they fall ill.

3 Standardization of Essential Services

The health system in Nigeria is fragile due to underfunding and limited infrastructure. Even before the pandemic, annual health spending in Nigeria was low, at only USD 27.84 per capita, far below other Economic Community of West African States' economies such as Ghana and Ivory Coast. Low spending can often infer that demand for health services will exceed capacity during a health emergency [25–28]. A Reuters survey found that African countries with COVID-19 cases, including Nigeria, have less than one hospital bed and one ventilator per 100,000 people [29]. In 2017, Nigeria had only 120 intensive care unit (ICU) beds for the whole country, i.e., about 0.07 ICU beds for 100,000 people [30]. According to the World Health Organization (WHO), the most critical COVID-19 patients need intensive care and a ventilator [31, 32]. According to less recent data, in 2004 Nigeria had 0.5 hospital beds per 1000 people, placing it among the countries with the lowest rate of beds per capita (i.e., less than 1.7 per 1000 people) [33]. In some areas of the country, hospitals and health centers are understaffed. Although this is not the case across the whole country, COVID-19 poses a threat to the Nigerian health system, especially in conflict-affected areas. Two-thirds of health facilities in the BAY states are not functioning because of conflict-related damage [34]. COVID-19 has put a strain on health facilities in states that record high numbers of cases, including Lagos, Kano, and Zamfara. The Nigeria Centre for Disease Control reported an overburden of isolation facilities in these states with not enough ICU beds for patients [35, 36]. Looking back at the last 2 years, as the number of COVID-19 cases in Nigeria continued to increase, the health system risks became quickly overwhelmed. In a country regularly affected by disease outbreaks, it will be important to integrate the COVID-19 health response into the existing health programs to adequately respond to the pandemic, including future shock events, while also treating patients affected by other epidemics such as measles, malaria, cholera, Lassa fever, and meningitis. Cholera, malaria, and Lassa fever are particularly common during the rainy season, normally spanning from February to July [37–39]. During these months, additional care and attention should be stressed (Fig. 3).

On another front, the COVID-19 pandemic forced schools to remain closed to allow for social and physical distancing. This resulted in over 46 million students to not attend classes because of government-led school closures. Children from poor households, children living in conflict-affected areas, and displaced children often do not have access to tools that enable home-schooling and distance learning [40, 41]. Access to education was already particularly challenging in Nigeria, especially in the BAY states, where schools have been damaged, looted, or attacked as a result of conflict or used as temporary shelters by the IDP population. Inadequate school infrastructure, insufficient number of teachers, and lack of learning material also hamper access to education in the BAY states [37, 38]. Before the pandemic, about 27% of children between 6 and 11 years old did not attend school and more than 25% of children between 12 and 17 years old did not have access to education [42–44]. As a result, more children are at increased risk of dropping out of school

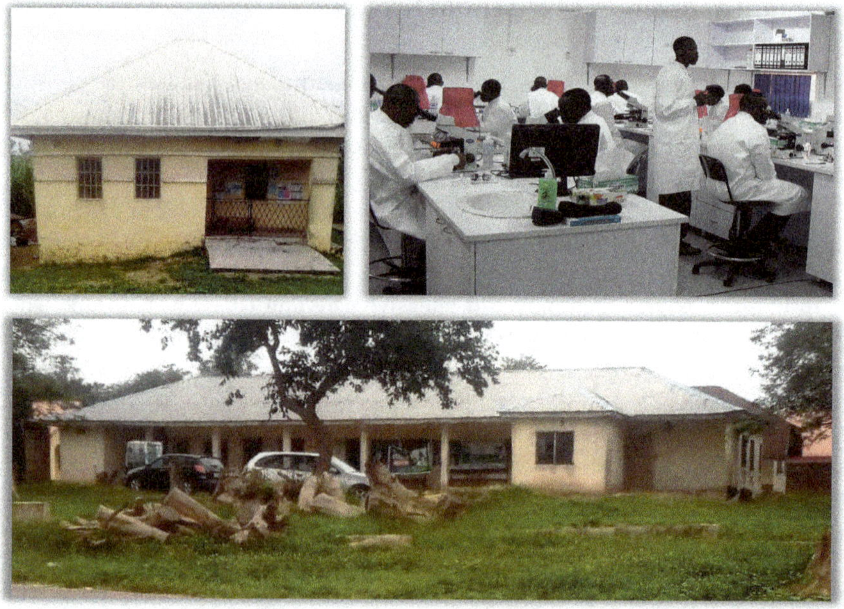

Fig. 3 Health clinics and health training in Nigeria: (*top left*) small walk-in health clinic in Iyin Ekiti (top right) Nigerian lab technicians undergo malaria microscopy mentoring at a Nigerian Air Force hospital near Lagos, and (bottom) health center in Iyin Ekiti. Source: (*top left* and *bottom*) Photographs by Olajumoke I. Omodara, 10 August 2022; (*top right*) photography by Rick Scavetta on Flickr, Creative Commons Public Domain, 22 September 2009

because of the pandemic. Pushed by the need to avoid any "nonessential" costs or the need to have additional family members engaged in labor activities, heads of these households suffering negative economic effects from the pandemic might decide not to send their children to school after containment measures have been lifted and economic strife takes over. For many children, not attending school portends to not having access to essential school services. For instance, some schools offer students, particularly those from poor households, free nutritious meals. Moreover, school closures also cut vulnerable children off from social protection programs, often implemented as part of humanitarian-oriented support [45]. Particularly in North-East, schools normally offer protection services such as psychological care and distribution of hygiene kits [38]. As such, the complexity of the crisis has resulted in an accumulation of several different crises, i.e., a combination of both natural and manmade causes. In this case, multiple overlapping crises affect the most vulnerable and the housing environments these people must sustain.

4 Housing Quality Concept, COVID-19, and Social Equity and Justice

The concept of housing quality has been addressed by the United Nations (UN) in a series of seminars on the social areas of housing, with the use of several terms like adequate housing, suitable housing, and standard and good housing. As it is impossible to have a globally accepted definition for quality and good housing, housing that satisfies residents' needs while promoting their safety is referred to as a good house [46]. It is also important for human dignity, in accordance with the UN Principles on Housing and Property Restitution for Refugees and Displaced Persons, to sustain family and community life by sheltering households, promoting family ties, their participation, and access to community facilities, as well as economic stability [47]. More so, the quality of houses, in a geographic location, provides essential information on the prevailing state of housing stock, delivers essential information for an inclusion in future projects undertaken, and offers insight into the current desires and needs of end-users [13]. This quality can be divided into subjective and objective. The subjective aspect relates to user characteristics which are led by specific desires, needs, and expectations. The objective aspect, on the other hand, involves the notion of "precise significance," i.e., the number of rooms, dwelling type, presence of relevant amenities, and dwelling condition. In other words, assessing the quality of a house at any given time involves the consideration of the housing environment, such as the characteristics of the physical environment as well as that of the community and local residents [48]. A house can be satisfactory when the gap between user needs, aspirations, and the reality of the prevailing residential context is harmonized [49]. Housing may also be viewed as quality and satisfactory when users experience pleasure and wellness. This can indicate the level of success of housing by measuring occupier effectiveness and mental responses to any high points as well as unpleasant aspects of the dwelling, its environment, and predicaments with future events. This can also assist in identifying the contribution to several factors including satisfaction, the difference between diverse factors, and link between the different dimensions of housing [50]. As important as user satisfaction is to the assessment of environmental quality, it is also essential in determining the quality of a house, as existing amenities and services contribute to the productivity of people residing in a particular location [51]. Hence, the higher the quality of the environment and the dwelling, the higher the satisfaction and safety expected from the residents [52]. In the context of the pandemic, the housing quality concept is an idea that, if correctly implemented beforehand, could have alleviated a lot of the distress, especially in informal settlements, during the lockdown measures (Fig. 4).

In terms of coronavirus, it has been globally reported as a strain virus that infects humans [53, 54]. Bats have been identified as the natural hosts of this virus alongside side other animals like civets, cats, and camels [50, 54]. Within the family of coronaviruses is SARS-COV-1 which emerged in 2002; since then, the current pandemic has globally prompted a myriad of studies, discussions, and reports with

Fig. 4 Empty streets in informal settlements during the COVID-19 lockdown measures in Nigeria: (*left*) Oja-Oba area in Osogbo—16 March 2020 and (*right*) market area of Idiaraba in Lagos—23 May 2020. Source: Photographs by Adewale O. Yoade

lots of concern for housing sector operations. Due to several governments' concerns on the transmission of the pandemic, COVID-19 has undergone notable lockdown measures over the last 2 years [55]. During this time, the level of homelessness, environmental quality, and housing location became increasingly recognizable and problematic in Nigeria. By definition, a house naturally divides the internal structure and space of the house from the external environment. For a while, scholars in the discipline of housing and planning have been faced with diverse challenges relating to housing quality, standard, inadequacy, and poverty. Various indicators for housing importance in the environment, to the economy, and individual well-being calls for effective enquiry into how quality and safe homes can be promoted during the pandemic, and beyond. As such, there is a need for housing quality and standard that promotes citizen safety in terms of space and the availability of necessary facilities. Issues like the level of crowding in a house, design type, and facilities need to be addressed in view of the pandemic as well as future events.

Housing generally is a major area where the pandemic is experienced [56]. COVID-19 continues to impact housing in several ways, aside from the fact that it will impact an individual's experience of a home and ability to regularly meet household expenses (e.g., rent), it also stimulates the need to promote quality and standard. Hence, housing policy and related procurements need to be better veered toward the curbing of disease spread, especially within low-income groups. Correspondingly, since Nigeria's population is predominantly urbanized, in which the better part of its housing development is occurring in cities and urban limits, this makes housing-related policy extremely important for the future of the country. During the COVID-19 measures, physical distancing and isolation were used as a major preventive measures; however, it is believed that this could have only been fully fulfilled if people had access to secure and safe housing environments with adequate food in reserve [57, 58]. Self-isolation or the restricting of the individual in their home changed their habitation dynamics, politics, and rhythm which may have

Fig. 5 Dilapidated buildings in informal settlements in Nigeria during the COVID-19 lockdown measures: (*left*) Beere area in Ibadan—5 April 2020 and (*right*) core area of Osogbo—26 March 2020. Source: Photographs by Adewale O. Yoade

stimulated several issues such as putting one's life in danger—especially when the environment of the house was not habitable.

Domestic violence around the housing environment was reported to increase across Nigeria due to the lockdown, especially in the environment when no security measures were available (e.g., the use of neighborhood police). In Nigeria, this made for an unsafe and unsecure formulae—especially within slum areas and at night [38, 59]. Moreover, homelessness across the country grew and live-in slums with no adequate understanding of the pandemic did not prevent themselves from getting ill [57, 58]. As a result, this caused informal settlement residents a lot of health problems such as risk of exposure and risk of disease spread [60]. More so, there has been a huge income loss for households as almost all sectors have faced a reduction in their income as well as some been laid off, i.e., businesses were pushed to operate with limited staff due to limited capital. As a result, a large portion of the population has turned to working remotely from home—partly to care for their family, e.g., to look after their children who are not able to attend schools, and partly to continue to earn a living. Of course, this is pertinent to work that can be done in a remote manner and if the worker had the facilities to work from home. This further highlights the importance of housing quality and standard and brings to the forefront how household health can be affected if improper planning is mismanaged. From the standpoint of informal settlements, this should be underscored as many areas in Nigerian cities have huge tracts of informal housing developments that have not respected any formal policy changes in addressing the pandemic. Self-isolation and physical distancing in such areas may not be totally possible, especially where there is a high percentage of low-income and underserved who have to struggle daily for their survival. As a result, people of all ages were commonly seen roving around the streets even when the total lockdown policy was employed—partly because of their substandard homes as well as the need to search for something to eat [60, 61]. The linkage between health and housing cannot be more visible than it is across Nigeria (Fig. 5). WHO ascertained this by justifying the essential needs of housing in promoting health and productivity [31]. This factor is fundamental to the curbing of COVID-19 and other diseases, as the lack of quality and adequate affordable housing can delay or abate the swift containment of shock events such as the pandemic. It suffices to say that the long-term structural deficits in Nigeria's housing systems need to be urgently fixed, as this will have a long-term and wide-reaching effect on the entire housing sector.

In terms of social equity and justice, urban and intercity housing has often been interconnected with the issue of poverty which mainly affects the poor people living in such areas. As the main goal of housing policies is to meet the basic need of all groups of people, when it comes into practice, poor people are, unfortunately, left for last and behind in getting access to a better quality of life. In Nigeria, for instance, affordable housing has been provided for by the government to cater to the need of low- and medium-income people but when it comes to the quality of housing and the environment within the community; the result, however, is quite disappointing. It should be expected that no one should be marginalized in the development process, and the poor also need to benefit rather than to give advantage to the upper group [12]. Therefore, a stepwise housing system that shapes a better future for the poor should be seen as sustainable, responsible, and carefully grown for a better Nigeria. This will include not only new houses, but new homes, in communities that work, where people are pleased to come home at night and happy to raise their children. Nigerians must build not to turn a quick profit, but to create a legacy that lasts for generations to come.

5 Challenges Moving Forward

Whether COVID-19 is creating new housing challenges or simply revealing or exacerbating the deep structural flaws in its existing housing systems, it is an open question that will require more nuanced conceptual and empirical attention as the country moves beyond the pandemic. Housing researchers will need to trace these changes as they play out across the immediate and long term. What worked and what did not? What were the effects of emergency housing policies and provisions? What were the consequences in places where changes were not made? Finally, how might these studies augment how the country understands and theorizes housing? Housing scholars have a wealth of knowledge to draw on. A large collective knowledge about the housing experiences of lower income and vulnerable households, about the connections between housing and health, and about how economic downturn affects all households across income groups and tenures is for future study. It is clear from collective research efforts that the global financial crisis was used by some to further exploit, marginalize, and disadvantage the already marginalized in our society [62]. We have a responsibility to draw on our existing knowledge to prevent this from happening again, i.e., to turn research into advice that can support rapid policymaking and help housing systems, such as in Nigeria, adapt to the short- and long-term reforms that are required to deal with the pandemic.

The COVID-19 pandemic is first and foremost an emergency with severe consequences for health and the economy; it has, however, also served as an example that changes in travel and production quickly and distinctly can improve air quality [63–65] as well as reduce the carbon footprint which translate into improved environmental health [66–68]. It remains to be seen to what extent the changes brought on by the pandemic, such as increases in telecommuting and reduced travel, will remain once the pandemic has completely passed. Obviously, the dramatic actions taken during the pandemic cannot be directly copied in non-pandemic times. However, it is believed that lessons can be learned, and that inspiration can be gained from the fact that quick positive feedback is seen when action is taken. The swift actions against the pandemic imposed by governments have been, to a certain extent, effective and lasting. However, as most of the African population is living from hand to mouth, these measures cannot sustain themselves in the long term. Since countries in Africa started lifting or relaxing their restrictions due to the high impact on their economies, other mitigation strategies to improve their economies and provide basic benefits to the public have been implemented. Based on past experiences, there is the possibility of further suppressing COVID-19, provided governments and the public do not change their behavior as they did previously for Ebola, human immunodeficiency virus, poliomyelitis, and other outbreaks. However, it comes as no surprise that Africans cannot confront this alone, and therefore global support in any form can assist Africa to step ahead of the pandemic. Three recommendations from a top-down perspective should be addressed. First, "vulnerable human settlements need to be [urgently] supported to reduce human suffering, [i.e.,] governments should create special task forces and establish permanent communication with informal settlements" [69]. Second, basic services, e.g., WASH, need to be accessible to the "informal sectors of society [...] with special funds to support [future] emergencies" [69]. Third, at a continental level, Africa by way of fiscal assistance needs "multilateral action that integrates central governments, multilateral organizations, and civil society [to cohesively establish] a regional public health emergency fund and coordinate debt relief and deferral of debt repayments with other countries" [69]. By applying these measures, African economies can expect to fast track their economic and social well-being post-COVID-19. To end, the UN should mitigate how urban economies are broken down, understanding that in Africa they represent most of the gross domestic product and have been, in general, worst hit—especially considering the recent upsurge in food insecurity in relation to the Russia-Ukraine conflict [70]. As a result, this conflict's trickle-down effect amplifies the need, especially within informal settlements, of rudimentary upgrades to the built environment "with access to adequate housing and basic services" [69]. These developments will help alleviate distress and hardship and offer the most vulnerable a chance to live better and a more dignified life—post-pandemic.

References

1. ILO (2020) COVID-19 and the world of work: impact and policy responses
2. Brookings Institute (2022) Foresight Africa: top priorities for the continent in 2019. Brookings Institute. https://www.brookings.edu/multi-chapter-report/foresight-africa-top-priorities-for-the-continent-in-2019/. Accessed 14 Jul 2022
3. Anaemene B (2018) Health and diseases in Africa. Dev Africa 71:207. https://doi.org/10.1007/978-3-319-66242-8_12
4. Ricco J (2020) For a govern mentality of ethical distance. Unbecoming Community. https://johnpaulricco.com/2020/03/17/for-a-governmentality-of-ethical-distance/. Accessed 13 Jun 2022
5. Nicola M, Alsafi Z, Sohrabi C et al (2020) The socio-economic implications of the coronavirus pandemic (COVID-19): a review. Int J Surg 78:185. https://doi.org/10.1016/J.IJSU.2020.04.018
6. Richardson S, Hirsch JS, Narasimhan M et al (2020) Presenting characteristics, comorbidities, and outcomes among 5700 patients hospitalized with covid-19 in the New York city area. JAMA 323:2052–2059. https://doi.org/10.1001/JAMA.2020.6775
7. Ricco J (2019) The COVID-19 pandemic returns us to our potentiality and hence to our capacity to resist. Unbecoming Community. https://unbecomingcommunity.wordpress.com/2020/04/03/the-covid-19-pandemicreturns. Accessed 13 Jun 2022
8. World Bank (2022) Nigeria: development news, research, data. World Bank. https://www.worldbank.org/en/country/nigeria. Accessed 14 Jul 2022
9. OECD (2001) OECD Glossary of Statistical Terms—informal settlements definition. Organization for Economic Co-operation and Development. https://stats.oecd.org/glossary/detail.asp?ID=1351. Accessed 14 Jul 2022
10. Richter F (2021) How the COVID-19 crisis has affected international tourism|World Economic Forum. World Economic Forum. https://www.weforum.org/agenda/2021/12/covid-crisis-drags-on-for-international-tourism. Accessed 8 Jul 2022
11. Chandran R (2020) Grow your own: urban farming is flourishing during the coronavirus lockdowns. United Nations, London
12. Olotuah AO, Bobadoye SA (2009) Sustainable housing provision for the urban poor: a review of public sector intervention in Nigeria. Built Hum Environ Rev 2:51–63
13. Sanderson D (2020) Coronavirus an "existential threat" to Africa and her crowded slums. Conversation. https://theconversation.com/coronavirus-an-existential-threat-to-africa-and-her-crowded-slums-135829. Accessed 13 Jun 2022
14. Wagers S (2020) In-depth analysis, research, news and ideas from leading academics and researchers. Conversation. https://theconversation.com/global. Accessed 13 Jun 2022
15. Wagers S (2020) Domestic violence growing in wake of coronavirus outbreak. Conversation. https://theconversation.com/domestic-violence-growing-in-wake-of-coronavirus-outbreak-135598. Accessed 13 Jun 2022
16. NRC (2022) NRC in Nigeria. Norweigen Refugee Council. https://www.nrc.no/countries/africa/nigeria/. Accessed 14 Jul 2022
17. Anyanwu MU, Festus IJ, Nwobi OC et al (2020) A perspective on Nigeria's preparedness, response and challenges to mitigating the spread of COVID-19. Challenges 11:22. https://doi.org/10.3390/CHALLE11020022
18. Obiwulu O, Abia B (2020) COVID-19 in Nigeria—Internally Displaced Persons (IDPs) as vulnerable populations at risk. CSEA AFRICA. https://cseaafrica.org/covid-19-in-nigeria-internally-displaced-persons-idps-as-vulnerable-populations-at-risk/. Accessed 14 Jul 2022
19. Cantor D, Swartz J, Roberts B et al (2021) Understanding the health needs of internally displaced persons: a scoping review. J Migr Heal 4:100071. https://doi.org/10.1016/J.JMH.2021.100071

20. Ajakaye OG, Ibukunoluwa MR (2020) Prevalence and risk of malaria, anemia and malnutrition among children in IDPs camp in Edo state. Nigeria Parasite Epidemiol Control 8:e00127. https://doi.org/10.1016/J.PAREPI.2019.E00127
21. Niyi-Gafar OL, Adelakun OS (2022) The impact of viral diseases on the rights of vulnerable population: Covid-19 and the Nigerian internally displaced child. Soc Sci Humanit Open 6: 100268. https://doi.org/10.1016/J.SSAHO.2022.100268
22. Guilbert K (2017) Nowhere to go: Nigeria's crowded camps fuel disease fears from open defecation. Thomson Reuters Found. https://reliefweb.int/report/nigeria/nowhere-go-nigerias-crowded-camps-fuel-disease-fears-open-defecation. Accessed 14 Jul 2022
23. Etikan İ (2019) Health and social assessment of internally displaced people (IDP) in Nigeria. Ann Biostat Biometric Appl 2:23–28. https://doi.org/10.33552/ABBA.2019.02.000543
24. Ngwa MC, Wondimagegnehu A, Okudo I et al (2020) The multi-sectorial emergency response to a cholera outbreak in internally displaced persons camps in Borno state, Nigeria, 2017. BMJ Glob Heal 5:e002000. https://doi.org/10.1136/BMJGH-2019-002000
25. Kruk ME, Gage AD, Arsenault C et al (2018) High-quality health systems in the sustainable development goals era: time for a revolution. Lancet Glob Heal 6:e1196–e1252. https://doi.org/10.1016/S2214-109X(18)30386-3/ATTACHMENT/A2BF7355-12DC-4249-A000-251067558931/MMC2.PDF
26. Blanchet K, Alwan A, Antoine C et al (2020) Protecting essential health services in low-income and middle-income countries and humanitarian settings while responding to the COVID-19 pandemic. BMJ Glob Heal 5:e003675. https://doi.org/10.1136/BMJGH-2020-003675
27. Khan JR, Awan N, Islam MM, Muurlink O (2020) Healthcare capacity, health expenditure, and civil society as predictors of Covid-19 case fatalities: a global analysis. Front Public Heal 8:347. https://doi.org/10.3389/FPUBH.2020.00347/BIBTEX
28. ODI (2022) The ODI website. Open Data Institute. https://theodi.org/. Accessed 14 Jul 2022
29. Houreld K, Lewis D, McNeill R (2020) Exclusive: virus exposes gaping holes in Africa's health systems. Reuters. https://www.reuters.com/article/us-health-coronavirus-africa-response-ex-idUSKBN22J1GZ. Accessed 14 Jul 2022
30. McKinsey (2021) Coronavirus' business impact: evolving perspective. McKinsey Company. https://www.mckinsey.com/business-functions/risk/our-insights/covid-19-implications-for-business#. Accessed 30 Jan 2021
31. WHO (2021) Guideline clinical management of COVID-19 patients: living guideline. World Health Organization, Geneva
32. Hajjar LA, Costa IBSS, Rizk SI et al (2021) Intensive care management of patients with COVID-19: a practical approach. Ann Intensive Care 11:1–17. https://doi.org/10.1186/S13613-021-00820-W
33. World Bank (2022) Hospital beds (per 1,000 people): Nigeria. World Bank Data. https://data.worldbank.org/indicator/SH.MED.BEDS.ZS?locations=NG. Accessed 14 Jul 2022
34. UN OCHA (2019) Nigeria: 2019 humanitarian needs overview. United Nations Off. Coord. Humanit. Aff. https://www.humanitarianresponse.info/en/programme-cycle/space/document/nigeria-2019-humanitarian-needs-overview. Accessed 14 Jul 2022
35. NCDC (2022) NCDC Coronavirus Covid-19 microsite. Nigeria Centre for Disease Control. https://covid19.ncdc.gov.ng/. Accessed 14 Jul 2022
36. Jacobs ED, Okeke MI (2022) A critical evaluation of Nigeria's response to the first wave of COVID-19. Bull Natl Res Cent 46:44. https://doi.org/10.1186/S42269-022-00729-9
37. UN OCHA (2021) Humanitarian needs overview: Nigeria. United Nations Office for the coordination of humanitarian affairs, Abuja
38. ACAPS (2020) COVID-19 in Nigeria: vulnerabilities to COVID-19 and containment measures. H2H Network and UK aid, Abuja
39. Eromosele F (2022) Rainy season: Nigerians at high risk of cholera, pneumonia, others. National Emergency Management System. https://www.vanguardngr.com/2022/05/rainy-season-nigerians-at-high-risk-of-cholera-pneumonia-others-nema/. Accessed 14 Jul 2022

40. GEC (2022) Nigeria: global education cluster. Global Education Cluster. https://educationcluster.net/country/nigeria. Accessed 14 Jul 2022
41. Egielewa P, Idogho PO, Iyalomhe FO, Cirella GT (2021) COVID-19 and digitized education: analysis of online learning in Nigerian higher education: E-learning digit. Media 19:19–35. https://doi.org/10.1177/20427530211022808
42. UNICEF (2022) Prospects for children in 2022: a global outlook. United Nations International Children's Emergency Fund, Geneva
43. Meinck S, Fraillon J, Strietholt R (2022) The impact of the COVID-19 pandemic on education: international evidence from the responses to educational disruption survey (REDS). United Nations Educational Scientific and Cultural Organization, Paris
44. UNICEF (2022) COVID-19 and school closures: are children able to continue learning. United Nations International Children's Emergency Fund. https://data.unicef.org/resources/remote-learning-reachability-factsheet/. Accessed 14 Jul 2022
45. Ishaku J, Adeniran A, Onyekwena C, Castradori M (2020) Building the resilience of internally displaced persons in Nigeria. Centre for the Study of the Economies of Africa, Abuja
46. Rogers D, Power E (2020) Housing policy and the COVID-19 pandemic: the importance of housing research during this health emergency. Int J Hous Policy 20:177–183. https://doi.org/10.1080/19491247.2020.1756599
47. Hassine K, Leckie S (2016) The United Nations principles on housing and property restitution for refugees and displaced persons ("the Pinheiro principles"): a commentary. Brill, Leiden
48. Sylla M, Lasota T, Szewrański S (2019) Valuing environmental amenities in Peri-urban areas: evidence from Poland. Sustainability 11:570. https://doi.org/10.3390/SU11030570
49. Streimikiene D (2015) Quality of life and housing. Int J Inf Educ Technol 5:140–145
50. Garber M (2020) Homes actually need to be practical now: one of the ironies of social distancing is that it can put privacy in short supply. Atlantic. https://www.theatlantic.com/culture/archive/2020/03/finding-privacy-during-pandemic/608944/. Accessed 13 Jun 2022
51. Wu K (2019) Housing reform, life course and urban housing acquisition (1980-2010). J Chinese Sociol 6:1–24. https://doi.org/10.1186/S40711-019-0101-5/TABLES/4
52. Ibem EO, Amole D (2013) Residential satisfaction in public core housing in Abeokuta, Ogun state, Nigeria. Soc Indic Res 113:563–581. https://doi.org/10.1007/S11205-012-0111-Z
53. Shereen MA, Khan S, Kazmi A et al (2020) COVID-19 infection: emergence, transmission, and characteristics of human coronaviruses. J Adv Res 24:91–98. https://doi.org/10.1016/J.JARE.2020.03.005
54. NIH (2022) Coronaviruses. National Institute of Allergy and Infectious Disease. https://www.niaid.nih.gov/diseases-conditions/coronaviruses. Accessed 14 Jul 2022
55. Davies W (2020) The last global crisis didn't change the world: but this one could. Guardian. https://www.theguardian.com/commentisfree/2020/mar/24/coronavirus-crisis-change-world-financial-global-capitalism. Accessed 13 Jun 2022
56. Chen W, Wu X, Miao J (2019) Housing and subjective class identification in urban China. Chin Sociol Rev 51:221–250. https://doi.org/10.1080/21620555.2019.1601012
57. Adediran AO, Oladejo SO, Ijagbemi CO (2020) The fundamentals to affordable home-ownership in Nigeria. J Multidiscip Eng Sci Technol 7:11659–11665
58. Adediran AO, Ali HM (2019) Nigeria housing finance operation: a review of key factors affecting housing finance. Glob Sci Journals 7:174–185
59. Afolayan A (2017) Housing as the fundamental link to tackling COVID-19 in Nigeria. UNILAG Cent Hous Stud
60. Farha L (2020) COVID-19 Guidance Note: protecting renters and mortgage payers. UN Special Rapporteur. http://www.unhousingrapp.org/user/pages/07.press-room/%0AGuidance Notes—Rent and Mortgages Arrears FINAL.pdf%0A. Accessed 13 Jun 2022
61. Farha L (2020) COVID-19 guidance note protection for those living in homelessness. UN Special Rapporteur. http://www.unhousingrapp.org/user/pages/07.press-room/. Accessed 13 Jun 2022

62. Fields D (2019) Automated landlord: digital technologies and post-crisis financial accumulation. Environ Plan A Econ Sp 54:160–181. https://doi.org/10.1177/0308518X19846514
63. Mehmood K, Mushtaq S, Bao Y et al (2022) The impact of COVID-19 pandemic on air pollution: a global research framework, challenges, and future perspectives. Environ Sci Pollut Res 1:1–17. https://doi.org/10.1007/S11356-022-19484-5/FIGURES/7
64. Venter ZS, Aunan K, Chowdhury S, Lelieveld J (2020) COVID-19 lockdowns cause global air pollution declines. Proc Natl Acad Sci U S A 117:18984–18990. https://doi.org/10.1073/PNAS.2006853117/SUPPL_FILE/PNAS.2006853117.SAPP.PDF
65. Ravindra K, Singh T, Vardhan S et al (2022) COVID-19 pandemic: what can we learn for better air quality and human health? J Infect Public Health 15:187–198. https://doi.org/10.1016/J.JIPH.2021.12.001
66. Venkatesh R, Gurnani B, Kaur K (2022) Impact of COVID-19 pandemic on carbon footprint and strategies to mitigate waste generation. Indian J Ophthalmol 70:690–691. https://doi.org/10.4103/IJO.IJO_2945_21
67. Ray RL, Singh VP, Singh SK et al (2022) What is the impact of COVID-19 pandemic on global carbon emissions? Sci Total Environ 816:151503. https://doi.org/10.1016/J.SCITOTENV.2021.151503
68. Le Quéré C, Jackson RB, Jones MW et al (2020) Temporary reduction in daily global CO2 emissions during the COVID-19 forced confinement. Nat Clim Chang 10:647–653. https://doi.org/10.1038/s41558-020-0797-x
69. UN-Habitat (2020) COVID-19: socioeconomic impacts on Africa. United Nations Human Settlements Programme, Nairobi
70. Odiwuor F (2022) The price of Russia's Ukraine invasion: Africa's food security. Africa Up Close. https://africaupclose.wilsoncenter.org/russia-ukraine-africa-food-security/. Accessed 19 Aug 2022

Influence of the Big Brother Naija Lockdown 2020 Edition Reality TV Show on Nigerians' Value Orientation During the COVID-19 Lockdown Measures

Blessed F. Ngonso, Peter E. Egielewa, Giuseppe T. Cirella, Felix O. Iyalomhe, and Christian Orobello

1 Introduction

Since the advent of television as a mass medium, its impact has always been a concern to media researchers. Owing to its clamorous nature, television programs attract a large audience, particularly young people. The primary influence of television stems from the fact that television provides many entertainment programs for young people, such as football, music, drama, and more recently reality television shows. Reality television shows, however, seem to be the most appealing TV program for youths, possibly because the program allows them to participate while viewing the program from the comfort of their home by way of voting for housemates' eviction or retention. According to Olley et al. [1], in Nigeria, reality television programs are gradually becoming a dominant genre in television programming. Some of the reasons for the transition are that many programs on television now revolve around reality television chiefly because they now provide audience members, advertisers, and producers with certain entertainment gratification and benefits. On the other hand, some people see reality programs on television as another way of exploiting the minds of the young audiences of the programs without morally impacting their lives. These researchers also averred that the craze for

B. F. Ngonso (✉) · P. E. Egielewa
Department of Mass Communication, Edo State University Uzairue, Iyamho, Edo State, Nigeria
e-mail: ngonso.frederick@edouniversity.edu.ng; peter.egielewa@edouniversity.edu.ng

G. T. Cirella · C. Orobello
Faculty of Economics, University of Gdansk, Sopot, Poland
e-mail: gt.cirella@ug.edu.pl; christian.orobello@ug.edu.pl

F. O. Iyalomhe
Polo Centre of Sustainability, Imperia, Italy
e-mail: fo.iyalomhe@polocentre.org

G. T. Cirella (ed.), *Uncertainty Shocks in Africa*, Advances in African Economic, Social and Political Development, https://doi.org/10.1007/978-3-031-21885-9_10

Fig. 1 Big Brother Naija Lockdown, 2020 edition reality TV show in Nigeria: (*left*) first day of the show—19 July 2020 and (*right*) last day of the show—27 September 2020. Source: Photographs taken by Felix O. Iyalomhe

instant fame is yet another issue that attracts a large proportion of the youth audience to reality television shows, because many youths now suddenly discover their supposedly hidden talents and reality television programs provide a platform to stardom with little or no hard work. The assumptions of these researchers formed the baseline for this chapter which seeks to explore the moral value orientation of the Big Brother Nigeria reality TV show on Nigerians during the onset of the COVID-19 pandemic (Fig. 1).

2 Big Brother Naija Lockdown 2020 Edition

Reality television shows have become the leading television programs for TV audiences, particularly the youth [2–6]. In Nigeria, one of the leading reality television shows is Big Brother Naija. This annual program is premised on young men and women living together for at least 3 months in a confined environment where they are denied access to the outside world. The environment, popularly known as the "Big Brother House" with the participants being known as "housemates," brings together young men and women who are viewed by the audience as celebrities. The housemates spend their time sharing emotions, values, life experiences, playing "house" games, and other activities scheduled for their participation. During the period of living together, some housemates develop a strong emotional attachment to one another, while some of the housemates, before their eviction, indulge in outright sexual intercourse with marriage promises in full view of the audience. However, some are much more reserved and focus on the social life in the house with their prime target of winning the NGN 85 million (i.e., USD 220,000) at stake for the overall winner in the competition. The peculiarity of the 2020 edition of Big Brother Naija Lockdown is that it took place amidst the COVID-19 lockdown period which led many Nigerians to criticize this particular edition. Many felt it was a waste of funds and immoral to gather young adults in a confined environment for no serious reason. Despite this labeling of Big Brother Naija Lockdown as immoral, the organizers went ahead to host the 2020 edition of the program. It was expected that people would keep themselves busy during the lockdown, i.e., they would spend part of their time watching the program. However, it was not established if they spent more time watching the 2020 edition given the fact that some people during the period were engaged in online studies and other activities. As a result, five research questions (RQs) were explored to ascertain what would likely be the influence of their viewership on their moral values. The questions asked were:

RQ1: Which gender spent more time watching the Big Brother Naija Lockdown 2020 edition?
RQ2: Which age range spent more time watching the Big Brother Naija Lockdown 2020 edition?
RQ3: To what extent did the lockdown measures influence viewership of the Big Brother Naija Lockdown 2020 edition?
RQ4: What kinds of audience members' activities limited the viewership of the Big Brother Naija Lockdown 2020 edition?
RQ5: What kinds of influences did the Big Brother Naija Lockdown 2020 edition have on Nigerians' moral values?

3 Television and Value Orientation

3.1 Psycho-social Development of Young People

Television is a value transmission medium. Sometimes, new ideas and information that shape the lives of people are direct consequences of the media messages they consume. This implies that these messages are sometimes responsible for some of the adjustments in the behavioral patterns of people in society. From the early days of television broadcasting to today, television has been the most influential medium among other forms of mainstream mass media. Boon and Lomore [7] cited in Omokhua [8] that the value of television as a medium of mass communication is esteemed all over the world. The influence of the medium on the psycho-social development of young people can be profound. Television can be a powerful teacher. This medium, as a secondary agent of socialization, can to a very large extent, influence the lives of many, cutting across different socio-cultural and economic statuses. Television has many impacts on its audience. One of the ways is brand consciousness, especially among adolescents who are exposed to a variety of programs. Huston and Wright [9], Huston et al. [10], and Valkenburg and Vroone [11], in their separate studies, argue that there is a broad consensus about the crucial role played by television in shaping the beliefs, attitudes, and values of young people. Their thesis is premised on the fact that citizens typically turn to television for entertainment but also acquire a considerable amount of information from what they watch. Alawad and Kambal [12], while examining the impact of media information, state that "the strength and power of information resides in its content, but the observer of modern communication organization observes the way it busies itself with something else other than carrying the message," entering into the conflicting position of whether the information is useful or not. This also implies that what people prefer in real life is what shapes their values. In Ngonso and Egielewa's [13] writing on how values are acquired through communication, they opine that "in communication philosophy, it is believed that the primary access to the realm of values is through acts of feeling and preference that are directed upon objects and persons bearing [those] values." This also aligns with the idea expressed in human psychology, that structural cognition and emotional feelings contribute to building the directions which affect the behavior of the person.

Television, as a medium with fantasy programs, such as reality television shows, can arouse the emotional feelings of television viewers. Hoffner et al. [14], cited in Omokhua [8], sees it from another perspective, i.e., "television is an important source of occupational information for youths and has the potential to introduce them to careers they may not have previously considered. Jobs or careers of television characters may appeal to youths and serve as role models in the development of their occupational aspirations." However, this is dependent on the construction and perception of the media messages. Alawad and Kambal [12] put it succinctly, stating "the impact of media communications on attitude formation and change depends on how the messages are comprehended." Alzoubi [15] states that "media language has a very important role in influencing people's attitudes and opinions towards certain political, economic, and social issues. This is because the media language has psychological and social roles, in which it conveys a social message for all individuals in society. This social message is based on a psychological basis that reflects the writer's psyche towards certain issues." Olley et al. [1], in their assessment of the content of reality television programs, state that the program has been criticized for being overly provocative and a disquieting representation of the society. The South African version of Big Brother proved to be highly controversial for its overt sexual content. However, Hyde-Clark [16] notes that people perceive reality programs to be a reflection of their culture. Adults may see reality TV as a reflection of the attitudes and behavior exhibited in society. They may see the comments made by contestants as an accurate expression of how they are viewed by society, and adjust their perception of themselves accordingly." This assertion appears to support the assumption by media scholars that, the media in our society as a whole is a powerful "director and moulder" of public opinion and a powerful means of creating a general attitude of thought and feeling.

3.2 *Television Conditioning*

Besides being influenced by the characters on television, people are also prone to be influenced by the presenters of the program. Television carries great value-oriented influence by way of penetrating the minds of the population with powerful messages which sometimes leave them without defense. Without sounding fallacious, to further buttress this claim, if we avert our thoughts to the internal responses that we would get if we asked adults who are constantly exposed to a reality TV show or other entertainment-oriented TV programs that use celebrities, the following questions. Are you sometimes tempted to dress like celebrities? Do you ever feel tempted to imitate the stunts of sportsmen on television? If their internal responses to these questions are in the affirmative, then you can rightly assume that television has an enormous effect on their lives. No wonder, Nwachukwu [17] describes the strength of television as "a medium with creativity and impact with dramatic and life-like representations of inanimate objects as well as embellishment and manipulation of life." Other research findings have also shown that television has become a popular source of information because of its audiovisual power which makes it easy to convey information, explaining trends and possibilities and educating people, see Burzyńska et al. [18] and Egielewa et al. [19]. Another unique characteristic of television is that it is a live medium which allows for the transmission of a live event instantly as it unfolds.

Television is also seen as a domestic medium which allows viewers to view programs from the comfort of their home without going to the cinema. Television is seen as having a powerful influence on its audience partly because of its audiovisual advantage over and above other forms of mass media such as the radio, newspapers, books, billboards, and magazines. Television is also called a glamorous medium. According to Baba [20], "while radio has sound, television content includes both sound and visuals. This audiovisual character of television makes it a magic medium which allows us to watch the world from our drawing rooms. This powerful visual nature helps television to create vivid impressions in our minds which in turn leads to emotional involvement. The audiovisual quality also makes television images more memorable." From a psychological point of view, it is assumed that when a particular trend is consistently aired on television, the human mind unconsciously begins to form opinions based on the information constantly seen on television. The psychological mechanism is therefore activated which is potent in influencing our attitudes and values. The more we see a particular thing on television being portrayed in a particular manner, the higher the tendency for our minds to begin to align and form an attitude in the manner it was portrayed. This assumption, therefore, provides researchers with the platform to anchor this concept on value change theory. This sociological theory believes in personal values people hold. According to Ngonso and Egielewa [13], "philosophers like Max Weber, Emile Durkheim, and Talcott Parsons in their early studies on ethics espoused this theory and based their argument on how, why, and to what extent or degree the values of a person hold." The theory asserts that humans hold on to a value which changes under certain conditions. It also uses the technique of "comparative feedback" to induce attitudinal and behavioral change. It is appropriate for this chapter because it emphasizes how values held by members of the community change as a result of intervening variables. It is equally important to note that every communication conveys value(s) held by the communicant, i.e., heavy television viewers are assumed to behave in a similar way to the celebrities portrayed on TV, therefore, share their values consciously and unconsciously assimilating the new values shared.

Minimal effects theory states that media alone cannot make people change their attitudes or behaviors. In other words, media functions, to large extent, to reinforce people's existing attitudes and beliefs [21–25]. The theory posits that people generally tend to interpret messages and information they receive from the media based on their existing beliefs and to strengthen and confirm their weltanschauung (i.e., worldview). This position, referred to as the "confirmation bias" by minimal effects theorists, becomes a factor in how people choose which media to consume and how they engage with such chosen media. On social media, this theory evolves into what has been termed "echo chambers" in which people of like minds with similar viewpoints and beliefs circulate their ideas and become less tolerant of opposing views and beliefs [21–23]. However, critics of minimal effects theory have argued, coming from the perspective of American voters' behavior [25–27], that there are factors that the theory did not take into consideration in explaining the minimal effects of the media. Chen [28] posits that even if the media reinforce and confirm one's existing beliefs and views, that in itself, still has an effect. He argues that a personal view may not be changed entirely but can be strengthened or weakened when applied to politics, in which media advertisements may or may not change people's choices but the media may make people's belief in a candidate weakened even if they would not change their minds to vote for a rival candidate.

4 Data Presentation and Analysis

The researchers created and distributed, primarily via WhatsApp and Facebook, an online survey using Google Forms, i.e., an online software that allows researchers to administer instruments (i.e., in this case a questionnaire) to a large number of respondents who cannot be assessed physically. This software also analyzed the data automatically giving accurate results. Moreover, the instrument was designed using a Likert scale and in a dichotomous response format. The study used Nigeria's entire population in 2020 of 206,130,000 million [29]. Based on Krejcie and Morgan's [30] formula for determining sample size, a population of over 200 million requires a sample size of 384. However, the sample size for this chapter is 400. The Google Forms questionnaire link collected responses to five RQs from 7 October to 26 November 2020, i.e., during the height of the COVID-19 outbreak in Nigeria.

4.1 RQ1: Which Gender Spent More Time Watching the Big Brother Naija Lockdown 2020 Edition?

Figure 2 illustrates that there were more females who watched the Big Brother Naija Lockdown 2020 edition reality show. The data shows that approximately three out of every five viewers were female.

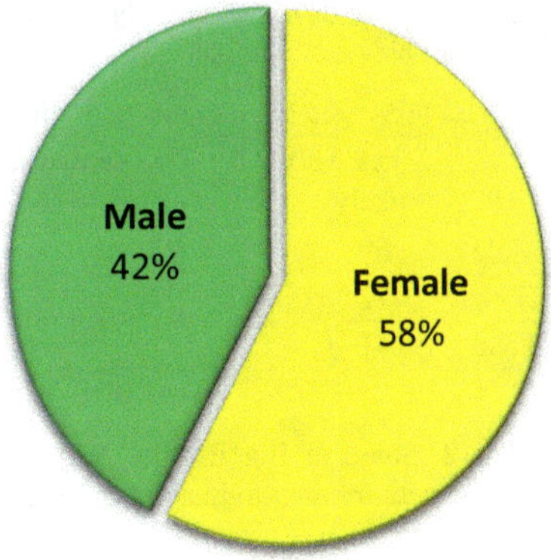

Fig. 2 Share of gender that frequently watched the Big Brother Naija Lockdown 2020 edition

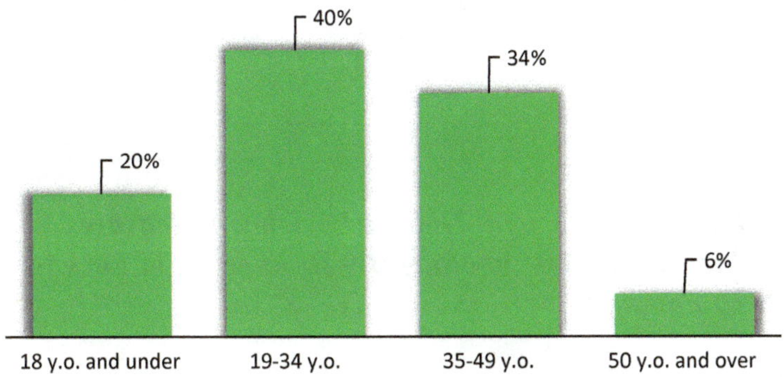

Fig. 3 Share of age ranges that frequently watched the Big Brother Naija Lockdown 2020 edition. Note: *y.o.* years old

4.2 RQ2: Which Age Range Spent More Time Watching the Big Brother Naija Lockdown 2020 Edition?

Figure 3 illustrates that the Nigerians who watched the Big Brother Naija Lockdown 2020 edition reality show the most were in the age range of 19–49, i.e., 74% of viewers. In other words, about three out of every four viewers of the show were likely to be people between 19 and 49. Also, older people above the age of 50 years were the least interested in watching the show.

Table 1 Share of Big Brother Naija Lockdown 2020 edition viewers who increased their viewership from previous editions

Do you think you have spent more time watching this edition than the previous editions?						
Gender	Yes, very likely	Yes, somewhat likely	I do not know	No, I do not think so	Not at all	Total
Male	69	77	22	0	0	168
Female	72	94	55	6	5	232
Total	141	171	77	6	5	400

Table 2 Share of Big Brother Naija Lockdown 2020 edition viewers who said the lockdown measures contributed to increasing their viewership in 2020

Do you think lockdown measures contributed to spending more time watching Big Brother Naija Lockdown in 2020?						
Gender	Yes, very likely	Yes, somewhat likely	I do not know	No, I do not think so	Not at all	Total
Male	126	9	12	10	11	168
Female	154	27	8	15	28	232
Total	280	36	20	25	39	400

4.3 *RQ3: To What Extent Did the Lockdown Measures Influence Viewership of the Big Brother Naija Lockdown 2020 Edition?*

Table 1 illustrates that more females (i.e., $n = 166$) than males (i.e., $n = 146$) agreed that they increased their viewership of the Big Brother Naija Lockdown 2020 edition compared to previous editions. In Table 2, more females (i.e., $n = 181$) than males (i.e., $n = 135$) said the lockdown measures contributed to increasing their viewership of the Big Brother Naija Lockdown 2020 edition.

4.4 *RQ4: What Kinds of Audience Members' Activities Limited the Viewership of the Big Brother Naija Lockdown 2020 Edition?*

The greatest inhibitions that the majority of viewers (i.e., $n = 257$) did not watch the Big Brother Naija Lockdown 2020 edition was online studies and reality TV shows were boring to watch (Table 3). Moreover, nearly a quarter of the viewership noted power failure as a factor for not watching the program regularly.

Table 3 Inhibitions from watching the Big Brother Naija Lockdown 2020 edition

What kind of audience members' activities limit the viewership of Big Brother Naija Lockdown reality TV program in 2020?

Age	Online studies	Power failure	Boring at watch reality TV shows	Distracted due to house chores	Total
18 y.o. and under	27	17	23	13	80
19–34 y.o.	61	38	44	17	160
35–49 y.o.	52	34	38	12	136
50 y.o. and over	7	10	5	2	24
Total	147	99	110	44	400

Table 4 Influences from watching the Big Brother Naija Lockdown 2020 edition

What kind of influences does the Big Brother Naija Lockdown 2020 edition reality TV program have on Nigerians' moral values?

Age	The show arouses my sexual emotions	The show arouses my interest to become a celebrity	I feel like I should be the winner of the prize money	The show makes me want to work hard in what I do	The show makes me want to become a millionaire as quickly as possible	Total
18 y.o. and under	1	14	10	50	4	80
19–34 y. o.	9	26	12	112	1	160
35–49 y. o.	7	15	23	83	7	136
50 y.o. and over	0	2	2	20	0	24
Total	17	57	47	266	13	400

4.5 *RQ5: What Kinds of Influences Did the Big Brother Naija Lockdown 2020 Edition Have on Nigerians' Moral Values?*

Data in Table 4 shows an overwhelming number of respondents (i.e., $n = 266$) feel motivated by the reality show to work harder in their respective work. This represents 67% of the total responses. This also indicates that the respondents feel positively influenced by the reality show to pursue the virtue of hard work. Only an insignificant number (i.e., $n = 13$ representing only 3.3% of all responses) feel motivated to become rich quickly by seeking to be millionaires as soon as possible. However, in Fig. 4, data shows that both genders found the reality show offensive to

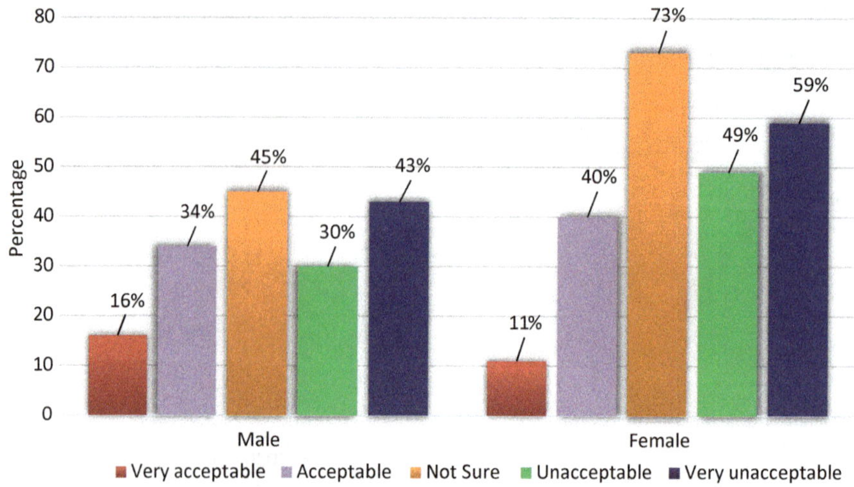

Fig. 4 Moral level of the content rated by the Big Brother Naija Lockdown 2020 edition viewers

Table 5 Chi-square tests used to determine the status of the null hypothesis

Test	Value	Degrees of freedom	Asymptotic two-sided significance
Pearson's chi-square	4.239	4	0.0375
Likelihood ratio	4.199	4	0.0380
Linear-by-linear association	2.404	1	0.0121
N of valid cases	400		

their values, although more female respondents (i.e., 45%) found the show distasteful compared to 37% of their male counterparts. Conversely, males found the show more acceptable (i.e., 28%) than their female counterparts (i.e., 26%). Thus, there is no significant relationship between genders of Nigerian viewers of the Big Brother Naija Lockdown 2020 edition and their perception of the moral content in the show, this will be known as the null hypothesis (H0).

If a predetermined alpha level of significance is given at 0.05 with 4 degrees of freedom, the chi-square results indicate the *p*-value is above 0.05 at 0.0375 (Table 5). Thus, with a *p*-value of 0.0375, which is higher than the conventionally accepted significance level (i.e., $p > 0.05$), i.e., H0 is accepted. In other words, there is no significant relationship between the gender of Nigerian Big Brother Naija Lockdown 2020 edition viewers and their perception of the moral content in the show. This means that respondents' perception of the moral content in the show does not depend on their gender. This aligns with the findings of this research which show that both genders found the reality show offensive to their values.

5 Discussion

In all, the results show that more females watched the Big Brother Naija Lockdown 2020 edition than males. In terms of viewership, Nigerians between the ages of 19 and 49 years old watched reality TV show the most—representing 74% of all respondents. Moreover, more females than males noted they watched the 2020 edition more than previous editions and that the COVID-19 lockdown measures made them increase the time they spend viewing the show. The key barriers to not watching the reality TV show were online studies and it being a boring (i.e., not interesting) program. Power failure also contributed to respondents not watching the program regularly. Interestingly, the reality TV show motivated a large number of respondents to state that they worked harder at their jobs as a result of the show. This finding aligns with studies by Hoffner et al. [14], and cited by Omokhua [8], who argue that prolonged exposure to television programs, i.e., especially to television role models, can motivate viewers to develop their occupational aspirations. This indicates a partial positive influence from the Big Brother Naija Lockdown 2020 edition during the height of the COVID-19 pandemic in Nigeria. However, even though more female respondents, i.e., 45%, saw the realty TV show as distasteful compared to 37% of their male counterparts, it can be implied that the show did not negatively affect the beliefs and values of the viewers. This agrees with the minimal effects theory as amplified by Ansolabehere [25], Neuman and Guggenheim [22], McFadden [24], and Woolley and Sharif [23]. The finding, however, contradicts the conclusions by Alzoubi [15] and Chen [28] who argue that media only confirms people's existing beliefs and values and hardly changes them in what has been referred to as the "confirmation bias." On the other hand, males found reality TV show more acceptable than their female counterparts. Finally, the chi-square test denoted that gender does not affect how they perceived the moral content of the reality TV show.

In a nutshell, both genders found reality TV show distasteful to their moral values. Based on the findings of this chapter the following is recommended for further research: (1) to probe why males did not watch the show as much as their female counterparts during the pandemic; (2) to explore if Nigerian viewership got better or worse after the lockdown measures were lifted; and (3) to understand why males found the show more acceptable even though they watched it less than their female counterparts. Since the COVID-19 outbreak dramatically changed the way people live, the effects of television regarding COVID-19 on healthy behaviors still has much to be explored [31]. Gong et al. [32], interestingly, states with "prolonged social isolation, media exposure [correlates with] collectivist norms." This may suggest that, inclusive of cultural factors, since reality TV shows, such as the Big Brother Naija Lockdown 2020 edition, are collectivist by nature, they may also be used to reduce anxiety and increase well-being during future public health crises. Further research into this matter is needed because apart from the heavy economic burden from the COVID-19 pandemic, the psychological impacts and any future lockdown measures have shown themselves to be equally harmful.

References

1. Olley W, Nwabara G, Olley J (2019) Nigeria university students' perception of reality programmes on television. Glob Media J 17:1–9
2. Ligocki DT (2018) The drama of reality television. Brill, Leiden
3. Peek HS, Beresin E (2015) Reality check: how reality television can affect youth and how a media literacy curriculum can help. Acad Psychiatry J Am Assoc Dir Psychiatr Resid Train Assoc Acad Psychiatry 40:177–181. https://doi.org/10.1007/S40596-015-0382-1
4. Vander Schee C, Kline K (2013) Neoliberal exploitation in reality television: youth, health and the spectacle of celebrity "concern". J Youth Stud 16:565–578. https://doi.org/10.1080/13676261.2012.733812
5. Ferguson CJ, Salmond K, Modi K (2013) Reality television predicts both positive and negative outcomes for adolescent girls. J Pediatr 162:1175–1180. https://doi.org/10.1016/J.JPEDS.2012.11.067
6. Patino A, Kaltcheva VD, Smith MF (2011) The appeal of reality television for teen and pre-teen audiences. J Advert Res 51:288–297. https://doi.org/10.2501/JAR-51-1-288-297
7. Boon SD, Lomore CD (2001) Admirer-celebrity relationships among young adults. Hum Commun Res 27:432–465. https://doi.org/10.1111/J.1468-2958.2001.TB00788.X
8. Omokhua S (2020) Television as a tool for attitudinal change: case study of "vote not fight" campaign on Edo University Iyamho students. Edo University Iyamho, Iyamho
9. Huston AC, Wright JC (1998) Television and the informational and educational needs of children. Ann Am Acad Pol Soc Sci 557:9–23
10. Huston AC, Wright JC, Marquis J, Green SB (1999) How young children spend their time: television and other activities. Dev Psychol 35:912–925. https://doi.org/10.1037/0012-1649.35.4.912
11. Valkenburg PM, Vroone M (2016) Developmental changes in infants' and toddlers' attention to television entertainment. Communic Res 31:288–311. https://doi.org/10.1177/0093650204263435
12. Alawad M, Kambal Z (2018) The world-view and its implications in media discourse: building and analyzing. Glob Media J 17:1–10
13. Ngonso BF, Egielewa PE (2018) When values change values: assessing how social media changes Nigerian youth communication patterns and values. JNMMC 68:1–8
14. Hoffner CA, Levine KJ, Sullivan QE et al (2006) TV characters at work: television's role in the occupational aspirations of economically disadvantaged youths. J Career Dev 33:3–18. https://doi.org/10.1177/0894845305282768
15. Alzoubi S (2019) The socio-stylistic variation of the media language of Jordan. Int J Int Relations, Media Mass Commun Stud 5:1–10
16. Hyde-Clarke N (2004) "But it's not real": perceptions of reality TV by south African youth. In: von Feilitzen C (ed) Young people, soap operas and reality TV. Nordicom, Gothenburg
17. Nwachukwu C (2011) Advertising's media sphere and effective deployment of options. Benin Mediacom J 1
18. Burzyńska J, Binkowska-Bury M, Januszewicz P (2015) Television as a source of information on health and illness—review of benefits and problems. Prog Heal Sci 5:174–184
19. Egielewa P, Ate A, Ngonso B (2020) COVID-19, television audience's programme choices: an analysis of how Nigerians consume television programmes during the pandemic. Working Paper
20. Baba JP (2012) Characteristics of television as a medium. Journal Communication. https://wecommunication.blogspot.com/2012/03/characteristics-of-television-as-medium.html. Accessed 13 Jun 2022
21. Oliver MB, Raney AA, Bryant J (2020) Media effects: advances in theory and research. Routledge, New York

22. Neuman WR, Guggenheim L (2011) The evolution of media effects theory: a six-stage model of cumulative research. Commun Theory 21:169–196. https://doi.org/10.1111/J.1468-2885.2011.01381.X
23. Woolley K, Sharif MA (2022) Down a rabbit hole: how prior media consumption shapes subsequent media consumption. J Mark Res 59:453–471. https://doi.org/10.1177/00222437211055403
24. McFadden B (2019) A theory of media consumption and demand, with implications for media industry structure and firm strategy. SSRN Electron J 50. https://doi.org/10.2139/SSRN.3097558
25. Ansolabehere S (2006) The paradox of minimal effects. Capturing Campaign Eff 1:29–44
26. Bartels LM (1993) Messages received: the political impact of media exposure. Am Polit Sci Rev 87:267–285. https://doi.org/10.2307/2939040
27. Ansolabehere S, Iyengar S (1997) Going negative: how political advertisements shrink and polarize the electorate. Free Press, New York
28. Chen KW (2020) Limitations of minimal effects model. Media Studies. 101. https://ecampusontario.pressbooks.pub/mediastudies101/chapter/limitations-of-minimal-effects-model/. Accessed 13 Jun 2022
29. Worldometer (2020) Nigeria Population—2020. https://www.worldometers.info/world-population/nigeria-population/. Accessed 30 Nov 2020
30. Krejcie RV, Morgan DW (1970) Determining sample size for research activities. Educ Psychol Meas 30:607–610. https://doi.org/10.1177/001316447003000308
31. Scopelliti M, Pacilli MG, Aquino A (2021) TV news and COVID-19: media influence on healthy behavior in public spaces. Int J Environ Res Public Health 18:1–16. https://doi.org/10.3390/IJERPH18041879
32. Gong J, Firdaus A, Said F et al (2022) Pathways linking media use to wellbeing during the COVID-19 pandemic: a mediated moderation study. Soc media + Soc 8(1). https://doi.org/10.1177/20563051221087390

COVID-19 Television Audience Program Choices: Analysis of How Nigerians Consume Television During the Pandemic

Peter E. Egielewa, Blessed F. Ngonso, Andrew A. Ate, Giuseppe T. Cirella, Felix O. Iyalomhe, and Christian Orobello

1 Introduction: Program Choices and Television

During the first year of the COVID-19 pandemic in Nigeria, Nigerians were confined to their homes due to lockdown measures. In their confinement, Nigerians resorted to television for their entertainment [1, 2]. To properly contextualize this chapter, a grasp of the basic concepts becomes imperative. These include COVID-19, media choices, program choices, and television. The novel coronavirus disease, otherwise known as COVID-19 is a strain of coronavirus discovered in China in 2019. The name "COVID-19" was derived as follows: "CO" stands for corona, "VI" stands for virus, "D" stands for disease, and "19" stands for 2019, i.e., the year it was discovered [3]. In Africa, the coronavirus outbreak was first reported in Egypt on February 12, 2020 [4]. The first case in Nigeria was reported on February 27, 2020 [5]. Authors such as Ngonso and Chukwu [6] found that television was the most trusted media for getting information on COVID-19 while Ngonso and Egielewa [1] found that the Nigerian audience relied more on television for their entertainment during the COVID-19 lockdown. According to Moemeka [7] p.141), "one basic issue to tackle when a decision [is made] to use the media of mass communication, the right way, is that of identifying and choosing the right medium or media."

P. E. Egielewa (✉) · B. F. Ngonso · A. A. Ate
Department of Mass Communication, Edo State University Uzairue, Iyamho, Edo State, Nigeria
e-mail: peter.egielewa@edouniversity.edu.ng; ngonso.frederick@edouniversity.edu.ng; ate.asan@edouniversity.edu.ng

G. T. Cirella · C. Orobello
Faculty of Economics, University of Gdansk, Sopot, Poland
e-mail: gt.cirella@ug.edu.pl; christian.orobello@ug.edu.pl

F. O. Iyalomhe
Polo Centre of Sustainability, Imperia, Italy
e-mail: fo.iyalomhe@polocentre.org

G. T. Cirella (ed.), *Uncertainty Shocks in Africa*, Advances in African Economic, Social and Political Development, https://doi.org/10.1007/978-3-031-21885-9_11

Moemeka [7] attributed this claim to the fact that the choice of the medium determines whether or not the target audiences are, in the first instance, reached with the right messages. The choice of medium or media also affects what people learn and how quickly and well they can learn it. In Africa, it has been observed that the predominant medium for information dissemination over the years is radio. Myers [8] states "that radio is still the dominant mass medium in Africa with the widest geographical reach and the highest audiences compared with television, newspapers, and other information and communication technologies." Egielewa and Dauda [9] in their study of prevention of child mortality in Nigeria and media use, found that women sought information on child mortality more on radio than on TV. Radio has been seen as a powerful means of disseminating information on all subject matters to the mass media audience. The powerful influence of the radio over other media includes the ability of radio waves to traverse national boundaries, its portability, ability to translate messages into local languages and dialects, affordability, and alternative use of power. Sambe [10] states that radio "is very effective in mobilizing people; hence it bypasses illiteracy and appeals to every person." Although radio has remained an acceptable medium for information dissemination in Africa, television has come to compete with it in the media space. Moemeka [7] and Ngonso and Chukwu [6] in separate studies have found that television has very significant advantages over both the radio and newspapers in the field of education. These findings contradict already known facts on rural people's media consumption which favors radio.

Television viewers' choices of media programs to consume refers to the decision of audiences to select what they see or hear from available content [11]. The media contents, from which audiences select, are usually diverse and have many distinct attributes. These attributes include pace and stimulation level, theme, and the type of characters featured. Próchniak [12] enumerates the factors that determine viewers' preferences for media channels to include: age, gender, motivation, personality, and a sensation-seeking trait. These choices may be made to fulfil certain goals or gratification of the audience which can include combating loneliness, need for activation, shyness, sensation seeking, task orientation, and a tendency to approach or withdraw from new stimuli [11]. Generally, the mass media perform four basic functions, i.e., information, education, persuasion, and entertainment. Amongst the various media platforms that carry out these functions, namely books, newspapers, magazines, radio, television, and new media platforms, television remains the most dynamic and probably still the most influential mass media for the global audience. According to Pugalendhi [13], new media platforms have not significantly reduced the premium position of television. Habermas and Cooke [14] also averred that this is even more so since TV became a digital medium and adopted 24-h non-stop viewing. However, a study by Global Web Index [15] found that there is a gradual decline in daily viewing of linear TV as a result of the shift towards online forms of TV content. In fact, in countries such as Australia, Germany, the Netherlands, the Philippines, Saudi Arabia, South Africa, the UK, and the USA, there is an over 70% increase in time spent watching online TV. Viewers' lifestyles and cultures can be greatly influenced by television, such as the variety of TV channels and how they make their choices on what TV channels to watch. Viewers make choices of what TV channels to choose from. The choice of viewers is usually based on the viewers' prior knowledge of the TV program schedule or after looking up the programs for the day or the week ahead, and that viewers will often reject certain types of programs that do not fit their taste [16]. The Nielsen people meter, cited in Rust et al. [17], has classified such channels into different program types, including children's news, instructions, advice, official policy, sports academy, amongst others. However, Headen et al. [18] and Rust and Alpert [19], cited in Rust et al. [17] developed a version of such channels into ten program types, namely: serial drama, action drama, psychological drama, game show, talk show, variety shows, movie, news, comedy, and sports. In modern times, viewers can choose between many different TV channels, national and international, thematic news, music, sport, talk shows, serials, soap operas, movies, games, and sitcoms which provide the viewers with an escape from their daily routine [12].

Certain factors influence viewers' selection and consumption of TV programs. Singhal et al. [20] in a study carried out on 100 youths between the ages of 15 and 29 in Haryana, India, found that there was a two-to-one preference for TV over the internet and an overwhelming percentage of the youth in the study got their news and entertainment from TV while other information was obtained from the internet. Also, Pugalendhi [13] researched what TV channel women in Chennai, India, watch daily. Using a sample size of 350 respondents divided into two groups of women, namely, working-class women and homemakers, the research found that most working women watched more cookery shows, horoscope programs, and TV soap operas than homemakers, who spent less time watching them daily. In a similar study, the Nielsen people meter found that the monthly TV consumption of American women is 16 h more than that of their male counterparts. In the study, while women spend an average of 166 h monthly watching TV, men watch only about 150 h [21]. Similarly, Gollust et al. [22], in a study, conclude that television news, and especially local TV news, remains an important vehicle through which Americans obtain information about health-related topics. The researchers found that in 2017 more Americans (i.e., 50%) stated that they more often get their news from TV than from any other source and local TV news reaches more Americans than national networks or cable news. Studies have also shown that some people depend on television for health information, such as COVID-19, because they also see television as the most popular source of information. In a critical review of 47 papers published in Polish and international scientific journals from 2010 to 2014, researchers found that television is the medium of choice for information on the topic of health and illness [23]. Also, during COVID-19, TV has become an escape from self-isolation with viewers increasing their screen time, and sourcing for programs that will uplift their moods [24]. In a new Nielsen people meter data report, the study shows that 60% of Americans increased their TV viewing during the period of stay at home during the COVID-19 shutdown [25]. The study further showed that American's increased their consumption of TV to 12 h daily. The study found that because of working from home recommendations, people increased their viewership by 3 h weekly in which feature films, news, and general entertainment programs were the most frequently watched during the shutdown. Ultimately, television viewers are motivated or influenced by personal gratification derived from the program. Banks [26] in his research found out that in the UK viewers prefer traditional news channels to other channels while Burzyńska et al. [23] concluded that people rely mainly on television for news. Though television studies have shown that viewers watch a variety of programs including health-related programs, it is not yet known if Nigerians during the COVID-19 outbreak, and subsequent lockdown measures were motivated to watch health-related programs or other programs. Therefore, the intention of this chapter is to ascertain their choice of TV programs during the lockdown measures occasioned by the pandemic.

2 Theoretical Framework

2.1 Hypothesis Development

The basic goals of this chapter are essentially derived from the tenets of the uses and gratifications theory and tied to three objectives. (1) The audience is active and its media use is goal oriented. Specifically, this objective examines the types of programs consumed by Nigerian TV viewers during the COVID-19 lockdown measures and examines the extent of Nigerian's TV consumption during the lockdown period. (2) The audience has enough self-awareness of their motives in media use to make the information collected useful in the research. This objective examines the TV program that is the most preferred by Nigerian viewers during the COVID-19 lockdown period. (3) Value judgments of media content can only be assessed by the audience. To understand this objective, it was necessary to explore the reasons for viewers' choices of TV programs during the COVID-19 lockdown period. This objective, however, has no relationship with the tenets but became necessary because of the peculiarity of Nigeria with regard to television viewership. To formulate the hypothesis (H1) of this chapter five accompanying research questions (RQs) are used.

RQ1: What are the types of programs consumed by Nigerian TV viewers during the COVID-19 lockdown measures?

RQ2: To what extent do Nigerian TV viewers consume programs during the COVID-19 lockdown period?

RQ3: What are the most preferred TV programs Nigerian viewers consumed during the COVID-19 lockdown period?

RQ4: What are the reasons for viewers' choices of TV programs during the COVID-19 lockdown period?

RQ5: What are the challenges faced by Nigerian TV viewers during the COVID-19 lockdown period?

The researchers linked the types of gratification, i.e., personal identity, self-confidence, personal stability, integrity, social status, and the need for self-respect, to form H1.

H1: There is a significant relationship between the gender of Nigerian TV viewers and the amount of time spent watching TV during the COVID-19 lockdown period.

2.2 *Television Viewing in Times of a Health Crisis*

During any crisis, whether health, environmental, social, or even political, citizens rely on the media to provide comprehensive information on the situation that is unfolding or already happened. It is the task of mass media to inform the citizens as quickly as they can since such information delivered quickly can "save their lives, health, and property, and even the environment" [27]. Víchová [27] argues that television is the most patronized media in terms of providing information on emergencies. She states that TV is the prime media during a crisis because it uses a combination of moving images, sounds, and spoken words to communicate most effectively and also because television news is usually short and brief and contains accurate information on the crisis that occurred most recently usually in the last 24 h. Burzyńska et al. [23] state that the audiovisual power of television makes it easy to convey health information, explaining trends and possibilities, educating people, and improving the health awareness of the viewers. Gollust et al. [22] posit that viewers trust information on health received in a crisis apart from consulting a doctor and family. However, Burzyńska et al. [23] argue that there is no clear evidence that information received on TV in emergencies influence the behaviors of viewers. Gollust et al. [22] also note that although TV remains the most popular for health information in a crisis or any other situation at that, local TV stations were preferable to national TV because is it geographically bound and air such news more frequently than national TV stations.

Since the COVID-19 outbreak, Nielsen people meter data has shown that TV viewing increased in South Korea, Italy, and the USA, predicting television viewing would rise during the pandemic because live shows, festivals, and leisure venues had been closed. The study further elucidates that TV became an escape from self-isolation and uplifted the moods of people shattered by the pandemic [24]. In the USA, for instance, Americans view television for an average of 2.8 h daily because it is seen as a popular form of leisure activity. Common Sense Media data, cited in Sussman and Moran [28], concludes that the average American teen spends 7 h 22 min on screens daily (i.e., excluding time spent for school or homework). There is generally no agreement amongst scholars as to what constitutes addictive viewing [28, 29]. However, some scholars argue that addiction should be examined from the angle of how it interferes and disrupts normal life tasks rather than the number of daily hours of viewed [28, 30]. Addictive television increases in crises periods with

American TV viewing increasing by 60% to 12 h of viewing daily [25]. Lafayette [25] found that television viewing increased 49% during the major snowstorm of January 2016 and 56% during Hurricane Harvey in August 2017. In the era of COVID-19, lockdowns in many parts of the world follow that same trend, and television viewing is becoming the escape route for self-isolation. The "stay at home" recommendation created an atmosphere for the television audience to connect with the variety of programs on TV and familiarize themselves with the talents both behind and in front of the camera. However, addictive television viewing can lead to negative consequences. Ngonso [31] in his study of football fans' behavior at viewing centers, found out that fans who viewed football 4 h and above a day and followed all televised European football could be defined as heavy viewers (i.e., addicted) and tended to exhibit aggressive behavior. Some of the negative consequences of addiction to television viewing include increasing social isolation, financial loss as a result of spending less time for income-generating activities, weight gain and obesity as a result of excessive TV viewing, aggressive behavior, and decreased school performance [28, 29]; however, there is no general prescription for this addiction a part from turning off the TV.

2.3 *Uses and Gratification Theory*

The uses and gratification theory was pioneered by Katz et al. [32] in 1974. It states that adults need satisfaction from media sources which includes surveillance, excitement, guidance, relaxation, tension reduction, social integration, entertainment, escape, self and personal identity, social contact, and information acquisition. This theory places emphasis on how and on which motives audiences use the mass media and what gratification is obtained from the consumption of such media [33, 34]. The uses and gratification theory counters other theories such as the magic-bullet and hypodermic needle theory which emphasize that media audiences were passive recipients of media programs and can consequently be easily manipulated. However, the uses and gratification theory posits that the audience is indeed an active consumer of media content and that they use such media content to gratify their individual needs [33–35]. The attention of uses and gratification theorists were initially (i.e., in the 1950s–1980s) focused on the traditional media of radio, newspaper, and television but with the advent of the internet and social media, the focus of the theory has been expanded to include those new media [33, 36]. The uses and gratification theorists Katz et al. [32] list five basic assumptions of the theory. (1) The audience is active and its media use is goal oriented. (2) The initiative in linking need gratification to a specific medium choice rests with the audience member. (3) The media compete with other resources for need satisfaction. (4) People have enough self-awareness of their media use, interests, and motives to be able to provide researchers with an accurate picture of that use. (5) Value judgments of media content can only be assessed by the audience. In terms of the types of gratification that audiences can receive from consuming media content, Katz et al. [32] list another five factors:

(1) cognitive needs—i.e., acquiring information, knowledge, understanding our social environment, curiosity, and exploration; (2) affective needs—i.e., esthetic and emotional experiences and pleasure; (3) personal identity—self-confidence, personal stability, integrity, social status, and the need for self-respect; (4) integration and social interaction—family relations and friendship, connection with the outside world, and the need for affiliation; and (5) escapism—the need to escape, tension release, and shifting attention from the unpleasant to the pleasant.

From the mid-1980s, a new dimension was introduced into the theory between "gratification sought" and "gratification obtained" in which media audiences remain with a particular media when gratification sought is achieved and stop using the media when gratification sought is not achieved [33]. Studies have shown that Nigerians, as well as Africans in general, consume television content for several reasons, such as entertainment, education, health, agriculture, and information [6, 37–40]. Since COVID-19 is still unfolding and there are limited studies carried out on how the audience in Nigeria consumes television programs during the COVID-19 pandemic, this chapter, therefore, intends to apply the uses and gratification theory to explain how the audience is consuming television and the gratifications they achieved. Thus, the theory is very apt for this chapter.

2.4 Questionnaire and Sample Distribution

Using the quantitative survey research approach, this chapter looks at Nigeria's entire population of approximately 200 million [41]. Nigeria is made up of 36 states and the Federal Capital Territory (FCT), spread across six geopolitical zones. Since the survey was done online, as long as the respondent is a Nigerian citizen and resident in any part of the country and can have access to the internet to fill out the online questionnaire—they qualified to be a respondent. The survey was made up of 19 questions and promoted using WhatsApp and Facebook with a link to a Google Forms questionnaire page (Table 1). The survey was conducted between April 27, 2020, to May 21, 2020, i.e., the first phase of Nigeria's lockdown in 2020 [42]. The Taro Yamane [43] formula, i.e., Eq. (1), was used to determine an appropriate sample size in which there is a 95% confidence level and p-value of 0.05.

$$n = \frac{N}{1 + N * (e)^2} \tag{1}$$

Where: n = sample size, N = population size, and e = acceptable sampling error.

Thus, an estimated sample size of 400 is representative for a population of 200,000,000. The researchers, however, for more reliability oversampled by 57 and, therefore, used a sample size of 457. Data was analyzed using Google Forms statistics and the chi-square test.

Table 1 Online administered questionnaire

No.	Question and responses
1	*Enter age:* ☐18 years and under, ☐19–30 years old, ☐31–45 years old, ☐46–60 years old, ☐61 years and over
2	*Enter gender:* ☐male, ☐female
3	*Enter state of residence:* ☐Abia, ☐Adamawa, ☐Akwa Ibom, ☐Anambra, ☐Bauchi, ☐Bayelsa, ☐Benue, ☐Borno, ☐Cross River, ☐Delta, ☐Ebonyi, ☐Edo, ☐Ekiti, ☐Enugu, ☐FCT (Abuja), ☐Gombe, ☐Imo, ☐Jigawa, ☐Kaduna, ☐Kano, ☐Katsina, ☐Kebbi, ☐Kogi, ☐Kwara, ☐Lagos, ☐Nasarawa, ☐Niger, ☐Ogun, ☐Ondo, ☐Osun, ☐Oyo, ☐plateau, ☐Rivers, ☐Sokoto, ☐Taraba, ☐Yobe, ☐Zamfara
4	*What is your religion?* ☐Christian, ☐Muslim, ☐traditional believer, ☐atheist, ☐none
5	*Enter education level:* ☐primary school leaving certificate, ☐SSCE/WAEC/GCE, ☐OND/NCE, ☐bachelor/HND, ☐masters, ☐doctorate/Ph.D., ☐other
6	*Enter the type of job are you engaged in:* ☐public sector employee (employed mainly by government bodies), ☐private sector employee (employed mainly by private firms and companies), ☐self-employed (entrepreneur), ☐student, ☐unemployed
7	*Which of these media do you consume during the COVID-19 lockdown period?* (tick as many as you use) ☐TV, ☐radio, ☐newspapers, ☐social media (Facebook, WhatsApp, YouTube, etc.), ☐online (online news, Google search, etc.), ☐other
8	*How many hours per day did you spend watching TV before the COVID-19 outbreak?* ☐3 h or less, ☐3–6 h, ☐6–9 h, ☐9–12 h, ☐12 h or more
9	*How many hours per day did you spend watching TV during the COVID-19 outbreak?* ☐3 h or less, ☐3–6 h, ☐6–9 h, ☐9–12 h, ☐12 h or more
10	*Which of the following TV genres do you watch? (tick as many as apply to you)* ☐news, ☐movies, ☐comedy, ☐sports, ☐cartoons, ☐food networks, ☐Drama, ☐educational, ☐documentary, ☐religious, ☐music, ☐health
11	*Which of the following channels did you watch during the lockdown period? (tick as many as you watched)* ☐Nollywood channels (Nigerian movies), ☐foreign movies (Hollywood, Bollywood, Zeeworld, Telemondo, etc.), ☐local music channels, ☐foreign music channels, ☐foreign comedy channels, ☐local comedy channels, ☐foreign religious channels, ☐local religious channels, ☐local news channels (AIT, channels TV, TVC, etc.), ☐foreign news channels (Aljazeera, BBC, CNN, DW, France24, etc.)
12	*Which of these international NEWS channels are the best for information on COVID-19? (tick as many as you watch)* ☐Aljazeera, ☐BBC, ☐CGTN, ☐CNN, ☐DW, ☐FOX news, ☐France24, ☐RT, ☐other
13	*Which of these local NEWS channels are the best for information on COVID-19? (tick as many as you watch)* ☐NTA, ☐channels TV, ☐AIT, ☐TVC, ☐Arise TV, ☐Silverbird TV, ☐other
14	*What urges you to choose specific programs on watch on TV?* ☐to combat boredom, ☐to educate myself on the latest information on COVID-19, ☐to find out whether a cure for COVID-19 has been found, ☐to get spiritual inspiration from god in this difficult period, ☐to distract myself, ☐to fulfil my passion, ☐other
15	*Are you satisfied with the TV information you are getting from the federal government on COVID-19?* ☐very satisfied, ☐satisfied, ☐I do not know, ☐not satisfied, ☐not satisfied at all
16	*Are you satisfied with the TV information you are getting from your state government on COVID-19?* ☐very satisfied, ☐satisfied, ☐I do not know, ☐not satisfied, ☐not satisfied at all
17	*Do you think the information you are generally getting on TV gives you a better understanding of COVID-19?* ☐I am very sure, ☐I am sure, ☐I do not know, ☐I am not sure, ☐I am not sure at all

(continued)

Table 1 (continued)

18	*What type of TV do you use to watch your TV program? (tick as many as you use)* ☐digital TV (using decoder), ☐terrestrial TV (using antenna only), ☐online TV (using internet data), ☐other
19	*Which of the following challenges did you encounter watching TV during the lockdown period? (tick as many as affect you)* ☐lack of power (PHCN), ☐inability to subscribe to a paid TV, ☐uninteresting programs, ☐too much of noise, ☐hunger, ☐distraction by family members, ☐lack of motivation, ☐sheer laziness, ☐I do not know, ☐other

PHCN Power Holding Company of Nigeria

Respondents filled out the online survey based on the state of residence as shown in Table 2. A breakdown of the distributions indicates 27 out of the 36 states of Nigeria and FCT took part in the survey which represents 75% of Nigerian states' participation. The data shows that residents in Nigeria's 17 western states overwhelmingly took part in the survey, an indication that residents in Nigeria's western states dominated the social media space through which the questionnaire was distributed. In terms of north-south geopolitical divide, 18% of the respondents were from north states and 82% from south states.

3 Piecing Together how Nigerians Consume Television During the COVID-19 Lockdown Measures

Figure 1 indicates the types of media that Nigerians were exposed to during the COVID-19 lockdown period. When a comparison is made between respondents' traditional and digital consumption, data shows that while 59% of all respondents were exposed to new media (i.e., online and social media), only 38% of the respondents were exposed to traditional media (i.e., TV, radio, and newspapers)—and 3% other. The data, therefore, showed a drift from the consumption of traditional media products of TV, radio, and newspapers as main sources of information and entertainment to digital and social media. This does not, however, indicate that people are no longer consuming traditional media products.

Furthermore, the majority of the respondents, i.e., 77%, viewed television three or less hours and 16%—3–6 h per day before the COVID-19 lockdown period. Respondents rarely viewed television more than 6 h pre-COVID-19. On the other hand, during the COVID-19 lockdown period, the number of hours spent watching TV significantly increased, with 28% of Nigerians spending 3–6 h and 10%—6–9 h per day. Interestingly, people watching TV programs for 9–12 h per day jumped from 2% before to 6% during the lockdown measures. Overall, 23% of Nigerians spent more than 3 h watching TV before the COVID-19 lockdown period whereas the percentage who watched TV for more than 3 h during the COVID-19 lockdown period increased to 46%. This is a 100% increase from the pre-COVID-19 period. In other words, Nigerians doubled the time they spent on TV during the COVID-19 lockdown period (Fig. 2). Moreover, the data from Table 3 clearly shows that males

Table 2 Demographic distribution of the respondents

States in Nigeria	Population[a]	Respondents' population based on residence in the state	Percentage of respondents	North-south divide of geopolitical regions
Abia	3,727,300	9	2.0	South
Adamawa	4,248,400	1	0.2	North
Akwa Ibom	5,482,200	5	1.1	South
Anambra	5,527,800	2	0.4	South
Bauchi	6,537,300	0	0.0	North
Bayelsa	2,278,000	0	0.0	South
Benue	5,741,800	3	0.7	North
Borno	5,860,200	0	0.0	North
Cross River	3,866,300	9	2.0.	South
Delta	5,663,400	22	5.0	South
Ebonyi	2,880,400	0	0.0	South
Edo	4,235,600	169	38.0	South
Ekiti	3,270,800	5	1.1	South
Enugu	4,411,100	2	0.4	South
FCT (Abuja)	3,564,100	49	11.0	FCT
Gombe	3,257,000	0	0.0	North
Imo	5,408,800	3	0.7	South
Jigawa	5,828,200	1	0.2	North
Kaduna	8,252,400	3	0.7	North
Kano	13,076,900	2	0.4	North
Katsina	7,831,300	0	0.0	North
Kebbi	4,440,000	0	0.0	North
Kogi	4,473,500	5	1.1	North
Kwara	3,192,900	3	0.7	North
Lagos	12,550,600	88	20.0	South
Nasarawa	2,523,400	3	0.7	North
Niger	5,556,200	3	0.7	North
Ogun	5,217,700	7	1.5	South
Ondo	4,671,700	16	3.5	South
Osun	4,705,600	2	0.4	South
Oyo	7,840,900	17	3.7	South
Plateau	4,200,400	4	0.9	North
Rivers	7,303,900	13	2.7	South
Sokoto	4,998,100	0	0.0	North
Taraba	3,066,800	1	0.2	North
Yobe	3,294,100	0	0.0	North
Zamfara	4,515,400	0	0.0	North
Total	193,392,500	447	100	

[a]Population is adopted from the 2006 census and on the 2019 projected populations published by the National Bureau of Statistics

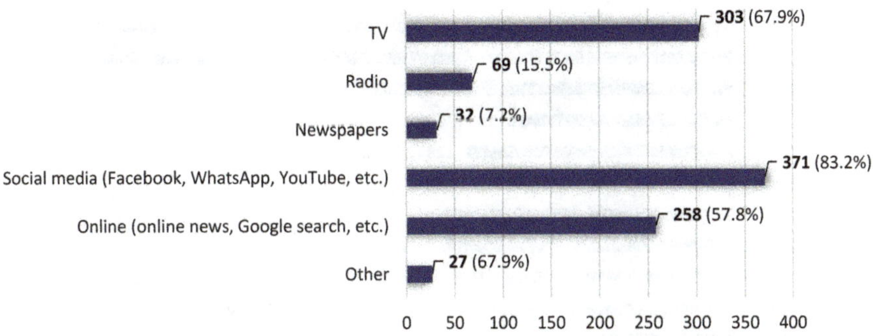

Fig. 1 Nigerians' distribution of media consumption during the COVID-19 lockdown measures

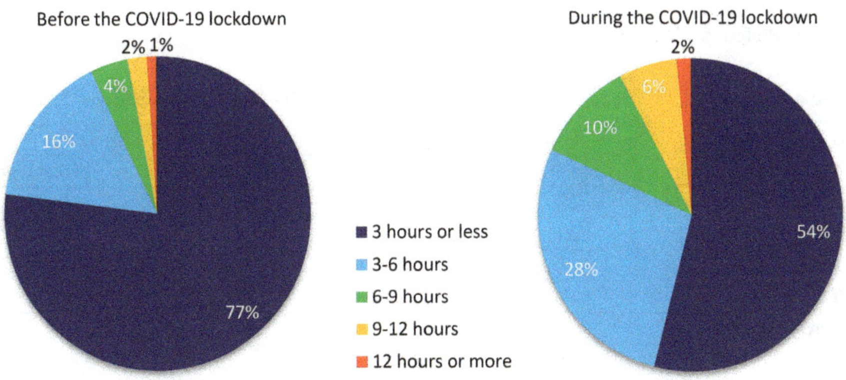

Fig. 2 Comparison of hours spent per day watching TV before and during the implementation of the COVID-19 lockdown measures

Table 3 Amount of time Nigerians spent watching TV during the COVID-19 lockdown period

Gender	3 h or less	3–6 h	6–9 h	9–12 h	12 h or more	Total
Male	158	92	27	22	4	303
Female	89	35	21	6	3	154
Total	247	127	48	28	7	457

spent more time watching TV during the lockdown period than their female counterparts. Indeed, it reveals that for every three people who watched TV for more than 3 h during the COVID-19 lockdown, two were males.

Figure 3 shows that most respondents preferred TV programs such as movies, news, and religion during the COVID-19 lockdown period compared to food networks, sports, and documentaries. Ironically, the data indicated that health programs, which should have proved to be relevant in the wake of the pandemic were not as preferred as the others. Only one out of every three respondents showed interest in health programs. To check if the most preferred programs were local or foreign, data in Table 4 showed that Nigerians preferred local channels to foreign

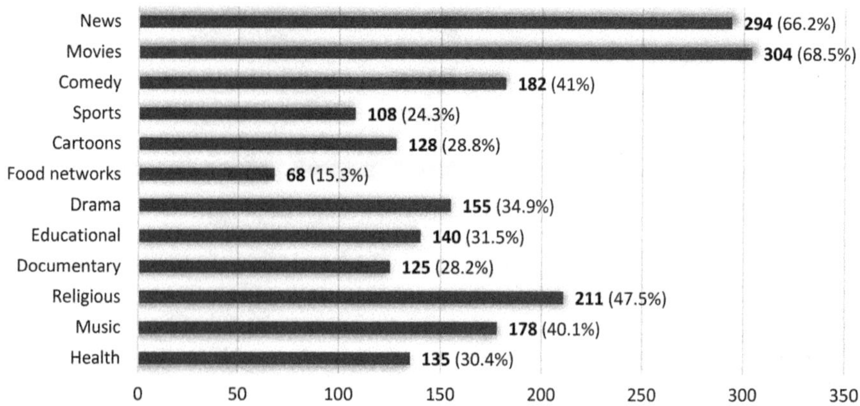

Fig. 3 Preferred TV programs by genre during the COVID-19 lockdown period

Table 4 Preferred TV channels by Nigerians during the COVID-19 lockdown period

TV program genre	Foreign TV channels		Local TV channels	
	Total	Percentage	Total	Percentage
Movies	200	46.2	218	50.3
News	204	47.1	282	65.1
Religion	86	19.9	150	34.6
Total	490	113.2	650	150
Percentage average		38		50

Table 5 Satisfaction of Nigerians with the Federal and State governments' handling of the COVID-19 crisis as watched on TV

Parameters	Federal government		State government	
	Total	Percentage	Total	Percentage
Very satisfied	32	7.6	38	8.7
Satisfied	124	29.5	114	26
I do not know	86	20.5	75	17.1
Not satisfied	124	29.5	159	36.2
Not satisfied at all	54	12.9	53	12.1

ones in all the programs. Approximately, three in every five respondents preferred local channels to foreign channels during the COVID-19 lockdown period.

Table 5 shows the satisfaction level of respondents regarding how their states and the Federal government handled COVID-19 as portrayed on TV. Data showed that respondents were more satisfied with the Federal government's efforts (i.e., 37.1%) than those of their respective state governments (i.e., 34.7%). More respondents expressed a higher dissatisfaction with their state governments' handling of the crisis (i.e., 48.3%) than that of the Federal government (i.e., 42.4%). This gives an indication that Nigerians are generally more impressed with the Federal

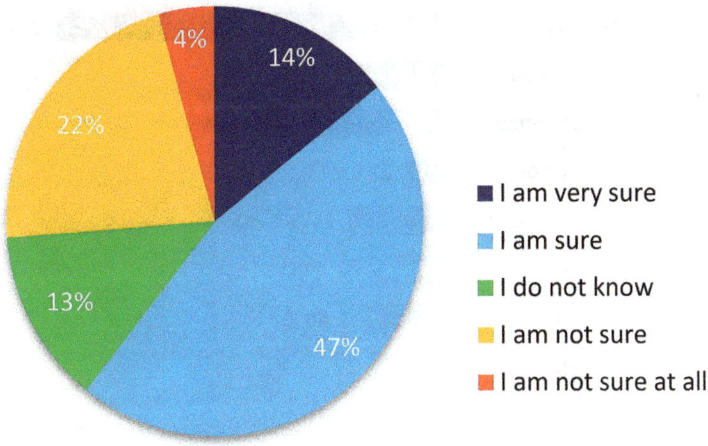

Fig. 4 Nigerians' level of satisfaction with information received on TV about the COVID-19 crisis

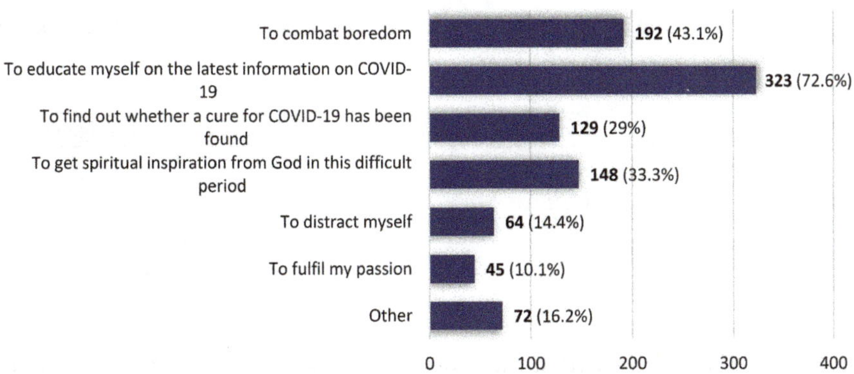

Fig. 5 Reasons why respondents chose a particular TV program to watch during the COVID-19 lockdown period

government's action as it relates to COVID-19 than their state governments. Figure 4 shows that, in general, Nigerians expressed a high satisfaction rate with the information they were getting on TV concerning COVID-19 (i.e., 61%), with only 13% unsure of it.

Figure 5 shows that most respondents chose TV programs for three major reasons: to get information on COVID-19 (i.e., 72.6%), to combat boredom (i.e., 43.1%), and to get spiritual inspiration from God (i.e., 33.3%). This indicates Nigerians were interested in their health and wanted to stay abreast of the latest information on COVID-19. In Fig. 6, an overwhelming percentage of Nigerians said that a lack of power, i.e., PHCN, was their major challenge during the COVID-19 lockdown period. In other words, approximately three out of every four peoples were unable to watch TV during the COVID-19 lockdown period due to a lack of

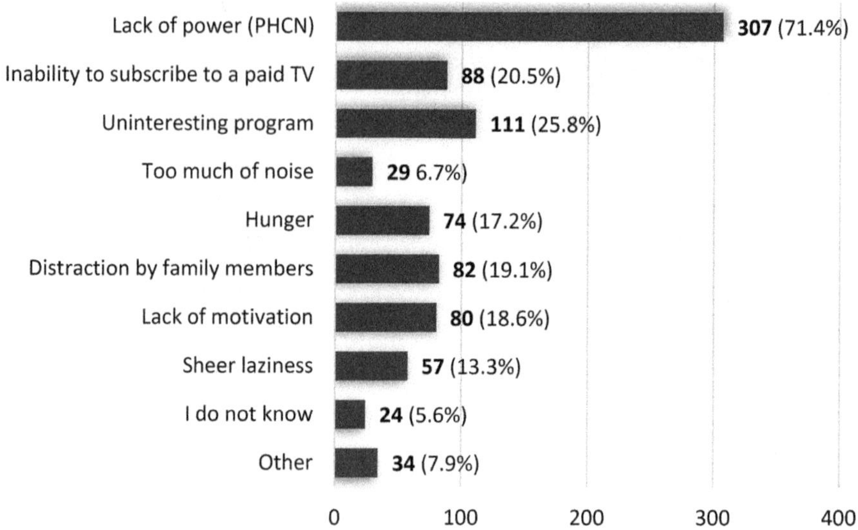

Fig. 6 Challenges faced by respondents in watching TV during the COVID-19 lockdown period

Table 6 Chi-square test results used to determine the status of H0

Test	Value	Degrees of freedom	Asymptotic two-sided significance
Pearson's chi-square	7.065	4	0.0133
Likelihood ratio	7.189	4	0.0126
Linear-by-linear association	0.354	1	0.0552
N of valid cases	457		

electricity. The data showed that lack of power alone accounted for 37% of all the eight challenges listed.

3.1 Hypothesis Test

H1 is tested using the chi-square test. This test is commonly used to assess relationships between two categorical variables. Usually, the null hypothesis (H0) of the chi-square test is used to establish whether the negative hypothesis should be accepted or discarded and the alternative accepted [44]. With a predetermined alpha level of significance at 0.05 with 4 degrees of freedom, the chi-square result is 0.0133 (Table 6). Consequently, with a corresponding probability level at about 1% and the *p*-value tested at 0.05 (i.e., $p > 0.05$), it can be concluded that H0 is accepted. In other words, there is no significant relationship between the gender of Nigerian TV viewers and the amount of time spent watching TV during the COVID-19 lockdown period.

3.2 *Deeper Examination of RQs*

The findings of this chapter were evaluated in-line with H1 and the five RQs to guide the execution of the work. A deeper examination of RQs is broken down to elucidate the findings in a more circumstantial manner, with a supplementary perspective from the researchers (i.e., as some of them are residents of Nigeria and experienced firsthand the 2020 lockdown period) as well on from supporting literature.

3.2.1 RQ1: What Are the Types of Programs Consumed by Nigerian TV Viewers During the COVID-19 Lockdown Measures?

These research findings show that most Nigerians preferred TV programs such as movies, news, and religion during the COVID-19 lockdown period and were least interested in food networks, sports, and documentary genres. This result also conformed to Ngonso and Chukwu's [6] study, conducted in 2021, on rural people's COVID-19 message consumption which concluded that rural dwellers of Iyamho community were exposed to COVID-19 messages on TV more than on radio. This collaborative data points towards a paradigm shift from radio to TV in the dissemination of information in Nigeria. The data also shows that three out of every five Nigerians preferred local channels to foreign channels during the COVID-19 lockdown period. This preference for local channels over foreign channels confirms the previous findings that 56% of British citizens prefer to watch the five local traditional channels of BBC One, BBC Two, ITV, Channel 4 and Channel 5 than other channels, including international ones [26].

3.2.2 RQ2: To What Extent Do Nigerian TV Viewers Consume Programs During the COVID-19 Lockdown Period?

The data of this study shows that the number of Nigerians who spend more than 3 h viewing TV daily increased by 100% from 23% before to 46% during the COVID-19 lockdown period. This finding implies that people tend to spend more hours watching TV when they are in a confined state than when they are free to move about. This result supports findings by Nielsen people meter data that 60% of Americans increased their TV viewing during this period of the COVID-19 shutdown [25]. Also, the study confirms the research findings by Burzyńska et al. [23] and Gollust et al. [22] that television is the most popular source of information during a health crisis such as COVID-19. Findings also show Nigerian males consume more TV media than their female counterparts. Indeed, for every three people who watch TV for more than 3 h during the COVID-19 lockdown, two were males. This negates a Nielsen people meter study that found that American women consume TV media more than their male counterparts [21]. However, on running a chi-square test, results showed that there is no significant relationship between the gender of Nigerian TV viewers and the amount of time spent watching TV during the COVID-19 lockdown period.

3.2.3 RQ3: What Are the Most Preferred TV Programs Nigerian Viewers Consumed During the COVID-19 Lockdown Period?

Data in Fig. 3 and Table 4 provide answers to this question. The implication, in this case, is that entertainment programs provide an escape from boredom. This underscores the fact that when people are bored, they look to television for relief [10, 32, 45, 46]. The data also shows that news on COVID-19 was ranked second in terms of program consumption during the lockdown measures. This conforms with several studies that highlight news as a key program watched throughout the COVID-19 era [47–49].

3.2.4 RQ4: What Are the Reasons for Viewers' Choices of TV Programs During the COVID-19 Lockdown Period?

Findings revealed that most Nigerians choose TV programs for three major reasons, namely, to get information on COVID-19 (i.e., 72.6%), to combat boredom (i.e., 43.1%), and to get spiritual inspiration from God (i.e., 33.3%). This finding implies that people still regard the TV as a reliable media source for health information. This also indicates that Nigerians were very much interested in their health and wanted to stay up to date with the latest information on COVID-19. This finding is also a justification that people use media for their personal uses and gratification, and that media consumers are active users of the medium [34]. In these cases, Nigerians have decided what media to watch and why they watch those programs as these findings show.

3.2.5 RQ5: What Are the Challenges Faced by Nigerian TV Viewers During the COVID-19 Lockdown Period?

Lack of power supply, i.e., from PHCN, which has been a recurring problem in Nigeria was confirmed as a major challenge for Nigerians during the COVID-19 lockdown period. Indeed, three out of every four Nigerians considered it the biggest challenge. This matches several studies that corroborate the need for proper preparedness and delivery of power supply during the COVID-19 era [50–54]. Moreover, not having electricity during a state of lockdown would likely exacerbate the interlinkage that some people felt imprisoned at home during the lockdown period [55–59]. Being in isolation without electricity, especially at night, would expectedly increase some people's anxiety levels [55, 56, 60–63].

4 Conclusion

From the supporting items related to the research instrument (i.e., the questionnaire, see Table 1), this chapter showed that 27 out of the 36 states of Nigeria and FCT participated in the survey—an indication that Nigerians using social media cuts across the entire country. However, the data shows that residents in Nigeria's 17 western states overwhelmingly took part in the survey, again an indication that residents in Nigeria's western states dominate social media. Figure 1 shows that 59% of all respondents consume new forms of online media sources and 38% still consume traditional forms. However, this data does not diminish people's consumption of traditional media, especially TV, i.e., in-line with findings from Singhal et al. [20] who stress socioeconomic level and access to the internet as possible barriers to being online. Nonetheless, Nigerians doubled their consumption of TV media (i.e., 3 h or more) during the COVID-19 lockdown period compared to the pre-COVID-19 era.

In terms of gender differences, male consumers were the heaviest consumers of TV media—constituting two-thirds of the total. In spite of this, the tested hypothesis result shows that there is no significant relationship between gender and the amount of time spent viewing TV during the lockdown period. The reason why this happened, in the opinion of the researchers, is that both male and female viewers were confined to their homes having equal time to spend viewing television. Another possible variable that may have influenced this result, though more applicable to married couples, is that the women (e.g., wives) may likely have watched TV alongside their male partners (e.g., husbands) which may end up in equal viewing hours. This assumption has been taken into consideration from the result that shows that, in general, Nigerians prefer to watch movies, news, and religious programs during the COVID-19 lockdown measures, showing only insignificant interest in food networks, sports, and documentaries. From the findings between preference for foreign versus local TV channels and the Federal versus state government handling of COVID-19, it can be concluded that Nigerians were dissatisfied at the state level but still relied heavily on local TV programs to get information on the COVID-19 crisis. From the findings of this chapter's research, it can be recommended that local media organizations should have offered Nigerians more information on the COVID-19 pandemic, as well as more movies, news, and religious programs. Likewise, the Federal government should work to overcome the recurring problem of power supply in the country to prevent any further decay and collapse infrastructure and availability of social amenities. Finally, additional research to find out the type of programs consumed on TV during the lockdown in the remaining nine states that did not participate in the online survey should be investigated.

References

1. Ngonso B, Egielewa PE (2020) Influence of Bigbrother Naija reality TV show, 2020 edition on Nigerian youth value orientation
2. Ewomazino A (2021) An assessment of private television broadcasting operations in Nigeria. Int J Commun Soc 3:1–11. https://doi.org/10.31763/IJCS.V3I1.184
3. UNICEF (2020) What is a "novel" coronavirus? United Nations International Children's Emergency Fund, Geneva
4. Africanews (2020) COVID-19: Egypt confirms first coronavirus case in Africa. https://www.africanews.com/2020/02/14/covid-19-egypt-confirms-first-coronavirus-case-in-africa/. Accessed 13 Jun 2022
5. Egielewa PE (2020) Effect of COVID-19 and social mediatisation of religious bodies among worshippers in Nigeria. MKAR J Media Cult 4:253–274
6. Ngonso BF, Chukwu OJ (2021) COVID-19 pandemic's broadcast media messages' consumption in rural community and behavioral change. Int J Commun Soc 3:12–19. https://doi.org/10.31763/IJCS.V3I1.185
7. Moemeka AA (2000) Development and mass communication: effective use of the mass Media in Rural (or Inner-City) development. In: Moemeka AA (ed) Development communication in action: building understanding and creating participation. University Press of America, Detroit
8. Myers M (2008) Radio and development in Africa. A concept paper prepared for the International Development Research Centre (IDRC) of Canada. https://www.comminit.com/media-development-africa/content/radio-and-development-africa-concept-paper. Accessed 13 Jun 2022
9. Egielewa PE, Dauda JA (2020) Mass media and the prevention of child mortality in Edo and Kaduna states, Nigeria. Benin MediaCom J 14:105–119
10. Sambe J (2005) Introduction to mass communication practice in Nigeria. Spectrum Publishers, Ibadan
11. Hall A (2005) Audience personality and the selection of media and media genres. Media Psychol 7:377–398. https://doi.org/10.1207/S1532785XMEP0704_4
12. Próchniak A (2017) Factors affecting Viewer's television preferences: a review. Int J Adv Soc Sci Humanit 5:1–6
13. Pugalendhi R (2015) A study on the television programmes popularity among Chennai urban women. J Humanit Soc Sci 20:1–18
14. Habermas J, Cooke M (1998) On the pragmatics of communication. MIT Press, Cambridge
15. Global Web Index (2016) Digital vs traditional media consumption: analyzing time devoted to online and traditional forms of media at a global level, as well as age and across countries. www.globalwebindex.com. Accessed 13 Jun 2022
16. European Commission (2004) Attitudes and expectations of viewers in terms of television programmes with a European content. European Commission Directorate-General Press and Communication, Gambais
17. Rust RT, Kamakura WA, Alpert MI (1992) Viewer preference segmentation and viewing choice models for network television. J Advert 21:1–18. https://doi.org/10.1080/00913367.1992.10673356
18. Headen RS, Klompmaker JE, Rust RT (1979) The duplication of viewing law and television media schedule evaluation. J Mark Res 16:333–340. https://doi.org/10.1177/002224377901600305
19. Rust RT, Alpert MI (1984) An audience flow model of television viewing choice. Mark Sci 3: 113–124. https://doi.org/10.1287/MKSC.3.2.113
20. Singhal PK, Gupta S, Malhotra S (2013) Media consumption habits of urban youth in Haryana. Acad An Int Multidiscip Res J 3:1–13
21. Bailey WS (2011) Women watch more TV than men. San Antonio Bus Journals. https://www.bizjournals.com/sanantonio/blog/2011/08/blog-women-watching-more-tv-than-men.html. Accessed 13 Jun 2022

22. Gollust SE, Fowler EF, Niederdeppe J (2019) Television news coverage of public health issues and implications for public health policy and practice. Annu Rev Public Health 40:167–185. https://doi.org/10.1146/ANNUREV-PUBLHEALTH-040218-044017
23. Burzyńska J, Binkowska-Bury M, Januszewicz P (2015) Television as a source of information on health and illness—review of benefits and problems. Prog Heal Sci 5:174–184
24. This Day (2020) The world of television and streaming during COVID-19 pandemic. This Day Newspaper. https://www.thisdaylive.com/index.php/2020/03/29/the-world-of-television-and-streaming-during-covid-19-pandemic/. Accessed 13 Jun 2022
25. Lafayette J (2020) Media usage expected to rise during crisis: Nielsen. Broadcast. https://www.nexttv.com/news/media-usage-expected-to-rise-during-crisis-nielsen. Accessed 13 Jun 2022
26. Banks A (2020) TV viewing audiences favour traditional channels despite the multitude of choices offered by digital services, EY study reveals. EY UK. https://www.ey.com/en_uk/news/2020/03/tv-viewing-audiences-favour-traditional-channels-despite-the-multitude-of-choices-offered-by-digital-services-ey-study-reveals. Accessed 13 Jun 2022
27. Víchová K (2016) The role of media in times of crisis. Univerzita Tomáše Bati ve Zlíně. http://www.posterus.sk/?p=18837. Accessed 13 Jun 2022
28. Sussman S, Moran MB (2013) Hidden addiction: television. J Behav Addict 2:125. https://doi.org/10.1556/JBA.2.2013.008
29. Hartney E (2020) The symptoms and risks of television addiction. In: Very Well Mind. https://www.verywellmind.com/television-addiction-22264. Accessed 13 Jun 2022
30. Horvath CW (2010) Measuring television addiction. J Broadcast Electron Media 48:378–398. https://doi.org/10.1207/S15506878JOBEM4803_3
31. Ngonso BF (2017) Television and football fans behaviour. Lap Lambert Publishers, Berlin
32. Katz E, Blumler JG, Gurevitch M (1974) The uses of mass communications: current perspectives on gratifications research. In: The uses of mass communications: current perspectives on gratifications research. Sage Publications, Beverly Hills, pp 19–32
33. Tanta I, Mihovilovic M, Sablic Z (2014) Uses and gratification theory-why adolescents use Facebook? Medijistraž 20:110
34. Musa AS, Azmi MNL, Ismail NS (2016) Exploring the uses and gratifications theory in the use of social media among the students of mass communication in Nigeria. Malaysian J Distance Educ 17:83–95. https://doi.org/10.21315/MJDE2015.17.2.6
35. Griffin EA, Ledbetter A, Sparks GG (2019) A first look at communication theory, 10th edn. McGraw-Hill, New York
36. Raacke J, Bonds-Raacke J (2008) MySpace and Facebook: applying the uses and gratifications theory to exploring friend-networking sites. Cyberpsychology Behav 11:169–174. https://doi.org/10.1089/CPB.2007.0056
37. Ndolo I, Eze VB, Nwodo JC (2015) Influence of cervical cancer media campaigns on the knowledge, attitude and behaviour of women in south-East Nigeria. ESUT J Media Stud 9:166–180
38. Odo N, Ekwe O (2015) The role of the media in managing flood disaster: an audience assessment. ESUT J Media Stud 9:216–225
39. Ezugwu M, Nzekwe N (2015) Influence of breast cancer broadcast media campaigns on the health behaviour of women in south-east Nigeria. ESUT J Media Stud 9:190–201
40. Didiugwu I (2015) Repositioning Nigeria's agricultural sector for sustainable development: the challenge of the media. ESUT J Media Stud 9:202–215
41. Worldometer (2020) Nigeria Population—2020. https://www.worldometers.info/world-population/nigeria-population/. Accessed 30 Nov 2020
42. Ibrahim RL, Ajide KB, Olatunde Julius O (2020) Easing of lockdown measures in Nigeria: implications for the healthcare system. Heal Policy Technol 9:399. https://doi.org/10.1016/J.HLPT.2020.09.004
43. Yamane T (1967) Statistics an introductory analysis, 2nd edn. Harper and Row, New York

44. Statistics Solutions (2020) Using chi-square statistic in research. https://www.statisticssolutions.com/free-resources/directory-of-statistical-analyses/using-chi-square-statistic-in-research/. Accessed 13 Jun 2022
45. Okunna CS (1999) Introduction to mass communication. ABIC Publishers, Enugu
46. Ndolo IS (2006) Mass media systems and society. Rhyce Kerex Publishers, Enugu
47. Ng R, Chow TYJ, Yang W (2021) News media narratives of COVID-19 across 20 countries: early global convergence and later regional divergence. PLoS One 16:e0256358. https://doi.org/10.1371/JOURNAL.PONE.0256358
48. Mihelj S, Kondor K, Štětka V (2021) Audience engagement with COVID-19 news: the impact of lockdown and live coverage, and the role of polarization. Journal Stud 23:569–587. https://doi.org/10.1080/1461670X.2021.1931410
49. Scopelliti M, Pacilli MG, Aquino A et al (2021) TV news and COVID-19: media influence on healthy behavior in public spaces. Int J Environ Res Public Health 18:1879. https://doi.org/10.3390/IJERPH18041879
50. Tingting XA, Weijun Gao B, Yanxue Li C, Fanyue Qian D (2021) Impact of the COVID-19 pandemic on the reduction of electricity demand and the integration of renewable energy into the power grid. J Renew Sustain Energy 13:26304. https://doi.org/10.1063/5.0045825
51. Rouleau J, Gosselin L (2021) Impacts of the COVID-19 lockdown on energy consumption in a Canadian social housing building. Appl Energy 287:116565. https://doi.org/10.1016/J.APENERGY.2021.116565
52. Su Y, Cheng H, Wang Z, Wang L (2022) Impacts of the COVID-19 lockdown on building energy consumption and indoor environment: a case study in Dalian. China Energy Build 263:112055. https://doi.org/10.1016/J.ENBUILD.2022.112055
53. Dawn S, Shree Das S, Gope S et al (2022) Global power and energy scenario during COVID-19 pandemic: lessons from lockdown. Int J Electr Power Energy Syst 137:107757. https://doi.org/10.1016/J.IJEPES.2021.107757
54. Bielecki S, Dukat P, Skoczkowski T et al (2021) Impact of the lockdown during the COVID-19 pandemic on electricity use by residential users. Energies 14:980. https://doi.org/10.3390/EN14040980
55. Grover S, Sahoo S, Mehra A et al (2020) Psychological impact of COVID-19 lockdown: an online survey from India. Indian J Psychiatry 62:354–362. https://doi.org/10.4103/PSYCHIATRY.INDIANJPSYCHIATRY_427_20
56. Dhami MK, Weiss-Cohen L, Ayton P (2020) Are people experiencing the "pains of imprisonment" during the COVID-19 lockdown? Front Psychol 11. https://doi.org/10.3389/FPSYG.2020.578430
57. BBC News (2021) Coronavirus: "Lockdown made me feel like I was in prison." https://www.bbc.com/news/av/uk-northern-ireland-55767704. Accessed 28 Jul 2022
58. The Guardian (2020) Concern for Britons feeling trapped and lonely during lockdown|Mental health|. https://www.theguardian.com/society/2020/apr/19/concern-britons-feeling-trapped-lonely-during-lockdown-mental-health. Accessed 28 Jul 2022
59. UNICEF (2021) Teens feeling trapped in lockdown turn to helpline for support|UNICEF. https://www.unicef.org/ukraine/en/stories/teens-feeling-trapped-lockdown-turn-helpline-support. Accessed 28 Jul 2022
60. Nawaz S (2020) How anxiety traps us, and how we can break free. Harv Bus Rev. https://hbr.org/2020/01/how-anxiety-traps-us-and-how-we-can-break-free. Accessed 28 Jul 2022
61. Price JS (2013) An evolutionary perspective on anxiety and anxiety disorders. In: Durbano F (ed) New insights into anxiety disorders. IntechOpen, London
62. İleri N (2017) Allure of the light, fear of the DarkNighttime illumination, spectacle, and order in fin-de-Siècle Istanbul. Comp Stud South Asia, Africa Middle East 37:280–298. https://doi.org/10.1215/1089201X-4132905
63. Bensch G, Peters J, Sievert M (2013) Fear of the dark? How access to electric lighting affects security attitudes and Nighttime activities in rural Senegal. SSRN Electron J. https://doi.org/10.2139/SSRN.2159712

Underlying Factors That Worsened the Vulnerability of Small-Holder Farmers During the COVID-19 Pandemic: Evidence from North-Central, Nigeria

Olalekan Ibitoye, Adedoyin L. Ibitoye, and Giuseppe T. Cirella

1 Introduction

Small-holder farmers in developing countries play a very critical role in food production, and by extension, remain a strong pillar in the food security structure of these countries. Evidence from the literature clearly indicates that small-holder farmers produce the bulk of the food in developing countries, estimated at 80% of the total food consumed in Asia and sub-Saharan Africa—combined [1]. Going by the internationally accepted standard and definition, farmers with land holdings of less than 10 ha are regarded as small-holder farmers. In Nigeria, more than 80% of farmers fall under this category. These farmers predominately cultivate arable crops, some cash crops, and rely exclusively on the basic production resources available at their disposal [2] (Fig. 1). Due to the exclusive reliance on personally owned production resources, several studies have reported that small-holder farmers in Nigeria are heavily vulnerable to all kinds of shocks, affecting both the demand and supply side of their production [3, 4]. Several attempts over the years, however, have been made (i.e., by successive governments) to boost agricultural production in Nigeria without much success [5, 6]. A review of the literature clearly indicates that efforts made towards improving agricultural production in Nigeria are concentrated on solving the manifested challenges which can best be described as "superficial." In practical terms, if the factors that worsen the vulnerability of small-holder farmers to various shocks is not well taken care of, the design of a sustainable approach and

O. Ibitoye (✉) · A. L. Ibitoye
School of Business and Management, Management Development Institute of Singapore in Tashkent, Tashkent, Uzbekistan
e-mail: oibitoye@mdis.uz

G. T. Cirella
Faculty of Economics, University of Gdansk, Sopot, Poland
e-mail: gt.cirella@ug.edu.pl

G. T. Cirella (ed.), *Uncertainty Shocks in Africa*, Advances in African Economic, Social and Political Development, https://doi.org/10.1007/978-3-031-21885-9_12

Fig. 1 Small-holder farm crops in North-Central: (*top left*) cassava farm at Afon village, Asa LGA, Kwara. (*top right*) cowpea farm at Sobi Ilorin, Kwara, (*bottom left*) maize farm at Afon village, Asa LGA, Kwara, and (*bottom right*) planting seeds in Jos Plateau. Source: (*top left* and *top right*) Photographs by Adedoyin L. Ibitoye, July 19, 2022; (*bottom left*) photograph by Olalekan Ibitoye, July 19, 2022; (*bottom right*) photograph by Tomiwa Ogunmodede on Upsplash, Creative Commons Public Domain, July 1, 2019

plan of mitigating the effects of such shocks will be extremely difficult to achieve. Therefore, a sustainable way of helping small-holder farmers overcome the effects of shocks will be to address, i.e., both the fundamental causes of such shocks and the underlying factors aiding their vulnerabilities to these shocks.

It is on this basis, using the first 2 years of the COVID-19 pandemic, that this chapter identifies the underlying factors that have worsened the vulnerability of small-holder farmers in North-Central, Nigeria. The pandemic has given rise to some lasting solutions to the problems of low productivity and limited capacity to cope with the shock. Two research questions are considered as a premise to this chapter. First, what is the socioeconomic characteristics of small-holder farmers in North-Central? Second, what are the underlying factors that worsened the vulnerability of them during first 2 years of the pandemic? Providing answers to these questions will, to a great extent, assist the relevant government departments and agencies, international organizations, and other interested parties to make informed decisions and policies that will address the issues that make small-holder farmers more vulnerable to shock events. By so doing, the capacity of small-holder farmers to withstand the effects of any kind of shock will be greatly enhanced, thereby ensuring the sustainability of food production and food security. Using socioeconomic characteristics, in combination with statistical means, this chapter attempts to untangle some of the complexities of the matter as well as provide a response to how small-holder farmers should move forward and, from an external viewpoint, be better respected.

2 Methodology

2.1 Study Area, Source of the Data, and Sampling Technique

The research study area is North-Central, Nigeria (Fig. 2). The North-Central part of the country comprises the states of Benue, Kogi, Kwara, Nasarawa, Niger, Plateau, and the Federal Capital Territory (FCT). According to Anderson et al. [7], the northern geographical zone is home to two-thirds of the small-holder farmers in the country (i.e., 25% in North-Central, 22% in North-West, and 20% in North-East). North-Central was selected because it is a major agricultural zone with the largest percentage of small-holder farmers in Nigeria (Fig. 3).

To piece together the research, primary data were used and collected directly from the small-holder farming households with the aid of a structured questionnaire and scheduled face-to-face interviews. The data collection period span over a period of 10 weeks between June and August of 2021. A well-coordinated data collection process was carried out. Data were collected simultaneously across the selected states and local government areas with the engagement of qualified and well-trained enumerators drawn from the study area. A multi-stage sampling technique was used for data collection. The first stage of the sampling process involves random selection of three states out of the seven states, i.e., FCT inclusive. The randomly selected states include Benue, Kwara, and Plateau. In the second stage of the sampling process, three local governments areas were purposively selected from each of the states. The purposive selection of the local government areas from each state was based on the number of registered farmers present in each local government council

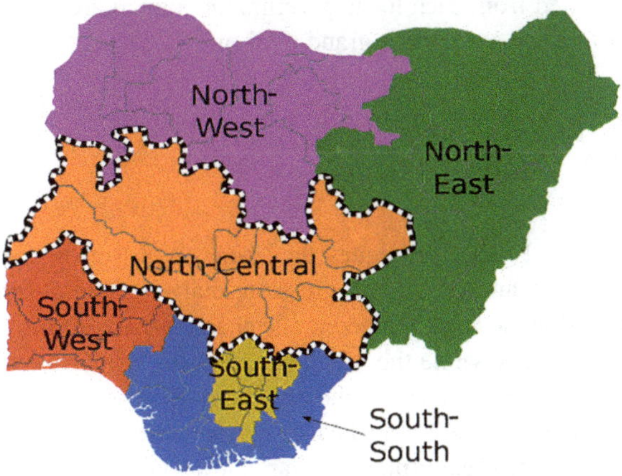

Fig. 2 Map of the six geopolitical zones of Nigeria with the study area highlighted. Source: Adapted from Wikipedia [8], Creative Commons Public Domain

Fig. 3 Example of small-holder farming settlements in North-Central: (*top*) Afon village settlement, Asa LGA, Kwara, and (*bottom*) Salama town, Busa Buji Street, Jos North LGA, Plateau. Source: (*top*) Photograph by Adedoyin L. Ibitoye, July 17, 2022; (*bottom*) photograph by Olalekan Ibitoye, August 10, 2021

area. This information was obtained from the list of registered farmers available at the Ministry of Agriculture of the respective states. In all, three local government council areas with the highest number of registered farmers were selected. This added up to a total of nine local government areas across the three states. In the fourth and the final stage of the sampling process, 40 farmers were randomly selected from each local government council area. This made a total of 120 farmers from each state and a grand total of 360 farmers across whole the study area.

2.2 Model Specification

The analytical techniques that were employed in the research include descriptive statistics and multiple regression analysis. The descriptive statistics were used to describe the key socioeconomic characteristics of the small-holder farmers and their households, while the multiple regression analysis was used to determine the actual factors that worsened the vulnerability of the small-holder farmers during the pandemic. Regression analysis shows the amount of change in the value of the dependent (i.e., explained) variable associated with a unit change in the value of independent (i.e., explanatory) variable(s). In this chapter, the multiple regression analysis using the ordinary least squares estimate was used to determine the actual factors that worsened the vulnerability of the small-holder farmers. The model specification utilized Eq. (1) to formulate the regression model.

$$Y = \beta_0 + \beta_i X_i + \varepsilon \tag{1}$$

Where: $Y =$ the dependent (i.e., explained) variable from the Economic Vulnerability Index (EVI), $\beta_0 =$ constant, $\beta_i =$ the regression coefficients, $X_i =$ the matrix of independent (i.e., explanatory) variables, $\varepsilon =$ the error term.

EVI is calculated as total expenditure divided by total income for every household. This follows the findings of Muhammad-Lawal et al. [9] who concluded that income and expenditure account for about 70% of the vulnerability of households to economic shocks in Nigeria. EVI suggests that the more income generated for a particular household, the less vulnerable it becomes to economic shocks, while, on the other hand, the more expenses a household incurs, the more vulnerable it becomes. The economic vulnerability of the small-holder farming households is dependent on the explanatory variables, i.e., X_1, X_2, X_3, ... X_n. Specifically, the model is looks for how much change is accounted for in EVI by each of the explanatory variables and how much is unexplained as measured by the error term. The independent variables of the regression model are specified as: $X_1 =$ age (i.e., years), $X_2 =$ sex of household head (i.e., female = 1, male = 2), $X_3 =$ educational level of respondents (i.e., number of years spent in school), $X_4 =$ household size, $X_5 =$ farm size (i.e., ha), $X_6 =$ farming experience (i.e., years), $X_1 =$ access to finance and credit facilities (i.e., no access = 0, limited access = 1, unlimited access = 3), $X_8 =$ adoption of improved technology (i.e., no = 0, yes = 1), $X_9 =$ access to inputs (i.e., no access = 0, limited access = 1, unlimited access = 3), $X_{10} =$ access to infrastructural facilities such as transportation facilities, storage facilities, processing facilities, etc. (i.e., no access = 0, limited access = 1, unlimited access = 3), and $X_{11} =$ access to extension services (i.e., no access = 0, limited access = 1, unlimited access = 3). For further reading on similar, concurrent regression modeling techniques see Zhong et al. [10], Begho and Begho [11], and Wu [12].

3 Results and Discussion

3.1 Socioeconomic Characteristics of the Respondents

From the 360 questionnaires administered, a total of 347 questionnaires were used. Thirteen questionnaires were discarded due to incomplete information being provided. Table 1 presents the socioeconomic characteristics of the farmers in North-Central. It reveals that the average age of the respondents in the study area is about 55 (i.e., $\sigma = \pm 15.49$) years, while the modal age is 60 years. This suggests that the

Table 1 Socioeconomic characteristics of the respondents, $n = 347$

Socioeconomic variables	Mean ($\overline{X}$)	Mode	Standard deviation (σ)
Age (i.e., years)	55.37	60.00	14.49
Sex of household head	–	Male	–
Years spent in school	6.26	6.00	5.92
Household size	7.38	8.00	2.34
Farm size (i.e., ha)	2.56	1.00	2.11
Farming experience (i.e., years)	18.27	20.00	10.67
Annual income (i.e., NGN)[a]	212,092.22	180,000.00	94,989.34

Source: Field survey, 2021
[a]USD 1 = NGN 415.00

majority of the farmers are fairly advanced in age. The result also reveals that most of the household head are male in agreement with a priori cultural expectation. The average and the modal years spent in school is six. The standard deviation is also found to be ±5.92 years. This is an indication that the level of formal education among the respondents is low since the majority of them only completed the first 6 years of elementary education. The result of the analysis further shows that the average household size is about seven persons (i.e., $\sigma = \pm 2.34$), with a mode of eight. Moreover, the average farm size is found to be 2.56 ha, mode is 1 ha, while the standard deviation is ±2.11 ha. This further confirms that the farmers are predominantly small-holder farmers. The average farming experience is revealed to be 18.27 years, σ ±10.67 years, and the mode is 20 years. This is an indication that most of the farmers are well experienced in farming-related activities. Finally, the average annual income among the respondents is NGN 212,092.22 (i.e., USD 515.00), with a standard deviation of ±94,989.34. This suggests that the annual income of the farmers from their farming activities is low.

3.2 *Factors That Worsened the Vulnerability of the Small-Holder Farmers During the Pandemic*

Table 2 illustrates the result of a multiple regression analysis for determining the factors that worsened the vulnerability of the small-holder farmers during the pandemic in North-East. The dependent variable is EVI, while the independent variables were age of the household head, sex of household head, educational level, household size, farm size, farming experience, access to finance and credit facilities, adoption of improved technology, access to inputs, access to infrastructural facilities, and access to extension services. The major factors that significantly worsened the vulnerability of the small-holder farmers during the first 2 years of the pandemic include educational level (i.e., measured by the number of years spent in school), farming experience, and access to finance. Other factors that had a lesser impact included the adoption of improved technologies and access to extension

Table 2 Factors that worsened the vulnerability of the small-holder farmers during the pandemic

Variables	Coefficients	Standard error	*t*-Value
Constant	0.312	0.222	1.405
Age	0.007	0.004	1.750
Sex	0.282	0.210	1.343
Educational level	−0.016**	0.007	−2.286
Household size	0.016	0.021	0.762
Farm size	0.033	0.018	1.833
Farming experience	−0.497**	0.209	−2.378
Access to finance and credit facilities	−0.380**	0.164	−2.317
Adoption of improved technology	−0.369**	0.171	−2.158
Access to inputs	−0.054	0.118	−0.461
Access to infrastructural facilities	−0.022	0.119	−0.185
Access to extension services	−0.253**	0.124	−2.040
R-squared	0.683		
Adjusted R-squared	0.497		

Note: The dependent variable is EVI; Source: Authors data analysis, 2020
**Coefficient significant at 5%

services. It was revealed that some variables had an inverse relationship on the level of vulnerability among the respondents. The negative relationship between the level of education and level of vulnerability to the pandemic is an indication that lower levels of education make the farmers more vulnerable. Hence, an increase in the educational level is expected to reduce the vulnerability level. That being said, a higher level of education is expected to boost one's chances of having other income-generating activities and, consequently, increase one's income level. A priori expectation also suggests that higher educational levels will increase the level of awareness of the farmers regarding the likelihood of a future shock and aid in their advancement in terms of wealth creation. Likewise, an increase in farming experience was found to significantly reduce the vulnerability of the farmers during the pandemic. This is also expected because higher levels of experience would have equipped the farmers with better coping strategies, thereby reducing their susceptibility to being able to cope with extended hardship. Access to finance also had a negative effect on the vulnerability of the farmers, suggesting that an increase in their access to finance and credit facilities could have significantly boosted their ability to cope better during the pandemic.

The analysis further discloses that the level of vulnerability to the pandemic reduces with every incremental increase in improved technological adoption. This agrees with the findings of Olalekan and Eyitayo [13] who reported that the use of technology (e.g., mechanized farming) significantly increases income of farmers in South-West which is believed to reduce vulnerability to pandemic-like shocks. Access to extension services also exhibits a negative effect on the vulnerability of the farmers during the COVID-19 pandemic, i.e., this is an indication that more extension services will significantly reduce the level of shock the farmers are

Fig. 4 Poorly kept roads and tracks found throughout rural North-Central: (*left*) Salama town, Jos North LGA, Plateau, (*middle*) Owu-Isin village, Isin LGA, Kwara, and (*right*) poorly kept track along Abuja-Lokoja Road. Source: (*left*) Photograph by Olalekan Ibitoye, August 11, 2021; (*middle*) photograph by Adedoyin L. Ibitoye, July 22, 2022; (*right*) photograph by Peace Itimi on Upsplash, Creative Commons Public Domain, May 26, 2019

exposed to. Further, this can be linked with the implication that more access to quality extension services will provide farmers with adequate orientation on coping strategies, early warning systems, information on modern production practices, and information on improved varieties, among others. The coefficient of multiple determination (i.e., R-squared) of the regression model is 0.683, implying that all the explanatory variables captured in the model jointly accounted for 68.3% of the variations in the factors that worsened the vulnerability of the small-holder farmers. However, after adjustment for the degree of freedom, the adjusted R-squared for the model is 0.497. This indicates that the model has 49.7% explanatory power regarding the variation of the factors that worsened vulnerability levels. Figure 4 illustrates some of the poorly kept roads and tracks found throughout rural North-Central.

4 Conclusion and Recommendations

This chapter, in summary, shows that the majority of the farmers are male, fairly advanced in age, with a relatively low level of formal education. In context, the average household size was about seven persons, with the majority of them having an average farm size of 2.5 ha. The study demonstrates that the farmers are well experienced in farming-related activities in which the average income is reported to be low for the North-Central region. It is noted that the major factors that significantly worsened the vulnerability of small-holder farmers during the COVID-19 pandemic is educational level, farming experience, and access to finance. On the other end of the spectrum, the factors, if acquired, that could better the farmers' situation is the adoption of improved technologies and access to extension services.

The regression model positively accounted for nearly two-thirds of the variations, indicating that the factors that worsened the vulnerability of the farmers is strongly founded. Based on these findings, the following three recommendations can be made. First, efforts should be made towards encouraging the small-holder farmers to acquire some level of formal education, and for those farmers that are fairly old, adult education should be encouraged. This is especially important as it was concluded that an inverse relationship exists between the level of education and the vulnerability index among the respondents. This also indicates that an increase in the educational level could have reduced the level of vulnerability during the height of the pandemic. Second, the government should increase access to finance and credit facilities directly with the actual small-holder farmers. This is expected to significantly boost their ability to cope with shock events and better allow them to prepare for future shocks. Third, more access to various improved farming technologies as well as quality extension services should be made available. This is because increased access to these factors would have potentially reduced the level of the shock during the pandemic and allowed farmers more time to adjust to the COVID-19 restriction measures implored in 2020 and 2021. Small-holder farmers in Nigeria makeup most of the country's local food production. Since this is crucial to a functioning society, these farmers should be better taken care of and better respected at all levels. An initial step to cementing this, would be to facilitate policies and interventions that prioritize the advancement of rural and agricultural communities—inclusive of social programs and infrastructure, to address volatility and limit market fluctuation, and to get rid of obstacles for local farmers to better facilitate the agricultural value chain. These steps would aid farming communities to better thrive as businesses and, indirectly, better prepare themselves for future shocks.

References

1. Sabo BB, Isah SD, Chamo AM, Rabiu MA (2017) Role of smallholder farmers in Nigeria's food security. J Agric Sci 7:1–5
2. Mgbenka RN, Mbah EN (2016) A review of smallholder farming in Nigeria: need for transformation. J Agric Ext Rural Dev Stud 3:43–54
3. Oluwatayo IB (2018) Vulnerability and adaptive strategies of smallholder farmers to seasonal fluctuations in production and marketing in Southwest Nigeria. Clim Dev 11:659–666. https://doi.org/10.1080/17565529.2018.1521328
4. Fan S, Rue C (2020) The role of smallholder farms in a changing world. In: Paloma SG, Riesgo L, Louhichi K (eds) The role of smallholder farms in food and nutrition security. Springer, Berlin, pp 13–28
5. Iwuchukwu JC, Igbokwe EM (2016) Lessons from agricultural policies and programmes in Nigeria. Department of Agricultural Extension, University of Nigeria, Nsukka
6. Ayoola GB (2001) Essays on the agricultural economy: a book of readings on agricultural development policy and Administration in Nigeria. TMA Publishers, Ibadan

7. Anderson J, Marita C, Musiime D, Thiam M (2017) National survey and segmentation of smallholder households in Nigeria: understanding their demand for financial, agricultural, and digital solutions. CGAP Working Paper, Geneva
8. Wikipedia (2022) Geopolitical zones of Nigeria. https://en.wikipedia.org/wiki/Geopolitical_zones_of_Nigeria. Accessed 15 Jul 2022
9. Muhammad-Lawal A, Omotesho OA, Kolade FT (2012) An assessment of household vulnerability to economic shocks in south western Nigeria. Int J Dev Sustain 1:701–713
10. Zhong Y, Zhang Z, Li S (2020) A constrained interval-valued linear regression model: a new heteroscedasticity estimation method. J Syst Sci Complex 336(33):2048–2066. https://doi.org/10.1007/S11424-020-9075-2
11. Begho T, Begho MO (2022) The occupation of last resort? Determinants of farming choices of small farmers in Nigeria. Int J Rural Manag:1–21. https://doi.org/10.1177/09730052221091343
12. Wu F (2022) Adoption and income effects of new agricultural technology on family farms in China. PLoS One 17:e0267101. https://doi.org/10.1371/JOURNAL.PONE.0267101
13. Olalekan I, Eyitayo OA (2015) Income distribution among arable crop farmers in Nigeria: evidence from Ekiti state, Nigeria. Focus 6(9)

Glossary

African Union The African Union is a continental union consisting of 55 member states located on the continent of Africa. The bloc was founded on May 26 2001 in Addis Ababa, Ethiopia, and launched on July 9 2002 in Durban, South Africa. The intention of the AU was to replace the Organisation of African Unity established on May 25 1963 by 32 signatory governments. The idea behind the African Union is to promote Africa's growth and economic development by championing citizen inclusion and increased cooperation and integration of African states [1].

Agenda 2063 Africa's blueprint and master plan for transforming Africa into the global powerhouse of the future. It is the continent's strategic framework that aims to deliver on its goal for inclusive and sustainable development and is a concrete manifestation of the pan-African drive for unity, self-determination, freedom, progress, and collective prosperity pursued under Pan-Africanism and African Renaissance [2]

Air pollution The presence of toxic chemicals or compounds, including those of biological origin, in the air, at levels that pose a health risk. Broadly speaking, air pollution means the presence of chemicals or compounds in the air which are usually not present and which lower the quality of the air or cause detrimental changes to the quality of life [3].

Atmosphere A layer of gases surrounding the planet made up of 99% nitrogen and oxygen plus other dry air gases such as argon, carbon dioxide, helium, neon, and other gases [4].

Biodiversity Biological diversity (i.e., biodiversity) is the variability among living organisms from all sources including, inter alia, terrestrial, marine, and other aquatic ecosystems, and the ecological complexes of which they are part; this includes diversity within species, between species, and of ecosystems [5].

Carrying capacity The maximum population that can be supported by a given set of resources [6].

G. T. Cirella (ed.), *Uncertainty Shocks in Africa*, Advances in African Economic, Social and Political Development, https://doi.org/10.1007/978-3-031-21885-9

Climate action Stepped-up efforts to reduce greenhouse gas emissions and strengthen resilience and adaptive capacity to climate-induced impacts, including: climate-related hazards in all countries; integrating climate change measures into national policies, strategies, and planning; and improving education, awareness-raising, and human and institutional capacity with respect to climate change mitigation, adaptation, impact reduction, and early warning [7].

Climate change Any change in the state of the climate that can be identified by changes in the mean and variability of its properties, and that persists for an extended period, typically decades or longer [8].

Conservation Refers to any form of environmental protection, including preservation [6]. The careful management and use of natural resources, the achievement of significant social benefits from them, and the preservation of the natural environment [9].

Consumption Refers to being fixed on a series of social and cultural issues in relation to the way that commodities and their meaning have become intertwined. Specifically, this refers to the extent to which a common global capitalist culture has been created by ever-increasing circulation of commodities and commodity meanings around the world. The salability and commodification of everything [10].

COVID-19 Coronavirus disease (COVID-19) is an infectious disease caused by the SARS-CoV-2 virus [11].

Development The economic, social, and institutional evolution of national states [9]. Can be interpreted to mean the process of becoming larger, more mature, and better organized, often in terms of economic criteria [6].

Economic development Programs, policies, or activities that seek to improve the economic well-being and quality of life for a community. This definition depends on the community you live in. Each community has its own opportunities, challenges, and priorities. Your economic development planning must include the people who live and work in the community [12].

Economic shock An economic shock refers to any change to fundamental macroeconomic variables or relationships that has a substantial effect on macroeconomic outcomes and measures of economic performance, such as unemployment, consumption, and inflation. Shocks are often unpredictable and are usually the result of events thought to be beyond the scope of normal economic transactions [13].

Entrepreneurialism Defined as starting new businesses, or getting involved with new ventures or ideas [14].

Environmental degradation Environmental degradation is the deterioration of the environment through depletion of resources such as quality of air, water, and soil; the destruction of ecosystems; habitat destruction; the extinction of wildlife; and pollution. It is defined as any change or disturbance to the environment perceived to be deleterious or undesirable [15].

Environmental pollution Defined as the contamination of the physical and biological components of the earth or atmosphere system to such an extent that normal environmental processes are adversely affected [16].

Food security Defined as all people, at all times, have physical, social, and economic access to sufficient, safe, and nutritious food that meets their food preferences and dietary needs for an active and healthy life [17].

Global South Represent the economically backward countries of Africa, Central and South America, the Indian subcontinent, the Middle East, amongst others. The Global South countries are agrarian based, dependent economically and politically on the Global North; the Global North has continued to dominate and direct the Global South in international trade and politics [18].

Green city A loose association of a city focused on sustainability, striving to lessen its environmental impact by reducing waste, expanding recycling, lowering emissions, increasing housing density while expanding open blue and green spaces, and encouraging the development of sustainable local businesses [19].

Green energy Green energy is any energy type that is generated from natural resources, such as sunlight, wind, or water. It often comes from renewable energy sources (see definition below) although there are some differences between renewable and green energy. The key with these energy resources are that they do not harm the environment through factors such as releasing greenhouse gases into the atmosphere [20].

Green infrastructure A strategically planned network of high-quality natural and semi-natural areas with other environmental features, which is designed and managed to deliver a wide range of ecosystem services and protect biodiversity in both rural and urban settings [21].

Habitation The state of living somewhere. When an area has no human habitation, it means that no people live there [22].

Human capital The term human capital refers to the economic value of a worker's experience and skills. Human capital includes assets like education, training, intelligence, skills, health, and other things employers value such as loyalty and punctuality. As such, it is an intangible asset or quality and is perceived to increase productivity and thus profitability [23].

Human ecology Concerned with the organizational aspects of human populations that arise from their sustenance-producing activities [24]. It interfaces with economic progress that meets all of our needs without leaving future generations with fewer resources than those we enjoy, hence, a way of living from nature's income rather than mining its capital account [25].

Human settlement A form of human habitation which ranges from a single dwelling to large urban center. It is a process of opening up and settling of a previously uninhabited area by people. The study of human settlement is basic to human geography as it examines the forms of settlement in any particular region reflective of the human relationship with the environment [26].

Infrastructure The basic physical and organizational structures and facilities (e.g., buildings, roads, and power supplies) needed for the operation of a society or enterprise. The underlying foundation or basic framework (as of a system or organization) [27].

Inequality Occurs when resources in a given society are distributed unevenly, typically through norms of allocation, that engender specific patterns along lines of socially defined categories of persons. It is the differentiation preference of access of social goods in the society brought about by power, religion, kinship, prestige, race, ethnicity, gender, age, sexual orientation, and class. Often referred to as social or economic inequality [28, 29].

Integration The two-way process of mutual adaptation between migrants and the societies in which they live, whereby migrants are incorporated into the social, economic, cultural, and political life of the receiving community. It entails a set of joint responsibilities for migrants and communities, and incorporates other related notions such as social inclusion and social cohesion [30].

Informal settlement An area where groups of housing units have been constructed on land that the occupants have no legal claim to, or occupy illegally. Unplanned settlements and areas where housing is not in compliance with current planning and building regulations (i.e., unauthorized housing) [31].

Internally displaced persons Someone who is forced to leave their home but who remains within their country's borders [32]. Note, they are often thought of as refugees, although they do not fall within the legal definition [33].

Livelihood Can be defined as the methods and means of making a living. The notion includes access to resources such as land or property, crops, food, knowledge, finance, social relationships, and their interrelated connection with the political, economic, and sociocultural characteristics of an individual community. A livelihood consists of capabilities, assets, and activities that are required for living [34]. A sustainable livelihood interlinks the definitions of resilience, sustainability, and offsets reducing vulnerabilities of the community, including reducing poverty levels, building capacities, and coping mechanisms, and focusing on community resilience [35].

Lockdown A period of time in which people are not allowed to leave their homes or travel freely, because of a dangerous disease, e.g. COVID-19. An emergency situation in which people are not allowed to freely enter, leave, or move around in a building, area, city, region, or country because of danger [36].

Macroeconomy The macroeconomy focuses on the performance of economies—changes in economic output, inflation, interest and foreign exchange rates, and the balance of payments. Poverty reduction, social equity, and sustainable growth are only possible with sound monetary and fiscal policies [37].

Marginalization A form of acute and persistent disadvantage rooted in underlying social inequalities [38].

Methodology Is a theory of producing knowledge through research and provides a rationale for the way a researcher proceeds. It is the philosophical underpinning of a given research practice. Methodology is the discussion of the theory upon which research is based and indicates how the experimentation is performed [39].

Opportunity cost Represents the benefits an individual, investor, or business misses out on when choosing one alternative over another [40]. The two definitions of opportunity cost differ in what is forgone. For the "quantity" type, it is the highest-valued alternative (i.e., the physical thing or things that otherwise would have been chosen). For the "value" type, it is the value of the highest-valued alternative (i.e., the value of the physical thing or things that otherwise would have been chosen) [41].

Pandemic A pandemic is an epidemic of an infectious disease that has spread across a large region, for instance, multiple continents or worldwide, affecting a substantial number of individuals [42, 43].

Policy A law, regulation, procedure, administrative action, incentive, or voluntary practice of governments and other institutions [44].

Poverty Poverty is about not having enough money to meet basic needs including food, clothing, and shelter; however, poverty is more, much more than just not having enough money [45]. Poverty is hunger, lack of shelter, being sick and not being able to see a doctor, not having access to school and not knowing how to read, not having a job, fear for the future, and living one day at a time. Poverty has many faces, changing from place to place and across time, and has been described in many ways. "Most often, poverty is a situation people want to escape. So poverty is a call to action—for the poor and the wealthy alike—a call to change the world so that many more may have enough to eat, adequate shelter, access to education and health, protection from violence, and a voice in what happens in their communities" [46].

Qualitative method Qualitative methods involve collecting and analyzing non-numerical data (e.g., text, video, or audio) to understand concepts, opinions, or experiences. It can be used to gather in-depth insights into a problem or generate new ideas for research [47].

Quantitative method Quantitative methods are a systematic investigation of phenomena by gathering quantifiable data and performing statistical, mathematical, or computational techniques. Quantitative research collects information from existing and potential customers using sampling methods and sending out, e.g., online surveys, online polls, and questionnaires [48].

Resilience The process of adapting well in the face of adversity, trauma, tragedy, threats, or even significant sources of risk. The act of bouncing back or resisting under pressure. Resilience theory is a set of ideas that discuss the impact of challenging events on individuals, communities, or any level of society and how well they have adapted to a traumatic experience [49, 50].

Resource A concept used to denote sources of human satisfaction, wealth, or strength. Labor, entrepreneurial skills, investment funds, fixed capital assets, technology, knowledge, social stability, and cultural and physical attributes may be referred to as the resources for a country. In a resource management context, natural resources, which are substances, organisms, and properties of the physical environment are valued for their perceived ability to satisfy human needs and wants [10].

Socio-demographic variables Socio-demographic variables include, e.g., age, sex, education, migration background and ethnicity, religious affiliation, marital status, household, employment, and income. Different index variables are formed on the basis of socio-demographic variables. They include, e.g., socio-economic status, which combines information on education and income. Socio-demographic details are often used to describe realized samples and to determine sampling error [51].

Sociocultural Related to the different groups of people in society and their habits, traditions, and beliefs [52].

Socioeconomics Socioeconomics (also known as social economics) is the social science that studies how economic activity affects and is shaped by social processes. In general it analyzes how modern societies progress, stagnate, or regress because of their local or regional economy, or the global economy [53, 54].

Survey A research method used for collecting data from a predefined group of respondents to gain information and insights into various topics of interest [55] .

Sustainability Development that meets the needs of the present without compromising the ability of future generations to meet their own needs [56].

Sustainable agriculture Ensuring the continuing availability to the consumer of adequate supplies of wholesome, varied, and reasonably priced food, produced in accordance with generally accepted environmental and social standards. Maintaining a flexible and competitive industry which contributes to an economically viable rural society. Ensuring effective protection of the environment and prudent use of natural resources. Conserving and enhancing the landscape, wildlife, cultural, and archeological value of agricultural land. Respecting a high level of animal welfare [57].

Trade regulations The removal or reduction of trade barriers in accordance with the former General Agreement on Tariffs and Trade and most recently the World Trade Organization presents opportunities for businesses. Likewise, multinational agreements that remove trade barriers to create largely duty-free and tariff-free trading zones allow for freer flow of goods and services between specific countries. These agreements create tremendous opportunities for businesses because they lower the costs associated with importing and exporting, which is a primary consideration for many companies [58].

Tourism industry The tourism industry, also known as the travel industry, is linked to the idea of people traveling to other locations, either domestically or internationally, for leisure, social, or business purposes. It is closely connected to the hotel industry, the hospitality industry, and the transport industry, and much of it is based around keeping tourists happy, occupied, and equipped with the things they need during their time away from home [59]. Equally, it is a comprehensive industry involving many industries such as hospitality, transportation, tourist destinations, travel companies, and more, by focusing on tourism, which is defined as people traveling and staying in places outside their usual environment for less than one year in a row for leisure, business, health, or other reasons [60].

Uncertainty shocks A mechanism that generates realistic micro dispersion (cross-sectional variance of firm-level outcomes), higher-order uncertainty (disagreement), and macro uncertainty (uncertainty about macro outcomes) from changes in macro volatility [61].

Urbanization The process through which cities grow, and higher and higher percentages of the population comes to live in the city [62].

Urban green space Urban space covered by vegetation of any kind, including smaller green space features (e.g., street trees and roadside vegetation), green spaces not available for public access or recreational use (e.g., green roofs and facades, or green space on private grounds), and larger green spaces that provide various social and recreational functions (e.g., parks, playgrounds, or greenways) [63].

Urban morphology Refers to the study of urban form that focuses on the formation and transformation of urban forms of cities, towns, and villages over time; their spatial patterns at different scales; and physical characteristics to inform appropriate urban interventions to promote sustainable urban development [64].

Urban sprawl Refers to urbanization and the migration of a population from populated towns and cities to low-density residential development over more and more rural land. The end result is the spreading of a city and its suburbs over such land. Urban sprawl can be low-density residential and commercial development moved to undeveloped land [65]. Largely unplanned expansion of an urban area; typically discontinuous, leaving rural enclaves [6].

Urban sustainability Based on positive interactions among three different urban substrates: physical, social, and economic. Urban sustainability predominately focuses on the city in which social well-being coexists with economic development and environmental quality [66].

Vulnerability Within a human context, it is the limited capacity to avoid, resist, cope with, or recover from harm. This limited capacity is the result of the unique interaction of individual, household, community, and structural characteristics and conditions [30].

Well-being The degree to which the needs and wants of a society are satisfied [6]. An individual's perception of their position in life in the context of the culture and value systems in which they live and in relation to their goals, expectations, standards, and concerns. It is a broad ranging concept affected in a complex way by the person's physical health, psychological state, personal beliefs, social relationships, and their relationship to salient features of their environment [67].

References

1. African Union (2022) About the African Union. https://au.int/en/overview. Accessed 12 Aug 2022
2. African Union (2022) Agenda 2063: The Africa we want. https://au.int/en/agenda2063/overview. Accessed 12 Aug 2022
3. Environmental Pollution Centers (2021) What is air pollution. In: Environmental Pollution Centers. https://www.environmentalpollutioncenters.org/air/. Accessed 24 Mar 2021
4. National Geographic (2021) Atmosphere. In: National Geographic Society. https://www.nationalgeographic.org/encyclopedia/atmosphere/. Accessed 24 Mar 2021
5. United Nations Convention on Biological Diversity (1992) Convention on biological diversity. https://www.cbd.int/doc/legal/cbd-en.pdf. Accessed 30 Oct 2019
6. Norton W (1998) Human geography. Oxford University Press
7. UNDP (2015) Goal 13: climate action. In: United Nations Sustainable Development Goals. https://www.sdfinance.undp.org/content/sdfinance/en/home/sdg/goal-13%2D%2Dclimate-action.html. Accessed 24 Mar 2021
8. IPCC (2007) Climate change 2007: The physical science basis. https://www.ipcc.ch/report/ar4/wg1/. Accessed 30 Oct 2019
9. De Blij HJ, Murphy AB (2003) Human geography: Culture, society, and space, 7th edn. Wiley, Hoboken, NJ
10. Johnston R, Gregory D, Pratt G, Watts M (2006) The dictionary of human geography, 4th edn. Gregory, Pratt Johnston: 9781405136044: Amazon.com: Books. Wiley, Malden, MA
11. WHO (2022) Coronavirus. In: World Heal. Organ. https://www.who.int/health-topics/coronavirus#tab=tab_1. Accessed 12 Aug 2022
12. Province of British Columbia (2022) What is economic development? https://www2.gov.bc.ca/gov/content/employment-business/economic-development/plan-and-measure/economic-development-basics. Accessed 12 Aug 2022
13. Investopedia (2021) Economic shock definition. https://www.investopedia.com/terms/e/economic-shock.asp. Accessed 12 Aug 2022
14. Your Dictionary (2018) Entrepreneurialism. In: LoveToKnow Corp. https://www.yourdictionary.com/entrepreneurialism. Accessed 30 Oct 2019
15. Johnson DL, Ambrose SH, Bassett TJ et al (1997) Meanings of Environmental Terms. J Environ Qual 26:581–589. https://doi.org/10.2134/JEQ1997.00472425002600030002X
16. Muralikrishna IV, Manickam V (2017) Introduction. In: Environmental management. Elsevier, pp 1–4

G. T. Cirella (ed.), *Uncertainty Shocks in Africa*, Advances in African Economic, Social and Political Development, https://doi.org/10.1007/978-3-031-21885-9

17. IFPRI (2021) Food security. In: International Food Policy Research Institute, United Nations' Committee on World Food Security. https://www.ifpri.org/topic/food-security. Accessed 24 Mar 2021
18. Odeh L (2012) A comparative analysis of global north and global south economies. Int J Curr Res Humanit 12:67–82
19. E/The Environmental Magazine (2009) What are "green cities"? In: Phys.org. https://phys.org/news/2009-03-green-cities.html. Accessed 24 Mar 2021
20. TWI (2021) What is green energy? https://www.twi-global.com/technical-knowledge/faqs/what-is-green-energy. Accessed 24 Mar 2021
21. Directorate-General for Environment (2013) Building a green infrastructure for Europe. In: European Commission. https://op.europa.eu/en/publication-detail/-/publication/738d80bb-7d10-47bc-b131-ba8110e7c2d6/language-en. Accessed 30 Oct 2019
22. Vocabulary.com (2019) Habitation. In: Vocabulary.com. https://www.vocabulary.com/dictionary/habitation. Accessed 30 Oct 2019
23. Investopedia (2022) Human capital definition. https://www.investopedia.com/terms/h/humancapital.asp. Accessed 12 Aug 2022
24. Poston DL (2015) Human Ecology. In: International encyclopedia of the social and behavioral sciences, 2nd edn. Elsevier, pp 283–288
25. Steiner F (2008) Human ecology: overview. In: Encyclopedia of ecology, five-volume set. Elsevier, pp 1898–1906
26. Josh J (2015) Human settlement. https://www.jagranjosh.com/general-knowledge/human-settlement-1448446636-1. Accessed 30 Oct 2019
27. Merriam-Webster (2022) Infrastructure definition and meaning. https://www.merriam-webster.com/dictionary/infrastructure. Accessed 12 Aug 2022
28. Wikipedia (2019) Social inequality. https://en.wikipedia.org/wiki/Social_inequality. Accessed 30 Oct 2019
29. Neckerman KM, Torche F (2007) Inequality: causes and consequences. Annu Rev Sociol 33: 335–357. https://doi.org/10.1146/annurev.soc.33.040406.131755
30. IOM (2019) Key migration terms. In: International Organization for Migration. https://www.iom.int/key-migration-terms. Accessed 30 Oct 2019
31. OECD (1997) OECD glossary of statistical terms - informal settlements definition. In: Glossary of Environmental Statistics, Studies in Methods, United Nations. https://stats.oecd.org/glossary/detail.asp?ID=1351. Accessed 24 Mar 2021
32. UNHCR (2021) Internally displaced people. In: United Nations High Commissioner for Refugees. https://www.unhcr.org/en-us/internally-displaced-people.html. Accessed 28 Mar 2021
33. Afolabi AO, Oluwatayo A, Oyeyipo O et al (2018) Assessment of designers' perception of post conflict housing schemes for internally displaced persons. Constr Econ Build 18:27–47. https://doi.org/10.5130/AJCEB.v18i1.5780
34. Islam T, Ryan J, Islam T, Ryan J (2016) Mitigation in the private sector. Hazard Mitig Emerg Manag 101–124. https://doi.org/10.1016/B978-0-12-420134-7.00004-7
35. UNESCAP (2008) Greening Growth in Asia and the Pacific. United Nations Economic and Social Commission for Asia and the Pacific, Bangkok
36. Cambridge English Dictionary (2022) Lockdown: Meaning, definition. https://dictionary.cambridge.org/dictionary/english/lockdown. Accessed 12 Aug 2022
37. World Bank (2022) Macroeconomics. https://www.worldbank.org/en/topic/macroeconomics. Accessed 12 Aug 2022
38. UNESCO (2010) Reaching the marginalized. Oxford University Press, Oxford
39. Zeegers M, Barron D, Zeegers M, Barron D (2015) Milestone 5: methodology. Milestone Moments Get your PhD Qual Res 61–74. https://doi.org/10.1016/B978-0-08-100231-5.00005-5
40. Kenton W (2019) Opportunity cost. In: Investopedia. https://www.investopedia.com/terms/o/opportunitycost.asp. Accessed 30 Oct 2019

41. Parkin M (2016) Opportunity cost: a reply. J Econ Educ 47:35–39. https://doi.org/10.1080/00220485.2015.1106366
42. Wingfield T, Cuevas LE, MacPherson P et al (2020) Tackling two pandemics: a plea on World Tuberculosis Day. Lancet Respir Med 8:536–538. https://doi.org/10.1016/S2213-2600(20)30151-X
43. Wikipedia (2022) Pandemic. https://en.wikipedia.org/wiki/Pandemic. Accessed 12 Aug 2022
44. CDC (2021) Definition of policy. In: Centers for Disease Control and Prevention. https://www.cdc.gov/policy/analysis/process/definition.html. Accessed 24 Mar 2021
45. Government of New Brunswick (2009) What is poverty? - Economic and social inclusion corporation. https://www2.gnb.ca/content/gnb/en/departments/esic/overview/content/what_is_poverty.html. Accessed 12 Aug 2022
46. World Bank (2016) Poverty. https://www.worldbank.org/en/topic/poverty. Accessed 22 Sep 2019
47. Bhandari P (2020) What is qualitative research? | Methods & examples. In: Scribbr. https://www.scribbr.com/methodology/qualitative-research/. Accessed 12 Aug 2022
48. QuestionPro (2022) Quantitative research: what it is, tips & examples. https://www.questionpro.com/blog/quantitative-research/. Accessed 12 Aug 2022
49. Richardson GE, Neiger BL, Jensen S, Kumpfer KL (1990) The resiliency model. Health Educ 21:33–39. https://doi.org/10.1080/00970050.1990.10614589
50. Greene RR, Galambos C, Lee Y (2004) Resilience theory. J Hum Behav Soc Environ 8:75–91. https://doi.org/10.1300/J137v08n04_05
51. Gesis (2022) Socio-demographic variables – survey guidelines. https://www.gesis.org/en/gesis-survey-guidelines/instruments/survey-instruments/socio-demographic-variables. Accessed 12 Aug 2022
52. Cambridge English Dictionary (2022) Sociocultural: meaning, definition. https://dictionary.cambridge.org/dictionary/english/sociocultural. Accessed 12 Aug 2022
53. Wikipedia (2022) Socioeconomics. https://en.wikipedia.org/wiki/Socioeconomics. Accessed 12 Aug 2022
54. Hellmich SN (2017) What is socioeconomics? An overview of theories, methods, and themes in the field. Forum Soc Econ 46:3–25. https://doi.org/10.1080/07360932.2014.999696
55. QuestionPro (2020) What is a survey | Definition, characteristics, examples of a good survey. https://www.questionpro.com/blog/surveys/. Accessed 24 Mar 2021
56. Brundtland GH (1987) Our common future: the world commission on environment and development. Oxford University Press, Oxford
57. DEFRA (2020) Sustainable agriculture. In: Department for Environment, Food & Rural Affairs. https://www.gov.uk/government/organisations/department-for-environment-food-rural-affairs. Accessed 24 Mar 2021
58. Saylor Academy (2012) Trade regulations, contracts, and prohibited activities in international business. In: Legal and Ethical Environmental Business. https://saylordotorg.github.io/text_the-legal-and-ethical-environment-of-business/s16-02-trade-regulations-contracts-an.html. Accessed 24 Mar 2021
59. Revfine (2022) Tourism industry: everything you need to know about tourism. https://www.revfine.com/tourism-industry/. Accessed 12 Aug 2022
60. IGI Global (2022) What is tourism industry |. https://www.igi-global.com/dictionary/economic-impacts-of-the-pandemic-on-the-tourism-of-the-developing-world/64553. Accessed 12 Aug 2022
61. Kozeniauskas N, Orlik A, Veldkamp L (2018) What are uncertainty shocks? J Monet Econ 100: 1–15. https://doi.org/10.1016/J.JMONECO.2018.06.004
62. National Geographic Society (2022) Urbanization. https://education.nationalgeographic.org/resource/urbanization. Accessed 12 Aug 2022
63. Hunter RF, Cleary A, Braubach M (2019) Environmental, health and equity effects of urban green space interventions. In: Biodiversity and health in the face of climate change. Springer International Publishing, Cham, pp 381–409

64. Chen F (2014) Urban morphology and citizens' life. In: Encyclopedia of quality of life and well-being research. Springer, Netherlands, pp 6850–6855
65. Conserve Energy Future (2019) Causes and effects of urban sprawl. In: Conserve Energy Future. https://www.conserve-energy-future.com/causes-and-effects-of-urban-sprawl.php. Accessed 30 Oct 2019
66. Diappi L, Bolchi P, Franzini L (1999) Urban sustainability: complex interactions and the measurement of risk. Cybergeo. https://doi.org/10.4000/cybergeo.1240
67. WHO (2014) WHOQOL: measuring quality of life. In: World Health Organization. https://www.who.int/healthinfo/survey/whoqol-qualityoflife/en/. Accessed 30 Oct 2019

Index

G. T. Cirella (ed.), *Uncertainty Shocks in Africa*, Advances in African Economic, Social and Political Development, https://doi.org/10.1007/978-3-031-21885-9

CPSIA information can be obtained
at www.ICGtesting.com
Printed in the USA
LVHW08081708022
738980LV00003B/1

9 783031 218842